BEYOND
THE LINE

BEN YOUNGS

BEYOND THE LINE

MACMILLAN

First published 2025 by Macmillan
an imprint of Pan Macmillan
The Smithson, 6 Briset Street, London EC1M 5NR
EU representative: Macmillan Publishers Ireland Ltd, 1st Floor,
The Liffey Trust Centre, 117–126 Sheriff Street Upper,
Dublin 1 D01 YC43
Associated companies throughout the world

ISBN 978-1-0350-6920-0

All images in the plate sections are the author's own, with the following
exceptions: p. 4 (bottom) © Warren Little via Getty Images; p. 5 (top and bottom),
p. 6 (bottom), p. 11 (top) © David Rogers, RFU/The RFU Collection via Getty Images;
p. 7 (bottom), p. 8 (bottom) © Dan Mullan RFU/The RFU Collection via Getty Images

1 3 5 7 9 8 6 4 2

A CIP catalogue record for this book is available from the British Library.

Typeset in Warnock Pro by Six Red Marbles UK, Thetford, Norfolk
Printed and bound in the UK using 100% Renewable Electricity by CPI Group (UK) Ltd

Visit **www.panmacmillan.com** to read more about
all our books and to buy them.

To Char, Boris, Billie and Ettie – thanks for all the love and support. I could never have done it without you.

CONTENTS

FOREWORD BY TOM YOUNGS

*'I guess earning an England call-up was
just a matter of time for him.'*

It is a minor source of salvaged pride to me that my brother Ben's England career ended after his 127th cap. I managed 28 so he only beat me by 99, not 100. Which is important.

You need many attributes to become England's most capped men's player. Clearly, you don't have to love the physical side of melting someone in a tackle, because Ben never had that in his repertoire. But he had pretty much every other gift a rugby player could have wished for.

When we were kids in Norfolk, it was obvious from the start how incredibly talented and skilful he was. When he ran with the ball, he would just glide through defences. He was always prepared to have a go, and always backed himself to make the difference.

He brought that fearlessness to Leicester. Some of the tries he scored in the early days at the Tigers were just maverick, off-the-cuff genius.

I guess earning an England call-up was just a matter of time for him. He certainly didn't have to wait long. To break into the national side at twenty years old was amazing in and of itself, but it's one thing reaching the top, and a whole other thing staying there. And Ben stayed there for thirteen years. Four different England coaches picked him as their scrum half.

It was his ability to change his game into something more scripted, as rugby evolved over the years, that enabled him to do so. He had an innate understanding of the game, for where it was going, and a gift for breaking it down that was like a sixth sense. Some say that awareness takes experience to develop, but Ben always had it.

It wasn't just the skills Ben brought to the teams he played for down the years that made them better. It was his personality too. He's great to have in any environment – he's fun, warm and good with people. He's also humble – I hate the word, it's so Kiwi. But it's true.

He can be sharp-tongued. If he feels that something is wrong, he will say so – but that's what you need and want in a professional sports team.

You don't carve out a career like his without being a really good person, and that's what he is to his core – a really incredibly good person. I know that more than anyone.

Thank you, Ben, from the bottom of my heart – and well played.

INTRODUCTION

*'I shook his hand and I told him I needed a bit
of time to myself to digest this. It was like
someone had punched me in the guts.'*

I had reached the point of no return. My head was ready to
explode.

France, November 2023 – my fourth Rugby World Cup repre-
senting England. I had travelled to the tournament knowing,
inwardly, that something was wrong, but I couldn't have known
that the eight weeks I spent there would end up changing my life.
They would force me to confront personal, painful truths and
take me to an emotional place I had never been before. Facing up
to those truths broke me – and then, miraculously, helped to put
me back together again.

I had pushed my issues to one side in the build-up to the World
Cup. England were in a mess, and as part of the team leadership
group I had a role to play in sorting it out. We had just lost to
Fiji at Twickenham for the first time in England's history. It had
been our final warm-up game, and there were plenty of pundits speculating that we would not even make it out of our World
Cup pool.

Sometimes, the solution to a team's problems feels miles away,
but I knew this situation was fixable. There were a good few of us

with experience of previous World Cups, and we knew the phoney war ahead of the tournament counted for nothing. If we could lift the standards in France, we knew we could turn it around for showtime.

A line in the sand was drawn as soon as we crossed the Channel. That first week at Le Touquet, where the English team was based, you could feel the difference. We were so much sharper, so much more intense than we had been. I'd trained well myself and I was an important voice in the squad, driving everyone else on. I felt like I'd really contributed. With our opening game against Argentina five days away, I was confident it was going to be all right on the night.

I was already preparing myself mentally for Marseille, my problems packed away and stored in a separate box.

It was the Monday morning of Test week and I was sitting in the team's private area at the Holiday Inn in Le Touquet when I felt a tap on the shoulder. It was Steve Borthwick.

'Can we go for a walk?' he asked.

Experience has taught me that whenever you get a tap on the shoulder and an invitation from a head coach to go for a walk, it never, ever means anything good. The reason they take you for a walk is twofold. It guarantees privacy for the difficult conversation that is about to take place, and it means that if things overheat, the row will happen side by side rather than face to face. Less confrontational, you see.

I'll never forget it. It was an overcast September day.

'Should we do a loop of the grounds?' Steve asked as we went outside. A loop? That meant he wanted to put some real distance between us and anyone else. This was definitely not good. 'Fucking hell,' I was thinking, 'I know what's coming. I've been here before.'

I want to make it clear: I always respected Steve hugely as a coach. I still do. I respect his work ethic and his desire for perfection. I thought he ran an incredible programme. But when it came to an emotional connection, I never felt anything. Nothing at all. It just didn't happen between us. I always thought there was something about me and the way I played that he just didn't fancy.

When Steve had been head coach at Leicester, he had a habit of leaving me out for big games for the club. We played Ulster in a Challenge Cup semi-final. He put me on the bench. We played Montpellier a few weeks later in the final. He put me on the bench. We played Saracens in the Premiership final. He put me on the bench. I was England's first-choice scrum half at the time.

Selection is so subjective, but with the national team I had gone from working under a coach in Eddie Jones, who I felt valued and understood me, to Steve who I felt really didn't.

We walked for a while in silence side by side and then he hit me with it.

'You're not going to be involved at the weekend against Argentina. I'm going to go with Alex (Mitchell) and Danny (Care).'

Not even on the bench this time, then. I didn't say anything for about ten seconds. I'd blown up at Steve before, at Leicester, and I knew you didn't get anything back – he just absorbed explosions like he was made of Kevlar – so I was calm when I eventually spoke.

'That is really disappointing, Steve. What are the reasons?'

'Speed of ball,' was his reply.

That old chestnut. Every dropped scrum half knows that the 'speed of ball' line from a coach is a cop-out. Unless your number 9 isn't reaching the breakdown in time, which I was, slow possession is down to issues with the ball carrier or the clearout. I had started against Ireland a few weeks beforehand and, while there had been a problem with the speed of ball, that was down to the breakdown being so messy, not how quickly I was arriving there.

I told Steve I strongly disagreed with his decision.

First games at a World Cup are never pretty. They are invariably nervy and scrappy. Our opening game against Argentina in 2011 was an arm-wrestle that we only just won at the death. Fiji and Tonga in 2015 and 2019 had taken some shifting too.

'I know what the first game of a World Cup is like, Steve, and it's tough. A week like this screams out for some experience,' I said. Steve countered that Danny had experience. No argument there, and he was a brilliant finisher so I had no issue with him being on the bench, but I was adamant I was the right guy to start. I made my points as we walked. Steve nodded, but I could tell that he had already decided what he was going to do and that was that.

We wrapped up the conversation, I shook his hand and I told him I needed a bit of time to myself to digest this. It was like someone had punched me in the guts. The Holiday Inn had its own training facility, which we were using. I walked off towards it alone and leaned against a barrier, staring across the athletics track towards the rugby pitch. 'Fuck me, I didn't see that one coming,' I thought.

I hadn't played much during the Six Nations that year – that was true. I had been left out after our opening game against Scotland. But Steve had explained that away by telling me he wanted to give the younger scrum halves more time on the pitch to get used to Test rugby. I could accept that. It made sense. I'd got 120-odd caps, while Jack van Poortvliet and Alex Mitchell were in single figures.

I had taken the precaution of checking in with Kevin Sinfield, Steve's assistant, though. 'Kev, am I done here, mate?' I'd asked him at the time. 'Because if I'm done, can you let me know? I don't want to be that guy who's still waiting at the port when the ship has sailed.' But Kev, who was a great sounding board, reassured me that wasn't the case, and at the end of the championship Steve backed that up. He told me that the squad needed my experience at the World Cup and that I would be part of his plans.

Now I was starting to see what those plans looked like.

I tried to tell myself it was only the opening game and that things could change, but there were a lot of other thoughts rushing around my head. Am I just here to be a support act? To train hard, to speak in meetings, to bring energy and life to the squad – all the things that I had done for more than a decade – but not to actually play? I had already spent a big chunk of time away from the family preparing for the tournament, and now it looked as if I could be in for another eight weeks as a training ground pawn.

Is that how it was destined to end? I felt my hackles rising.

I had almost quit England ten months earlier. I hadn't said a word to the coaches, or any of my teammates, but in my head I had come close.

We had just lost at home to Argentina, and I felt for the first time afterwards that I wasn't sure I wanted to play Test rugby any more. I had ticked off one hundred caps and gone past Jason Leonard's record as the most capped Englishman – wonderful milestones for those close to me – but I wasn't feeling the same buzz as I had done. In fact, I was wondering why I was still doing it.

I rang my brother Tom, whose own England career had ended after the 2015 World Cup, and told him how I was feeling. 'Look, you're less than a year away from the World Cup,' he said. 'Don't throw it away now.'

And I didn't. I stuck at it. But fast-forward to France, and here I was, left fearing the worst. 'I nearly called it last year and now look where I am,' I thought to myself.

Mitch – Alex Mitchell – hadn't even made the original World Cup squad. It was only because Jack van Poortvliet had picked up an injury that he had squeezed in. He'd had to rejoin the squad hot off a holiday in Croatia. But now here he was, the starting scrum half for the first game of the tournament.

It was a big call, and not just for me personally. It would inevitably be a major talking point in the media and, more importantly, among the squad. I'm not brilliant at hiding my emotions; I'm an open book, and it's pretty obvious if I'm up or I'm down. I knew I would have to deal with teammates coming up to me, asking why I wasn't playing and what Steve had said to me.

My instinctive reaction was to go back to my room in the hotel and hide away, but that wasn't an option. I had to help prepare the lads who would be involved against Argentina. They could not afford any distractions. I had to try to put a brave face on it and just get through that training day. But when training was over, I confided in my roommate George Ford and told him I was feeling hard done by, and this wasn't how I expected things to go. He listened, like a good friend would.

I got through training on Tuesday too, supporting the boys, doing the best I could to get them ready but I was still unsettled. Wednesday was our day off. It was also the day David Priestley, England's sports psychologist, arrived in camp. I had worked with him before at Leicester. I thought to myself that he might be a good guy to talk the situation through with.

How do I describe David? He's *intriguing*. He has this aura of quiet wisdom. He stands in a room, not saying much, but taking everything in. I don't know what it was about him, but I always felt

I could be extremely open with him. His room at the Holiday Inn was twelve doors down the corridor, so I walked down there and knocked.

He opened it, invited me in and we sat down. It was daytime but it was noticeably dark in his room – like a place of mourning. We made general conversation for a couple of minutes and then he asked: 'How are you, Ben, how are you feeling?'

I explained that I felt pretty pissed off. I didn't really understand why I'd been overlooked. The decision had really affected me. There was a piece or two out of place in the jigsaw puzzle and I needed some help putting it back together so that I could park what had happened and crack on.

David paused for a moment and then said to me: 'This is your fourth World Cup, right?'

'Yes, that's right.'

'And when you went to your first World Cup in 2011, what were you?'

'What do you mean?' I asked.

'Where did you sit within the squad?'

'I was first choice.'

'Right. And how old were you?'

'Twenty-two. Just.'

'Wow, twenty-two, starting in a World Cup. In 2015, what were you?'

'I was the starting nine.'

'Two World Cups in a row. Starting nine. Incredible. 2019 World Cup – how was that one?'

'Well, it was probably one of the best rugby experiences of my life.'

'Where did you sit in the squad then, Ben?'

'I was first choice.'

'So 2023, fourth World Cup – very few people get to do that. Where do you sit in the squad now?'

'Right now, third choice.'

'So you burst on the scene at Leicester, you were capped at twenty, you played in all these World Cups as first choice and now, at the back end of your career, you're third choice. You're just doing it the other way round to most people,' he said. 'They go to their first World Cup as third choice, then they maybe go to their second and third as first choice. Or maybe they don't get a third. Not many get four. I guess overall that's not bad, is it?'

I thought about that for a moment.

Then David said to me: 'You're England's most capped player.'

I looked at the carpet.

'I've noticed this about you,' he said, immediately. 'Why, whenever someone says to you, "You're the most capped England player", do you always look down? You never puff your chest out and take it in, you always shun it. Why is that?'

He knew there was something way deeper to this visit than just being dropped from a rugby team. And if I'm being honest, I did too – but I didn't know if I could allow myself to go there.

I wasn't looking at the floor now. I was looking directly into the eyes of the man sitting a couple of metres away. *It's OK*, his eyes seemed to say. *Let it go.*

I could feel a bubbling volcano of emotions begin to rise inside me.

'Let me ask you another question,' he said. 'If I gave you a pen and piece of paper and told you to write a letter to a sixteen-year-old Ben Youngs, what would it say? You're going to tell him about all the things you've done and achieved. Do you think he'd be happy with it?'

And that was the trigger. That was it; all it took for all my emotions to come out. I just broke down. It was as if someone had turned on a tap. The tears streamed down my face in a torrent. Suddenly, I was sobbing uncontrollably. Crying, crying and crying some more. It felt like I was never going to stop.

At one point, David leaned over and touched my shoulder. 'None of this is your fault,' he said. 'This didn't happen because of you. You didn't make the situation worse.'

That set off another bout.

I'm quite an emotional person, but I had never cried like that before. It came from somewhere cavernously deep within me. I don't know how long it went on for. Two minutes? Five minutes? It's hard to say. I just wept and wept.

When I had no more tears left to spill and I finally stopped, we began to talk. To talk about why.

I've always loved rugby, ever since I first picked up a ball. It's in my blood, you might say. And the sport had given me so much during my life. But by the time of the World Cup in France, my relationship with it had soured – more than I think I knew.

In 2014, Tom's wife Tiffany had been diagnosed with blood cancer, shortly after the birth of their daughter Maisie. In 2017, she was told that she might only have a short time left to live. I pulled out of the Lions tour that summer to be around to support them as best I could. Amazingly, she went into remission, but the cancer came back in late 2021. That season was meant to be the last one Tom and I would have together at Leicester, but he retired in November to look after Tiff.

She died eight months later. I still miss her terribly.

The previous June, I had also lost my brother-in-law Jake – who also happened to be one of my cousins – to motor neurone disease. It had been a horrible time for the family. Shattering for everyone. Yet rugby – *my* rugby – was their saviour back then. For eighty minutes, my family would be offered some brief respite and escapism from the grim reality they were facing. And for me, playing was something tangible I had to give to them when they were dealing with so much.

In very difficult times, as they were trying to piece their lives back together, rugby brought the people I loved more than anything in the world some kind of joy.

But not for me. The enjoyment the sport had always given me had disappeared.

I was carrying this burden – this sense of guilt – during that whole time. Why should I be the one still living my best life when everyone around me was trapped in this nightmare? There I was, playing professional sport for club and country, like nothing had ever happened. Winning the medals. Picking up the accolades. Revelling in my privileged existence.

From the outside looking in, I must have seemed bulletproof. Everyone just assumed that because I was playing for England, because I was winning a Premiership with the Tigers, because I was breaking records, I was all right.

But I wasn't all right.

I was far from all right.

The truth was that I was struggling. I wasn't thinking straight. In my head, rugby had become interconnected with tragedy. I couldn't separate it from what had happened to Tiff and Jake. Rugby, illness, death – everything had just merged into this vast, enveloping black cloud.

Where once I had been in love with the game, suddenly I could only think of it in negative terms. I had started to resent it. Hate it, even.

When I sat down with David, he knew that there was something buried inside. He knew I had some trauma that I didn't know how to express. The floods of tears were me starting to untangle the knot. That grieving session was the release I needed desperately, and I have to thank David for taking me there. I don't think I could have gone there with anyone else.

We had maybe an hour together and, as we unpicked my thoughts and feelings and he made sense of them for me, I could feel some of that cloud begin to lift. When I left David, I went back down the corridor to my room with my face a tear-streaked mess, hoping against hope George wouldn't be in. I hadn't the emotional energy left to explain myself to him at that moment. I felt exhausted. Thank God, he was out.

I went and lay on my bed. On the table next to it was a pen and the England notebook I used to jot down the game plans for match day. I turned to an empty page and started to write. What I wrote was pretty deep. This was it, word for word.

I felt nothing but guilt for achieving all I have, for seeming like I was the only one happy or having fun.

For it looks like my life just carries on as normal while others' fall apart.

When all that was a lie, I too was falling apart, broken and lost, driven on by the fact that if I stop, I, we, will all crumble.

At that time, I was the only one who could bring a smile or give the family hope.

I did it for them, not me. It was never for me.

By doing this, the game I once loved is now the game I hate.

Only, now I realize I wasn't selfish. I did bring them joy. I did the right thing.

On the opposite page I wrote some more, trying to move myself on.

How do I feel?

Relieved – it's not my fault.

I couldn't have done any more.

It's OK to achieve, have fun, without feeling guilty. I did the right thing.

They would be so proud. You are not selfish.

You did bring joy and hope.

They would have wanted you to carry on.

I don't need to feel like this any more.

Then I rang my wife and I read it to her. She was so happy that I'd been able to go to that place. I had bottled it all up and not shared how I felt inwardly with anyone, not even her. Or my brother. She said: 'You're going to feel so much better for that.' And I did.

Once I'd had the courage to be vulnerable, I was able to start to disconnect rugby from tragedy. I had more sessions with David at that World Cup.

My perspective shifted. Training became easier and I found a bit more joy in the sport again. I felt much more able to just accept rugby for what it is. When all is said and done, it is just a game. Even the World Cup. Just a series of games.

Had I not knocked on David Priestley's door, who knows where things would have ended up? I wasn't thinking rationally. Without those conversations, I just don't know how I'd have coped. I could still be sitting here now, not really understanding why I felt a seething resentment towards the game that had given me so much. It took David to bring it all out.

To this day, I still think I should have been picked against Argentina. But here's the thing. I wouldn't have been able to get to that place of self-awareness and understanding if I had been.

In a very personal sense, maybe that dispiriting walk with Steve in Le Touquet was for the best.

Mitch had a brilliant tournament. I had a couple of cameos off the bench against Japan and Chile, and a farewell send-off in the bronze medal match, but I remained, effectively, the third-choice scrum half for the 2023 World Cup. I wouldn't have chosen that path, but I dealt with it.

As for being introduced as England's most capped men's player, I'm getting better at looking people in the eye and accepting it.

But it's still a work in progress. And – I guess – so am I.

1

BUILDING BLOCKS

'I wasn't a naughty kid at school, but the sound of laughter was like a magnet for me. I liked to have fun wherever and whenever I could.'

So how did I manage to win 127 caps? How did I convince four different England coaches, with four very different outlooks on rugby, that I should be the one to wear the number 9 jersey for so long? For the answer to that, we have to go all the way back to the start of my life – to the undersized Norfolk farm kid who struggled to read and write.

An international rugby career presents many challenging situations. Taking on massive South Africans in the thin air of Loftus Versfeld, facing the haka at Eden Park, fronting up to Wales in Cardiff when every person in the stadium wants your blood – it's a life lived on the edge. Yet I can honestly say I never felt fear in any of those moments.

Ask me to write a few words on a whiteboard, though, and I'm terrified.

Standing up in front of teammates and verbally presenting tactics in a meeting isn't an issue. Talking through video clips with absolute detail and clarity, I can always deliver information in a way that they engage with and listen to. But try to get me to write up there? Not a chance. I would feel inadequate, uncomfortable and embarrassed.

Dyslexia does that to you.

Academically, I always found school really difficult because of it. Exams were always stressful because I didn't have the skill set to spell out certain words. While I had my way of writing things down that I understood, something I would go on to use in team meetings in later years, I always worried that if something was spelled so badly (and my work was), then the examiner would have no idea what I was trying to say.

Reading was also a problem for me. With the letters all mixed up, it would take me a lot longer to get through sentences than most kids. Growing up, I was put in the bottom set for English with some others who were in a similar boat and, when it came to reading out loud, it was a case of who was going to stand up and make a fool of themselves first. Sometimes, I would just suddenly hit a dead end. There'd be one word that would stop me in my tracks, usually one that was spelled weirdly or that started with a silent letter. If I couldn't sound it out, then I was done for. I was still trying to get through Biff and Chip aged fifteen.

My dad is dyslexic, and my brother is as well. Tom didn't get diagnosed initially. His reading issues were put down to a problem with his eyesight, so he was given these milk-bottle-bottom glasses that gave him banging headaches whenever he wore them. I remember there was a student from Hong Kong, Queenie, who joined his class with limited English and within two weeks could already spell better than him. By week three, Tom was copying Queenie's notes.

Our dyslexia was a real stumbling block for us both in the early years. If it hadn't been for the support we received at our school, it might have proved an insurmountable challenge.

Gresham's is a school in North Norfolk, set on a 200-acre estate, four miles from the sea. James Dyson, the inventor and industrialist, was educated there. Because it took boarders as well as day pupils, the intake included kids from all over the country, and from all sorts of different backgrounds too.

It was a public school, so we were lucky to have small class sizes and extra one-on-one tuition. One of my early influences was an amazing lady called Linda Rose, who helped me with my English. My God, she had her work cut out! But because of her, I ended up passing my GCSE with what must have been one of the lowest C grades possible. I also had a great history teacher called Mr Kinder, and his enthusiasm for the subject captivated me, but on the whole, I didn't enjoy being in the classroom. All I wanted to do was escape to the sports field – the place where all my struggles melted away, and I could properly prove my worth. It's funny though, because now I look back and I think that dyslexia actually helped me in becoming the rugby player I did.

I could always problem-solve. I think that was partly a product of having to be adaptable as a child; I had to figure out alternative ways around my difficulties in school. So often, the conventional way of doing things wasn't available to me, and I had to think out of the box. I don't know the science behind it, but I reckon the brain rewires itself a little when you are dyslexic. My son, who has it too, did a test with a question asking how he might fit an awkward sofa through a doorway space, and he scored amazingly. He could just see the solution really quickly.

I think there's something of that in my rugby. With thirty players on the field, rugby is a game of many moving parts. It's a puzzle that's always changing. Growing up, I could always see where the space was on the field and work out how to get the ball there in two moves instead of three. I just saw things differently to other players. Was dyslexia, which I always thought of as my curse, actually my superpower? Maybe.

Gresham's was only twenty minutes from where we lived on

the family farm, but somehow we managed to be late most mornings. My mum would be desperately trying to herd us into our increasingly battered red Audi A4 estate to get us there on time, but it was always touch and go.

Dad, in the meantime, would always be busy out at work on the farm. It was a mix of livestock and arable; we had cows and sheep at various times, and we had working sheepdogs as well. We also had a Jack Russell at one point – Roly. I don't know why, but this dog had a straight-up *vendetta* against my brother. Basically, any time Tom went near him, he would growl and go for him, which was obviously a great source of amusement to me.

The farm was a great environment to grow up in, with all that space available in which we could freely run around. My grandfather fashioned us some rugby posts out of broken and rusty irrigation pipes – being a farmer too, he didn't want to sacrifice any good ones. I'm pretty sure he didn't get the measurements right, though, because the crossbar seemed to be ridiculously high. A conversion was impossible until I was around thirteen – but hey, we effectively had our own pitch to play on. That was pretty handy if you had designs on becoming a rugby player.

As was having a dad who had played scrum half for Leicester and England.

Back in the days where Tigers scrum halves had letters on their backs rather than numbers, Nick Youngs was quite a player. So I'm told, anyway. I never saw him in the flesh. By the time I arrived, he had retired, so the only time I got to see him in action at Welford Road was during a veterans' game – and, being honest, by then all the players looked as if they had swapped training evenings for a night down the local pub and the fish and chip shop.

Still – he was good enough to play six times for his country and to be part of the England side that beat the All Blacks in 1983. You never would have known it from our house, though. There was no shrine to his achievements, no framed shirt on the wall. The only clue was in his office – a photo of him dive-passing the ball away in an England shirt. Dad was always very, very humble about his rugby, and never really talked about it himself. It was only when old teammates like Peter Winterbottom and Chris Butcher called round that Tom and I found out a bit more about his career.

So Dad wasn't a pushy rugby parent by any means. The total opposite, in fact. He did teach me how to pass off both hands – he obviously thought that skill might come in handy somewhere down the line – but for the most part he left me to develop at my own pace. He certainly didn't have me running up hills like the Vunipolas had to (in fairness, there weren't that many in Norfolk), nor did I spend my formative years in an elite changing room as Owen Farrell did with his dad at Wigan. Instead, when I think of my parents and our family, the first things that spring to mind are the love and laughter, rather than some hot-housing coaching environment. There was no sense that I was pre-programmed to follow in my dad's footsteps; I honestly think nurture had more to do with it than nature.

To succeed in international sport, you need many attributes – physical ones, for sure, but mental ones too. If you're not a competitor, you either don't survive very long, or you never make it in the first place. Luckily for me, growing up in an extended family like I did, I had to develop a competitive streak. Tom and I might have been the only two children under our roof, but the gang we rubbed along with was absolutely enormous.

My mum is one of six sisters. My poor grandfather kept trying to keep the family name (Hannant) alive; he got to six girls and then gave up! Every one of them had children – that meant an explosion of cousins on my mum's side. There are twenty-five first cousins in all and, of those, I'm the second youngest. Not only that, but I was small for my age. Very small.

A lot of my early interactions when it came to sport – or any competitive activities – were with all these older cousins, and there was absolutely no allowance made for age or size. We'd play rugby, football, hockey, British Bulldog, whatever – and I had to fight to survive. My grandparents lived at Barningham, a few miles away from us, and they had this lovely lawn that was basically our playground when we all got together during the holidays. The cousins, who called me Lenny for no better reason than it rhymed with Benny, liked to play this one game where we would stack ourselves on top of each other and build a sort of human pyramid. Five people would lie on the bottom one way, then four more across each other in the opposite direction, then three the other way, and so on. Right at the top would be Jake – the eldest cousin and the ringleader, like the mafia boss. He always put me at the bottom of the pile, which was akin to being pressed to death in medieval times.

The rules were that everyone had to grab hold of somebody else to link the whole heaving mass together and then, when the game started, everyone had to fight like hell to break free. If you managed to, then you raced to the finish line twenty metres away. The last-placed cousins would be put on the bottom in the next round. It was every child for himself. There was no sense of the older ones being gentle on the younger ones. Anything went.

These games could go on and on and there would inevitably be injuries. Run inside crying and you would be met with five aunts and your mother nattering away with a cup of tea in one hand

and a cigarette in the other. It was a Silk Cut fog in there, like a scene from *The Simpsons* with Marge's sisters, Patty and Selma Bouvier, puffing away. You would receive a cursory check-up and a 'there, there' but, basically, you'd be sent back out and told to get on with it. Between the wall of smoke and the tough love, the tears weren't usually worth it. So you'd opt to stay in the battle.

We also had the Norfolk coastline on our doorstep, and the cousins would get together there too on the sand at Sheringham Beach for mass games of anything. The same rules applied, i.e. none. You needed resilience to deal with those batterings. You had to be competitive. I reckon that, subconsciously, the desire and fight and all the inner essentials I would one day need to survive and thrive in Test rugby were being shaped in those rumbles.

It was an outdoor upbringing. My cousin Monty would come and stay for a couple of weeks during the summer holidays, and we would spend countless hours kicking a ball about together. Tom was more into helping Dad with the farm, but sometimes we would play one-against-one rugby together too.

Basically how that would unfold was that Tom would kick the ball out to me, I would catch it and take him on and, being little, quick and elusive, skin him. He would get so annoyed that, when it was his turn to receive the ball, he would just run straight at me and basically bulldoze me out of the way. He always had that natural farmer strength, even as a kid, and he was a lot bigger than me so he could hurt me very easily. Sometimes that happened and Tom got told off. We never physically fought – a result for me, I think, as I would have come off second best by a long way.

It was Tom who eventually got me into organized rugby, indirectly. A lot of my older male cousins had started playing locally at Holt Rugby Club, where one of my dad's best friends – a guy named Mike Bush – headed up the Sunday morning mini-rugby section. Dad wanted to start taking Tom down there but, aged five, I was still too young to play.

Dad decided to bring me along anyway. He enrolled me with the Under-6s and I ended up playing with the year above all the way through. I was the youngest and the tiniest but I loved it. The rugby was great – exhilarating, thrilling, free – but there was a whole lot more to it besides. It was like a family gathering, with all the cousins playing and the parents watching. The rugby would finish at twelve o'clock but we would all still be there a couple of hours later, running around outside, kicking a ball around, while the parents propped up the bar.

Eventually, we would head home to a Sunday roast that Mum had cooked, gorge ourselves on that and crash out in front of the fire.

Holt was a great community rugby club. It being Norfolk, there were lots of farmers, of course, but everyone else – from the postman to the butcher to the accountant to the tree surgeon – was there too. People from all different backgrounds. It just felt like a really welcoming place. I went back not long ago to watch my nephews play, and I instantly got that same warm feeling. I associate Holt with so many happy memories. It's a special place for me. I made friends for life there. James Knight was part of that first Holt team I joined, and he is still one of my best mates.

In a lot of ways, Holt was like any other local minis team in that it was a bit of a mish-mash. You had some kids who loved it and were good at it, some who loved it but didn't have a great deal of talent, and some kids who only did it because their parents just wanted them to do something on a Sunday. I remember one lad called Charlie, bless him, who would genuinely rather have been anywhere else. He used to wear every bit of protective kit possible, stand on the wing hoping not to get involved and drop the ball every time you chucked it to him.

I never minded the physical side of rugby – the cousin pile-ons had prepared me for that well enough – but the bit that really appealed was running with the ball. I wanted it in my hands all the time. Being so small, my point of difference had to be to move quickly and to step and I found I had a talent for that.

I soon realized that being good could have spin-offs too. One Sunday in the Under-9s, Mum offered me a chocolate try bonus. She said she would give me one of those really nice shell-shaped ones – Guylian seashells, I think they're called – for each try I scored in the two games we played. I managed thirteen so it was a decent payout.

A lot of us at Holt minis were into wrestling on the TV – WWF, as it was then. Triple H, 'Stone Cold' Steve Austin, all those guys. Mike Bush used to get so annoyed at our rugby games because it was all we would be talking about. Even at half-time. I remember him completely losing it before one game because we were all practising these wrestling moves on each other instead of paying attention. It was absolute chaos and Bushy couldn't get any control. He must have blown his whistle twenty times. Then he just said: 'That's it. You'll have to coach yourselves.' And he walked off into the clubhouse.

My initial reaction was: 'Brilliant, we can just carry on messing about.'

It took some maturity from James, who suggested we should probably go and apologize to Mike and ask him to come and coach us again, to get him back on board again. The wrestling stopped for a while after that.

The Sunday tournaments we played in were brilliant fun. Our biggest rivals were Braintree – we would always meet in the final and pretty much always end up drawing with them as well. We couldn't be separated.

When Dad came along to watch, he would stand on his own behind the posts rather than on the sideline where the other parents stood. People would want to chat to him, but I think he just enjoyed watching in peace. He would never shout anything during the game or try to influence what I was doing. If I wanted to talk about the game in the car on the way home, he would chat to me about it, but he would never initiate that conversation.

The only thing he might tell me was to pass a bit more to my teammates instead of going on one of my glory runs so they saw more of the ball. He wanted me to love rugby, yes, but because I loved it not because he loved it. You might have expected – with him being an ex-Tiger – that I would have gone along to Welford Road with him a few times as a kid, but I reckon we only went a couple of times when I was growing up.

I went to Twickenham to watch England more often than I did Leicester. The first time I went – to watch a Calcutta Cup game – I was awestruck by the sheer scale of the place. It was vast. Because Dad had played for England, we were allowed into the England Rugby Internationals Club room before the game, so I went around collecting autographs while Dad had a drink with his old mates. The game that really lit a spark inside was when New Zealand came to play. Seeing the haka in the flesh and feeling the electricity around the stadium as the England fans drowned it out was exhilarating.

It made me want to be out there one day.

As I grew older, rugby was starting to play a bigger and bigger part in my life. It was coming at me from all angles. Before I knew it, I was going to rugby training on a Monday, playing in a school fixture on Wednesday, training again on Thursday and then playing games on Saturday for school and Sunday with Holt. That was five times a week. But I couldn't get enough of it.

When it wasn't rugby in the flesh, it was *Jonah Lomu Rugby* on the PlayStation. And there was this old VHS I used to play over and over again – *Bill McLaren: The Famous Voice of Rugby* – in which he ran through some of his favourite players down the years.

Then there was the *Living with Lions* video, chronicling the 1997 tour to South Africa. That got some hammer too.

I used to absorb the Five Nations and Six Nations and the Tri Nations and Super Rugby from the southern hemisphere, and go out into the garden pretending to be Christian Cullen in a Hurricanes jersey. Then I would be Carlos Spencer in an Auckland Blues shirt. I was the easiest kid in the world to buy a present for, because all I wanted was rugby shirts. Every Christmas Auntie Lulu would get me a different one. One of my favourites was the France one that Émile Ntamack was wearing when Jonny Wilkinson upended him in Paris. I had loads. But what was really weird was that I never asked for an England shirt. Or a Leicester one.

I had a couple of great rugby coaches at prep school in Richard Brearley and Simon Worrall who, like Bushy, nurtured the talent I had and helped me to express it. Before school games on a Saturday, Mr Brearley used to gather us in his geography room and put on these old tapes of the Barbarians playing. We would be watching this vintage footage with no clue who these ancient players were. But the passion and enthusiasm for the game that he had was easy to recognize – he would deliver these brilliant Churchillian speeches that we loved.

At school, I would play at outside centre, which gave me the space to use my speed. Because I was quick, I also shone at athletics, which we did during the summer term. When I was ten years old, I was entered into the 400 metres at the junior regional championships, trying to win a place in the national finals. It was at a proper athletics track with a small stand beside it where all the parents were sitting watching.

Each event had two heats and I was running in the second heat. I was nervous because there was a lot on the line – the top three would go through to the nationals. Big stakes. Nerves can affect people in different ways, and for me on that day they manifested themselves in an urgent need to wee. 'Excuse me,' I said to one of the grown-ups organizing the race. 'Can I go to the toilet?'

The official said that I could but if I missed the race that was on me. It was a dilemma. I didn't want to miss my big moment, so I thought I had better just hang on. Unfortunately, the first heat took an age to get under way for some reason. We were left waiting for more than ten minutes. So by that point, I was absolutely bursting.

Finally, the race was called, but all I could think about as I walked towards the start line was my bladder.

'I need the toilet so, so badly. I'm just going to have to sprint this thing then just run to a bush,' I thought to myself. I was in lane one and my mum and Tom were nearby in the stand as we went down to our marks. I lifted up on 'get set' and then on 'go' I went.

Literally.

I just started wetting myself! I could feel it running down my leg. A puddle was forming on the start line as I remained there, frozen. It was at that point that Tom – helpful as always – stood up and shouted: 'Oh my God, he's pissed himself!' Humiliated.

I set off and ran like the wind – as quickly as I could in my desperate desire to get off that track. It was that, rather than my athletic ability, which took me to victory. Mum was there to meet me at the finish line and help me through it, but I've never quite lived that down with Tom.

I did actually win the prep school national 100 metres one year, but for some reason he talks less about that race than the pissy one.

I also played hockey at school in one of the winter terms. Auntie Lulu was an England international and, while I wasn't quite that good, I liked it. I did manage to play Norfolk representative schools hockey once. I think the exposure to hockey was beneficial for my rugby, certainly in terms of the position I ended up playing. In hockey, you are bent over, playing the ball with your stick while simultaneously trying to scan the peripheral picture. It's exactly what a scrum half does at a ruck. Your head is down but you've got to have a mental image of where there's space on the field and where the ball – or you – should be heading.

You'd imagine if I could play hockey then I'd be able to play cricket. I couldn't. I couldn't bowl, I couldn't bat, and I didn't like the thought of being whacked by a hard red ball. I made it to the dizzy heights of the C team, which basically consisted of all the kids who were terrible at it.

We only had about two fixtures a year, which was two too many in my book. There was one memorable incident when we were playing Uppingham. I was messing about in the slips with my mate Charlie, who was wicket-keeper, trying to make the best of it, when this guy came into bat for them. He asked for middle and leg, scraped his guard with his boot and then proceeded to do a load of gardening, prodding the pitch with his bat for ages like he was a Test player.

I thought: 'Does he think he's Joe Root or something? He's number six in the C team. What is he doing? We're all useless – that's why we're here.' So as the bowler ran up and released the ball, I shouted: 'Don't miss it!' just as it left his hand – which this Root wannabe promptly did. And he was bowled first ball.

Well, there was uproar.

The square leg umpire was one of our teachers and he bellowed at me: 'Youngs, come here.' I went over: 'Yes, sir?'

'That was absolutely unacceptable. Not in the spirit of cricket. He will carry on batting, and you can go and score for the rest of the game.' Charlie was in tears of laughter behind the stumps as I was dispatched from the field.

I was quite happy with the arrangement. Filling in the dot balls in the scorebook was definitely an improvement on having to play, as far as I was concerned. But I had to go see the headmaster on the Monday to explain myself and apologize for my unsportsmanlike behaviour.

So cricket was never my thing.

I wasn't a naughty kid at school, but the sound of laughter was like a magnet for me. I liked to have fun wherever and whenever I could. I can't say the teachers would always appreciate that.

I remember rehearsing for a play once in our drama lesson. I had to lie on the ground face down and then pop up and say my lines. Charlie came out onto the stage and delivered my cue, but I had an attack of the giggles and couldn't move for laughing. All you could see was my shoulders going up and down as this wave of laughter washed over me. Charlie delivered his line about five times, but there was nothing I could do. It was a proper corpsing. The drama teacher was just watching on, simmering.

If I was never going to make an actor, then there wasn't much hope for me as a farmer either.

While Tom loved everything about it, I wasn't interested in it at all. There was one incident when I was about eleven that summed up our contrasting attitudes.

Dad asked my brother and I to pull out the wild oats that were growing among the crop in one of the fields. He dropped us off in the morning, told us to clear the field and said he would pick us up at lunchtime. It was back-breaking work, walking up and down the lines, bending down every time you spotted a strand and pulling it out, but Tom went off like a man possessed. Soon I was fifty metres behind him. Then eighty metres. Then a hundred metres.

It was a really nice morning and, in the end, I just thought, 'Bollocks to this', and lay down in the sunshine, allowing the warmth to wash over me. As Tom marched on into the distance, I fell asleep. Unfortunately, Dad decided to check in on how we were doing mid-morning while I was kipping. When he turned up, Tom had done pretty much the whole field on his own and I was happily enjoying a siesta.

Dad just burst out laughing.

Another time, Dad – who by now was painfully aware of my limitations – gave me the job of topping. For any non-farmers (like me), topping is basically grass-cutting big fields with a glorified lawnmower on the back of the tractor. It's an idiot-proof job – or so he thought.

Everything started off OK, and I was going up and down the field on the tractor without a hitch, when in front of me this massive mound of soil came into view. I had the choice of driving around it or over it. Big decision. I turned around, looked out of the back of the tractor cab and saw the huge blades behind me. 'Those things will just chew that mound up and splatter the soil everywhere, no problem', I thought. It turned out they didn't. And there was a problem. The blades got stuck in the mound, there was a horrible screeching noise and suddenly there was smoke everywhere.

I did 1,800 quids' worth of damage in that incident.

'Why didn't you just go around it?' Dad asked afterwards. It was a reasonable question. Then, when he eventually gave me another chance at the topping, I managed to get the tractor stuck down a verge and needed towing out.

Basically, I was shocking with any sort of machinery.

Dad only ever turned to me when he was desperate. One year, he was short-handed for the sugar beet carting (ferrying the beets away from the field, in other words), and he called me in to lend a hand. He talked me through the process very carefully. I had to drive a tractor with a trailer behind it. My task was to pull the tractor up parallel to the harvester so the sugar beet could be dropped into the trailer and then, when it was full, drive off with the full load.

'Whatever you do, though, don't hit the front of the beet harvester with the tractor. The last thing we want is for that to be damaged,' he warned me. 'No problem, Dad,' I said confidently. 'Leave it to me.'

I put the radio on in the cab and waited my turn to load up. When it came, I pulled in perfectly. Like Lewis Hamilton coming in for a pit stop. Nice and parallel. Spot on. Into the trailer poured the sugar beet . . . I was loading like a champion. When it was full, all I had to do was drive off and deliver my precious cargo.

That was when things went wrong. I made to pull to the left thinking, for some reason, that the guy in the beet harvester – Ian – would turn right. But he didn't. He turned left too. And we collided. I drove straight into the front of him with a horrible thud. Exactly what Dad had told me not to do.

I had two options. Either get out and face up to my mistake like a man, and cop a face-full of fury from Ian, who was going mad in the beet harvester cab. Or drive off and hide.

I took the second option.

I scuttled away with my trailer full of beet and parked in the woods for an hour while the storm blew through. When I eventually went back, everything had calmed down, so it had been a smart move really. The front of the harvester was damaged but was fixable. It could have been worse.

In the end, the only job my dad trusted me to do on the farm was potato grading. This was basically the lowest role going. My job was to pick out the rotten ones on the conveyor belt and lob them away. That was it.

I will essentially go down as one of the worst farmers that the Youngs family has ever produced. I was absolutely incompetent.

If it hadn't been for the actual farming, living on a farm would have been perfect. For one thing, it enabled Tom and me to build our own race track. There was a local garage up the road, which used to scrap cars that had failed their MOTs, and Dad decided he would take some of these bangers for us to drive around the farm.

Jimmy the Jeep was our first banger, and he lived in the potato shed. We used a cultivator to make a track in the field to speed around in Jimmy. We wouldn't go on the public road, obviously – I was thirteen – but because the field ran parallel to one, we would sometimes race cars that were on it. We had lots of fun with that, although we were only ever allowed one banger at a time, to stop us from racing each other.

Sometimes we would drive off into the woods. I remember taking my cousin Bruce for a spin one time, losing control and ending up in this boggy ditch. The banger was on its side and there was water seeping in. It was balanced precariously, so it was a bit of a situation. Bruce wasn't keen on me moving and unbalancing it, but I wasn't going to stay there. I pulled myself out, and fortunately he got out in one piece too.

My worst scrape growing up was actually on a BMX bike rather than in a banger. I got whacked by a car near the farm, was knocked a fair distance and landed in a hedge. I was pretty bruised after that one. My underpants suffered collateral damage too – I crapped myself in mid-air. I don't know if the pain or the embarrassment was worse. I ended up waddling back to the house like John Wayne after a full day's filming on horseback.

Correction, the worst scrape could have been one Christmas when I set myself on fire. I was walking past a floating candle in the house. It was really hot in the lounge and Dad had opened up the side door to let some air in. A gust of wind caught the tail of my shirt and sent it into the candle flame. I panicked and ran when I saw it on fire but that made things worse as the flames spread up my back. Fortunately, the family were able to rip the shirt off, but I ended up spending the night in hospital. It was less Christmas, more Burns Night.

Ultimately, though, mine was a carefree and happy upbringing, with the only clouds around my schoolwork.

When I was fifteen, I predicted my school report was going to be a particularly bad one. It just was. I knew it. This was a concern, so I decided to do something about it. The school posted the reports out to our home addresses, so every day, when the postman came, I would run to the front door and intercept the mail, flicking through the letters in search of the report.

When it finally landed, I was ahead of the game. I took it away before my parents had the chance to see it, tore it open and read the whole report through. It was as bad as I had expected. I thought: 'They can't see this. Any parent who spends their hard-earned money on a private education for their son and reads this would go bananas.'

So I burnt it.

We had an oil drum at the bottom of the lawn that was used to get rid of rubbish, so I chucked it in there, followed it up with a lit match and watched it go up in flames. A couple of weeks went by, and Mum and Dad kept asking about the missing report. They rang the school, who assured them it had definitely been sent. They kept on at me asking if I was sure I hadn't seen the report and in the end I just cracked.

At dinner one night I announced to them that I had something to tell them. 'My report has been sent. I've seen it, read it, and I thought that you wouldn't enjoy reading it, so I burnt it,' I told them. Now, obviously, most parents would react negatively to this piece of news. It would be understandable in the circumstances.

But Mum and Dad's reaction was to burst out laughing. That's my parents for you. They are laid back and lovely. I think the greatest compliment I can give them is that I'd like to bring my kids up the way they brought up Tom and me. If I can look back and say I've done that, I'll be a very happy man.

My mum and dad make a good pair. Mum (Patricia – or Trot, as everyone calls her) is always up for a good time. Our kids call her Granny Cuckoo, which is about right. My dad is different – less bonkers, but he loves a laugh all the same.

I guess I adopted some of their same take on life; that the best way to live it is with a big smile on your face. Over the course of my career, I had so many teammates who were perplexed at how

I could be laughing and joking minutes before a big game, when others had their eyeballs lodged somewhere in the back of their heads, but that's just the way I was brought up to be.

By the time I was a teenager, rugby was starting to get more serious, even if I wasn't. Norfolk was in Leicester's academy catchment area and Tom had already been taken on. My career took its first significant shift with a move to North Walsham. Walsham and Holt had always had this rivalry, so it felt a little bit like joining the enemy, but I had no choice in the matter.

When Holt had moved up to fifteen-a-side games, we were struggling for numbers. We were fine for the first year, but then some of the team started moving away to other schools and others just stopped playing. We'd go to away games and have to borrow players, and of course, we were always given the crappest ones, or they would say they didn't have any spare, so we just had to play with twelve and things like that. Before we knew it, we had only ten players left. At that stage the decision was taken, with heavy hearts, to call time on the team.

It was no one's fault, just circumstances. It wasn't fair to have to keep on borrowing players. Those who were left had to find a new club. For James Knight and me, that meant North Walsham.

The coach was a guy called Bob Barringer, and his son Henry was the captain. In one of our first games together for our new team, James made a big impression by scoring four tries. He was the best player on the pitch by a mile. We won the game pretty easily and Bob got all the players together in a huddle at the end and congratulated us.

'Great game, Walsham, well done everyone,' he said. 'Man of the Match this week . . .' James was preparing his best modest smile . . . 'Goes to my son, Henry.' James, in disbelief, flapped his arms like a penguin. 'What? Were you watching the same game, Bob? I scored four tries and you're giving Man of the Match to your son? Are you being serious?'

He just wasn't having it. He was right, it was a total injustice. Blatant favouritism, it seemed to me. Overall, though, Bob was a lovely guy – as was Henry, for that matter. They made us feel very welcome.

James and I were a bit of a double act in the backline. There was one game where we were playing a team that wasn't very good, and everyone had scored a try except me. I was playing fly half and James was the outside centre. We had an attacking scrum, so I told him I was going out onto the wing and asked him to move to 10 and put a crossfield kick on the money for me. Which he did, and I scored to complete the set.

James was a really good player, and our shared dream of making it big together in rugby was slowly crystallizing. We had been picked for Leicester's Elite Player Development Group – the EPDG – which fed into the Tigers academy and were training with them on Monday nights. We were invited up to Leicester for trials.

I always imagined that we'd go on to make it together. I felt we were meant to. And I remember the elation of being told afterwards that I was in. But that feeling was wiped away when James rang to tell me that he hadn't been picked.

I was so upset. I lay on my bed and cried. We'd had this shared ambition, this dream, but only one of us was going to go on the adventure. I remember being absolutely gutted for him.

James genuinely couldn't have been happier for me. He turned out to be a rock for me during my career, the most supportive mate I could ever have wished for. Every sportsman needs a true friend they can rely on, and James was invaluable to me. I would ring him after a good game, I would ring him after a bad game, and he would always just give it to me straight.

A great guy.

Joining Leicester's academy was a big deal for me, obviously, but Dad made sure I didn't get above my station with the news.

He knew how rugby worked, and he told me all it meant was that I had got my foot in the door, and that I shouldn't think I had made it. He said I had been given an opportunity to train with a good team under good coaches, but it was up to me to make the most of it.

I got it. I knew nothing was written in the stars. I felt like I had to do everything in my power to make this work out. I would be leaving a great school, my friends, my family and a part of the world I loved, so I needed this to be a success.

I was all in.

2

TIGER CUB

*'I guess when your head is on the block
you are more wary about picking
an untried youngster.'*

Things happened very quickly for me at Leicester. So quickly, in fact, that I was told off for spraying victory champagne at Twickenham after we'd won the Premiership final, because I was only seventeen and legally too young to drink it.

I had arrived at the club with the Tigers having not won a trophy for four years. This was a famine for the best-supported club in the English game, after the glory years around the turn of the millennium. But it wasn't really any of my business as an academy kid. I was just there to learn the ropes as a junior professional.

I had signed a £12,000-a-year contract. Not a king's ransom, but a grand a month was more than enough for me. The idea that someone – not just someone, *Leicester Tigers* – was actually paying me to play this sport I loved so much was a joy.

I was still a kid really – all my mates were still in school – but here I was living the dream. All the same, being a professional rugby player did not excuse me from education. There was a guy at the club called Mike Harrison, who was in charge of making sure we kept on doing something academically as well as playing rugby. It was a precarious career, after all.

At first, I was sent to a place in Loughborough that was full of Nottingham Forest and Derby County football academy lads who basically couldn't give a monkey's. It was crap, and I told Mike I didn't want to do it. I was quickly packed off to Wyggeston and Queen Elizabeth I College, which was a state sixth-form college in Leicester.

There was nothing wrong with the place, really. But it was very different from the sheltered existence I'd been used to at a rural public school. I'd never seen a TV wheeled in with a padlock on it before. The hammers in design and technology classes were chained down too.

I couldn't believe that someone was likely to grab them and use them as weapons, but possibly that was just me being a bit naive. I liked it in Leicester, but after the safe bubble of North Norfolk and its slow-paced lifestyle two and a half hours away, it seemed like another world.

It didn't help that I couldn't get back home very often, because I couldn't drive. At least not on a public road. Even when I turned seventeen, I didn't pass my driving test for ages. I had no parent nearby to take me out to practise, so it was all driving instructor lessons. And I had picked up such bad habits from driving the banger cars that what should have happened in double-quick time just did not.

With Tom at Leicester too, Mum and Dad were empty-nesters ahead of schedule. That was definitely a very difficult adjustment – for my mum in particular. She always says she never got a chance to put her finishing touches on us both.

There were some simple things I hadn't had a chance to learn before I left. For instance, I'd never been on a bus before. Then, all of a sudden, I was living with my brother and another academy lad – Ben Pienaar – near the Tigers training ground in Oadby, so getting to college meant navigating the public transport system into Leicester.

There was a stop three minutes away from the house, and I had been told the number of the bus I needed to catch. I got on OK, but when I sat down I suddenly thought to myself: 'How do I know where it stops?' It sounds ridiculous, I know, but it was only when I saw someone press the stop button that I worked it out. I didn't know how many stops there were on the road to college and I was worried that, if I left it too long, I would end up over-shooting it. So, knowing what a stop button was now, I pressed it pretty much straight away. I ended up miles short of where I should have got off, and had to walk a further forty-five minutes to get to college.

There was other stuff too. I remember being given a cheque and taking it to the bank, but not having a clue what to do with it. I had to ring my dad and ask him to tell me how to pay it in. I was so badly lacking in life skills. Fortunately, my brother and Pienaar were OK at cooking, or I might have starved to death.

There wasn't much of me at that point. The first time I stood on a pair of scales at Leicester, I was only 76 kg. And the academy was a step up to what I was used to physically. If you were seven-teen, you'd be playing against nineteen-year-olds who had been on gym programmes for the previous two years, so they were maturing into adulthood.

Leicester's chief scout then was Dusty Hare, the former Eng-land international full back. He had come to watch me play in an Eastern Counties Under-16s game as a fly half, and he liked the amount of time I seemed to have on the ball. He told Simon Cohen, the club's head of rugby operations at the time, that he had to sign me.

Playing fly half against my own age group was one thing, but by now I was also starting to play men's A League rugby, and playing at number 10 put me in the firing line of some pretty chunky opposition ball carriers. I was tried in a few different positions – 9, 10, and even 15 sometimes – but the decision was taken quite early on that I should concentrate on playing at scrum half. There was a question mark over whether I had the build to survive the collisions elsewhere, and scrum half was one of the few positions where I could be a bit more protected. It also just so happened that the first team had suffered an injury crisis at scrum half at that time, so I found myself called in to train with the first team to make up the numbers.

That really was a leap.

I used to have to do the sessions with the forwards. What an education that was. Suddenly, I was rubbing shoulders with these amazing pros who had won World Cups and had great careers. Leicester at the time was very much the kind of environment where you only spoke when you were spoken to, and otherwise just put your head down and worked hard – but, that said, the senior players were welcoming.

Guys like Lewis Moody, Geordan Murphy and Benny Kay were really good to me – even Julian White, who was a scary guy. They had such a wealth of knowledge. I was like a sponge soaking it all in. There were so many things that I picked up – how to direct players at a defensive maul, how to manipulate lineouts, timing when to play the ball away from a scrum: stuff I had barely even thought about.

Benny would teach me to take the ball on the move from a lineout, Martin Corry would advise me where I should stand to give room for a number 8 pick-up, Moodos would let me in on little tricks to win breakdown penalties. If a scrum had collapsed, the front-row boys told me to put the ball in anyway. Why? To give the referee the impression that you are wanting to scrum so it couldn't have been your side that had caused the problem. They were like my lecturers at rugby university.

Except there were more fights than at university.

Training was mental then, when I think back. We had double sessions on a Tuesday and Thursday, when the forwards would basically scrum, maul, and beat each other up in the morning before we trained again as a team in the afternoon. The director of rugby, who oversaw the programme, was Pat Howard, but the shaven-headed training ground sergeant major was Richard Cockerill.

Cockers was about a bee's dick away – at any given time – from exploding at you for no particular reason.

He had been the B in Leicester's famous ABC front-row club, a fiery hooker who would never take a step backwards. He brought that same ominous rumble of a volcano ready to erupt to the training ground. There would often be a scrap on his watch, which he would do a whole lot of nothing to stop.

It wouldn't take much for the forwards to kick off. They didn't really need a reason. It was just what they did – upholding a proud Leicester tradition that went back to Dean Richards, Martin Johnson, and before then even. If there wasn't a fight in training, people thought that we weren't going to play well. It was like a reassurance for everyone that we were up for that weekend's game.

That's what made Leicester *Leicester*. It was in the DNA.

There was no chance of drifting in those early months. This was a real hothouse environment, and my standards had to be high all the way through the sessions with those guys. The training was of such high quality and intensity compared to what I had been used to.

Cockers liked to do this drill where one player would carry into a tackle bag held by a teammate, drive for five metres, and then present the ball on the floor. One time I ended up as tackle-bag holder to the giant Seru Rabeni – one hundred-odd kilos of flailing dreads and Fijian muscle.

But it wasn't going as expected. Seru was running into the bag, but it was hardly going anywhere. There was sweat pouring off him and he was grunting and groaning, but every time he collided with it he would just slide to the ground. He looked as if he was dying out there.

Cockers was exasperated.

'What the fuck's going on, Seru?' he said. 'Come on, get up Seru, go again. You should be smashing him. It's only Lenny.' (My Norfolk nickname had travelled with me to the Midlands.)

Seru just lay there. 'I cannot, Richard,' he gasped. 'I cannot get up.'

Cockers wasn't having any of that. He put his arms under each of Seru's armpits and scooped him up like an overgrown toddler who had fallen over. He chucked the ball in his gut and literally launched him back into me, like he was being fired out of a cannon. Seru hit the bag and just flopped to the floor again.

A fuming Cockers blew his whistle and announced that we would have thirty seconds of recovery and then it would be on to small-sided games of touch rugby instead.

Well, this was manna from heaven to Seru.

What a transformation. It was like the bloke had wolfed down twenty-five carb gels and sixteen Lucozades. He instantly recovered, and was up stepping, offloading, and doing the full Fijian thing. A minute before, he had been dead. The man just lived for playing with the ball in his hands.

I could see where he was coming from. I'd say I had a very

similar mindset. It wasn't that I was lazy, it was just there were some aspects of training that totally failed to push my buttons. I didn't mind training, but with a ball – not conditioning. I might have been quick, but ask me to run shuttles and I'd be pretty unimpressive. It was only when I was put into a game situation with a ball that I came alive.

I also had a really bad intolerance to lactic acid build-up and regularly threw up after conditioning sessions. The only player who suffered worse than me was Tom Croft. The number of times I saw him lying on the ground looking green or hanging over the balcony at the training centre, moaning and groaning, was unreal.

As for the gym, I just didn't like it. I understood that I had to be robust enough to play at the professional level – and I enjoyed sniping and taking on people around the fringes, and that meant going up against bigger men in those areas. So I knew I needed to be strong enough to shrug people off and wriggle out of tackles, and you couldn't do that unless you had some shape. But I didn't like it.

I did a one-on-one gym programme with one of the club's strength and conditioning guys, Alex Martin, to bulk up. But as soon as I'd built myself up to the level I needed to be at, my desire for lifting weights fell off a cliff. There were about three exercises I could tolerate. I enjoyed doing a squat. I enjoyed doing a back squat. And I enjoyed doing a pull-down, but that was it. The rest, I couldn't have cared less about.

Leicester had another strength and conditioning coach called David Cripps, and he used to get so frustrated with me, because I would manage to do three reps with a certain weight one week then, totally unmotivated, would only squeeze out half a rep with the same weight a week later. It would infuriate him.

He would ask my brother: 'How do I get Ben engaged in the gym?' And Tom would shrug and say: 'It's just not his thing.'

Tom, who was much more compact and powerful than me, was into it. But it wasn't for me. By the latter stage of my career, I had pretty much signed out. I hardly did any weights after the age of twenty-eight.

The training ground set-up at Oadby featured an academy changing room, and two other changing rooms in the main building for use by the first team squad. One of these changing rooms was a decent spot, but it was reserved for club legends and senior internationals, and access was on an invitation-only basis. The other one was nicknamed The Dungeon, for reasons that soon became obvious. This space – although there wasn't much of it – was for your rank-and-file club players. As a new squad member, this was where I had to move at the start.

It was very hierarchical. Even if you were an All Black with a bunch of international caps, you would have to start day one of your Tigers career in The Dungeon. You'd be promoted into the senior players' room pretty quickly, usually, but everyone started in the same place. The exception to the international fast lane was Jim Hamilton who, when he was capped by Scotland, was told he had to get to fifty caps first before he could move up – because, on the Tigers currency market, fifty Scottish caps equated to one English cap.

The Dungeon was a bit like the inside of a Mumbai commuter train, but you learned to love it to the point where you never wanted to leave by the end. After my first England cap, it took me a few seasons to move up to the senior changing room, but it was a sad day when I finally went. We had such a laugh in that hell-hole. The young lads kept you young because they'd be the ones who always had the best stories from the weekend.

Anyway, the rule was that – if you were a Dungeon dweller – you weren't allowed into the other changing room without express permission. One day, in that first season, after staying out to do some kicking practice, I found a pair of boots that had been left out on the field. I knew that they belonged to one of the international lads so, thinking I would helpfully return them to their owner, I scooped them up and took them inside.

The first door off to the right along the corridor in the changing area was The Dungeon. Three metres beyond that, on the left-hand side, was the door to the big dogs' changing room. I walked past The Dungeon and pushed open the door to the senior players' dressing room.

Honestly – before I could set foot inside the door, or even get a word out, about six rolls of tape had been lobbed at my head, water had been squirted in my face and several pairs of boots had been flung at me. 'GET OUT, GET OUT, GET OUT', yelled these guys who had all been so helpful to their young scrum half out on the training field half an hour earlier.

The door was slammed in my face.

Outside, wiping myself down, I wondered what had just happened. 'You knock', a voice from inside told me.

So, very hesitantly, I did. The door slowly opened. 'What's the matter, Lenny? What can we help you with?'

I was so confused! A moment ago, they had gone all Fergie/Beckham on me, and now here they were being polite once more.

'Err, one of the lads left his boots outside', I said. 'I've just come to return them.'

'Oh yes, those belong to Julian White. He sits there. Come in and just put them on his peg.'

I looked around at the faces in there, Graham Rowntree, Benny Kay, Martin Corry, Geordan Murphy, trying to read their expressions. Nothing. I edged into the room, bracing myself for the next assault, then padded softly across it with the boots in my hand. I placed the boots down carefully and walked back out, scanning for trouble all the while. There was none. That was it. Boots returned. Mission accomplished.

All it took was a knock and a granting of permission and you could cross the threshold. You just had to know the rules of engagement.

Because I was needed with the first team, Leicester soon offered to rip up my academy contract and hand me a better one to reflect the fact that I was training full time. It wasn't something Leicester normally did. They usually waited until you had done two years in the academy and then they made a decision on whether to keep you or let you go.

It meant that I never did complete my sixth-form studies. I was fine with that. I was happy to throw all my eggs into one basket, to forget the qualifications and go for it. My parents didn't try to stop me.

We were competing on three fronts that season, but our resources at scrum half were stretched. Scott Bemand had suffered a long-term injury, which left Harry Ellis, Frank Murphy and me. Ordinarily, that would have meant Harry and Frank with me in the shadows, but the games were piling up as the season reached its climax.

Having won the EDF Energy Cup with a victory over the Ospreys in the final in April 2007, we were fighting for the league title, and in Europe too, so Pat Howard had to juggle his resources. Our penultimate league match of the regular season at Bristol was sandwiched in between a Heineken Cup semi-final against Llanelli, and our last Premiership game at home against Wasps. Pat made the call to rest Harry at Ashton Gate and put me on the bench to cover Frank. I got on for the last ten minutes, which earned me the record of being Leicester's youngest Premiership player – until Ben White broke it eight years later.

Harry was back for the Wasps game, and that should have been that for me for that season, but a week later he hurt his knee really badly in the play-off semi-final against Bristol. Frank was promoted to start the final against Gloucester, and suddenly I found myself on the bench for Twickenham. It was crazy.

In training that week, we were running through one move where I had to pass the ball to Alesana Tuilagi, and I chucked an absolute pie out to him. Because he was so good, he scooped it off his toes and played on like nothing was wrong, but then he came up to me afterwards and said: 'Brother, do you want me to come a bit closer?' He was wanting to help. 'No,' I replied. 'I'm just a bit nervous, that's all.'

In truth, I felt way out of my depth.

We travelled down on the bus the day before the game, and the senior players made a point of giving me a special seat to sit in to make me feel comfortable. It was basically one row in front of the toilet, so not exactly the prime spot, but it was still a gesture of inclusion, a hint that they weren't totally pissed off at having a wet-behind-the-ears kid in the squad.

Warming up, Twickenham felt even bigger than it had done when I had been in the stands as a spectator with my dad. It felt like the place might swallow me up. Taking the short walk from the dressing room down the tunnel to the pitch, the whole stadium slowly revealed itself. First the lower tier, then the middle and finally, as we walked out, the top tier. The stadium just seemed to go up and up into the sky.

And the pitch was huge.

We cruised that final 44–16, largely thanks to Alesana, who was unplayable. Because we were so far clear in the closing stages, Pat decided he would put me on for the last eight minutes. He didn't have to do that, and I was really grateful to him but, honestly, I felt like a bit of a fraud when we went up to get our medals. I mean, how much had I really contributed to us lifting the trophy? Nothing.

The day ended back in Norfolk at a friend's eighteenth birthday party, thanks to a lift home from my parents. My mates could hardly compute that I had been playing in front of 60,000 people at Twickenham earlier in the day. To be honest, I felt exactly the same way.

We didn't manage the treble – Wasps beat us in the Heineken Cup final the week afterwards – but as a start to life at Leicester, and to professional rugby, it was pretty spectacular.

Pat Howard left at the end of my first season to return to his native Australia and the club appointed Marcelo Loffreda as his successor. He had done a great job with Argentina since taking charge in 2000 and had coached them to their first victory over England at Twickenham. He was finishing with the Pumas after the World Cup in the autumn of 2007, so in the meantime Cockers took temporary charge. He gave me a couple of starts during that period. I remember Richard Hill buying a dummy from me against Saracens at Vicarage Road, which – given he was a World Cup winner – was a bit of a wow moment for me. Although, in fairness, I think Hilly's knees must have been knackered by then.

But, when Loffreda eventually arrived, after guiding Argentina to their highest finish of third at the tournament, the opportunities dried up. Marcelo was actually keen for me to go back to studying again. One of my few appearances under him was against Toulouse at Welford Road in the Heineken Cup in December 2007 when Frank got knocked out. I was fully expecting just to sit on the bench all game, but Marcelo had to throw me on.

I've always had a thing about Toulouse – the jersey, the glamour, the style – so to suddenly be on the same field as French stars like Fabien Pelous, Yannick Jauzion, Thierry Dusautoir, Yannick Nyanga, Vincent Clerc – and an All Black scrum half in Byron Kelleher – felt surreal. I was just trying to survive in their company. That was one of the few times in my rugby career when I looked around me and just felt starstruck.

We won that game, but Toulouse had their revenge the following week in France, and we bombed out of Europe in the group stages.

We only just scraped into the Premiership play-offs, too, and although we made the final, we lost to Wasps at Twickenham.

It was clear it wasn't working under Marcelo. It wasn't a big surprise when he was sacked at the end of the 2007–8 season. He had done great things with the Argentina national team and there were big expectations surrounding his arrival, but unfortunately he didn't seem to understand the culture of the club at all. The senior players weren't impressed with him and, once you get into that situation at a club, you know a head coach is on dodgy ground.

Leicester appointed the South African Heyneke Meyer as his replacement for 2008–9, but he was only in post for a few months before he had to return to South Africa for personal reasons. Heyneke did do one amazing thing, though, in his short time at the club – at least for Tom and me. He picked both of us to start an EDF Energy Cup tie at Bath in October.

Tom and I had played some A League games together already,

including one at Welford Road that proved memorable. Tom hit this perfect spiral kick in the warm-up, right off the laces, which managed to strike an elderly fan on the head, poleaxing her. Tom was mortified and rushed over to apologize as the paramedics treated the patient.

But the Bath tie was significant as being the first Leicester first team game we had played together. Dad trailed down to The Rec from Norfolk to watch a fine Tigers win, which included a try for me on what was a proud day for the family.

When Heyneke left, the Tigers board took the plunge and put Cockers in charge. It was a bit like handing an arsonist a box of matches, but it turned out to be an inspired appointment, one that saw Leicester become serial winners again. Here's the thing: if you cut Cockers in half, you'd see Tiger stripes – he is Leicester through and through – and he thrived on the old-school mentality of the place. In fact, he drove a lot of it.

We were only allowed to wear black boots. That was a big thing for Cockers. It was as if any departure from this rule would mean the whole ethos of the club would be lost; the walls would come crashing down.

I must have been feeling particularly brave one day because I turned up for training in a pair of white and black boots – and, being honest, they were more white than black.

I was practising my goal-kicking with Paul Burke – a champion of a bloke who invested a lot of time in me. Anyway, I was kicking with Paul when Cockers spotted the boots. 'You better be fucking good wearing those,' he grunted to me. The kick I was about to take was from the sideline, but I struck it perfectly and over it went. I turned to look at Cockers with a 'what-do-you-think-of-that?' expression on my face.

He just glared at me.

A few of us did break him down on the boots in the end, but it took a while. His tolerance for deviation from this uncompromising approach was low. He never really lost that front-row mentality. I reckon – of all the things I did at Leicester – the proudest I've ever seen Cockers of me was when I was suspended for punching Jamie Gibson against London Irish.

Jamie Gibson's basic role in rugby, it seemed, was to spoil the game – he would do anything to make it worse. On this occasion, he tackled me about three seconds after I had passed the ball, and then he lay on top of me so I couldn't get up. I ended up losing my head a bit, caught him with a knee and threw a punch at him. Dean Richards, the referee, just gave a penalty, but I was cited after the game and suspended for a week.

It was the only ban of my career but it didn't bother Cockers one bit.

Cockers seemed more reluctant to pick me when he was the top man than he had been when he was a caretaker coach. I guess when your head is on the block you are more wary about picking an untried youngster. It's easier to go with someone you feel you can trust. Also, maybe because things had happened really quickly for me, I think he felt that he had to keep me grounded. He had no need to worry on that score, though. I had some really good people around me who would have made sure I stayed focused. But maybe Cockers felt that if he gave me an inch, I'd try to take a mile.

I was with the team every weekend as a travelling reserve but never played. I was involved with England Under-20s, which gave me some time on the pitch, and playing some A League, but not first team stuff. Eventually, Cockers recognized that I needed more opportunities to develop. So he agreed to release me for a fortnight with the England Sevens team at the back end of the 2008–9 season.

Cockers did not really like Sevens – it was not his sort of game – but I couldn't just stand there holding a tackle pad all season. So off I went. What a weird experience that was.

The chance to play in the famous Hong Kong event with an England side coached by Ben Ryan was an exciting one. Back then, England were using the Sevens team as a development squad, and I went out there with a few other promising prospects like Noah Cato, who was at Saracens at the time. There were also Sevens specialists, like Ben Gollings, along on the trip as well.

We lost to Samoa in the quarter-finals, but I learned in Hong Kong that defeat in international rugby need not be all doom and gloom. I've never seen a team get changed so quickly afterwards to drown their sorrows in the party central madhouse that was the South Stand.

Barely recovered, we flew on to Australia to play in the Adelaide Sevens. We played Fiji in our first group game, which was a tough start. William Ryder, who was an unbelievable Sevens player, basically just took the piss out of us. He was just jinking around everyone in his ankle socks, throwing these no-look passes, making it all just look so easy. He was phenomenal and we got battered.

Then we played Kenya. We lost to them too. I scored a length-of-the-field try, which turned into a genuine near-death experience, because the Kenyans' anaerobic fitness was off the scale. They all just kept on chasing me down and I had to sprint every inch of the way. It damn near killed me. I guess we might have expected they would be able to run, but they could play rugby too.

That loss was a terrible result for us and, when we lost to France as well in our last group game, we were out of the main tournament. It meant we would have to play in the Bowl instead – an add-on featuring the also-rans, which filled the day's entertainment out for the crowd. Gollings was so ashamed to be associated with the rest of us by this point that he was resting up what he claimed was a tight calf.

We were drawn against the USA in the Bowl, who had apparently never beaten England before, but we managed to lose to them as well. Twice. There was a scoreboard error the first time, which somehow turned what we thought was a loss into a draw, so back out on the field we trailed for golden-point extra time. We kicked off, the Americans caught it and went the length to score and win. Again.

We might have known it would not be the best week after losing to the Cook Islands – population 15,000 – in a warm-up game.

It was a disastrous event all round.

At the end of that season, I played with Leicester at the Melrose Sevens and we reached the final, but for me the circuit was a sideshow. I had been given snippets of exposure at fifteens in my first season, and now I wanted more. I was frustrated when the opportunities didn't come. Other clubs started enquiring about my availability.

I met Jim Mallinder, who was Northampton's director of rugby. He said the Saints could give me more first team rugby if I moved there. It was an important moment in my career, and I wasn't sure what I should do.

Little did I know that a big turning point was just around the corner.

It was a game against South Africa in November 2009, to mark the opening of the new stand at Welford Road. We had loads of top-line players missing, so I was given a go in a Tigers team that also included a teenage Manu Tuilagi. We played out of our skins in front of a crowd of 24,000 and we beat the Springboks 22–17.

Aaron Mauger was playing at number 10, but he had a bad back so I got the goal-kicking job and put over seventeen points, which made me the hero. My first kick nearly hit the corner flag though, from long distance. You could immediately sense the disquiet in the ground, but Aaron just came over, told me to forget about it and get into my flow. All my kicks sailed over after that.

I used to enjoy goal-kicking, but that element of my game died away as I got older. Maybe I should have kept chipping away at it – I had the ability and could give it a decent whack – but we had such good specialist kickers at the club, with guys like Paul Burke, Andy Goode, Jeremy Staunton, Toby Flood and George Ford that we didn't really need another one.

I had enough on my plate anyway, because from that game onwards Cockers handed me the number 9 shirt. Julien Dupuy, our French international scrum half, had bought himself out of his Leicester contract in the summer of 2009 to move to Stade Français, but up to that point Cockers had gone with James Grindal. After the Springboks game, though, he told me that I was going to play every week because I'd earned it.

You treasured it when Cockers said 'well done' because he didn't say that very often. You craved his respect, and that backing was priceless from a guy like him. We definitely had our moments of friction, because I was a young guy who wanted to play, but maybe Cockers holding me back for longer than I wanted was a stroke of genius. It didn't feel like it at the time, but perhaps he did know what he was doing after all. When he finally gave me the keys to the castle, I was absolutely ready for it and I flew.

That 2009–10 season was my true breakthrough year, not the flash in the pan of playing at Twickenham as a bewildered seventeen-year-old. That was when it all went bang. It was crest-of-a-wave stuff; a thrilling joyride that I never wanted to stop.

I wish now that I could have bottled how I felt at that time. I was twenty years old, doing the thing that I loved most in the world, and I just felt so free.

Inevitably some of that youthful exuberance dissipated as I progressed in my career. Some of it got coached out of me as I got older. I brought more to the team in other regards as I took on more responsibilities, but I also turned in on myself a bit. I developed more of an appreciation of the tactical side of the game, which was good, but maybe at the cost of that instinctive element.

Back then, everything was new and exciting. I was fearless. Thriving. Playing without consequences.

It helped that Leicester were a good side who won more than they lost, but even when we lost, I had a great night out with my mates to look forward to. I was sharing a place with Tom Croft – Crofty – by now, and we had such a laugh together. Basically, we were living as well-paid students, and just spent all our spare time – of which we had plenty – pissing about.

I remember we bought a Scalextric set from Toys R Us, set up the track in the lounge and did endless laps. We also had this table tennis table, which we squeezed into the hallway/stairs area. If you played the ball into a certain area, you didn't have any room to return it because of the wall. Tom had a great reach, so he was annoyingly good, but we would go at it for hours. Another time, Crofty bought this rusty old Land Rover from a farm auction and destroyed the pergola in the garden by attaching a chain to the back of it and pulling it over.

At one point, we decided to become entrepreneurs, and came up with a plan to open a food or drinks outlet of some sort at the stadium. Crofty's first thought was a little food truck serving duck wraps. 'Great idea,' I said. I mean, who doesn't love duck wraps?

Crofty told me he had a contact who could supply the ducks who was based an hour away.

We went to see this guy and he gave us these white uniforms to put on before we were taken on a tour of his farm. He was taking us through the process of boiling up the meat and all this, and we were listening intently, but after what must have been an hour and a half, we still hadn't seen any ducks.

Crofty said: 'Right, so where are the ducks?'

'I don't do ducks,' he said.

It turned out to be a turkey farm.

I told Crofty what an idiot he was all the way back to Leicester, where we nipped into Costa for a coffee to restore our shattered morale. And that's where we got the great idea of a coffee outlet instead. Coffee and doughnuts.

Unfortunately, because it was only open on match days, we struggled to get anyone to work in it. On the handful of occasions when it was open, it didn't make any money. It lasted a couple of years in the end before we gave up on the idea.

Later on, I bought a share in a racehorse – Leg It Lenny – which was another disastrous business decision. It ran nine times, costing all the teammates I'd urged to back it a packet, before being quietly put out to pasture after trailing in tenth out of ten in its final race at Lingfield Park.

Back then, Crofty and I were just two mates living together, having a great time, without a care in the world. One drunken night he made me sign a tenancy agreement that basically said I would never leave. He had it laminated and put on the fridge. On New Year's Eve, because he was such a loser and he had no plans of his own, he came back with me to Norfolk to a party I was going to. He met my cousin Harriett there and ended up marrying her.

You can imagine how happy Harriett was to see the sign on the fridge. I did eventually move out, but I took some shifting.

It was great living with him, but it did have its moments. One day he forgot to give me the lift into training that he had promised.

I didn't know what the time was until he rang from the training ground, asking where I was because there was a team meeting about to start. I quickly got ready and rang Cockers, but there was no answer because he'd started the meeting already.

By the time I got to the club, the meeting had finished. Cockers had told me that I was going to be playing at the weekend, but I was now dropped because I had been late. 'No one's late on my watch,' snarled Cockers. I tried to argue that it was Crofty's fault, that he had been meant to give me a lift in, but Cockers wasn't listening.

For the most part, though, all was good. Better than good, actually. I scored a try in the 2010 Premiership final win over Saracens, and I was Players' Player of the Year at Leicester that season – which was a decent effort given some of the company I was keeping – and also the league's Young Player of the Year.

Oh, and one other thing. I was called up by England.

3

JOHNNO'S ENGLAND

'Everyone says that you always remember your first cap – and you do – but it wasn't my career highlight or anything like that.'

The first time I ever met Martin Johnson was at East Midlands Airport before a flight to Portugal for England's 2010 pre-Six Nations training camp.

I remember being like a nervous fan. Sometimes supporters get a bit tongue-tied when they come up to you because they put you on some sort of pedestal – that was what I was like with Johnno. He just had that aura about him, that presence. Part of it was physical – he's a gigantic man and he towered over me. Then there was his default facial expression, which I can only describe as 'glowering'. He could be in the happiest mood ever, but you wouldn't really be able to tell because he gave so little away.

But I also was meeting someone I had grown up idolizing. I had watched him lead the Lions, I'd seen him lift the World Cup, I knew the regard in which he was held at Leicester and, all of a sudden, he was my boss.

The England call-up had totally blindsided me. Even though I had started to get my feet under the table in the Leicester first team, Test rugby just wasn't on my radar at that point. Harry Ellis was struggling with his knee again, but it seemed to me there were much more experienced scrum halves available.

On the other hand, my England Saxons appearance in January 2010 had gone really well. I had been called up to play for the A side in their game against Ireland A at The Rec. Stuart Lancaster was the Saxons coach, and Andy Farrell, who was at Saracens at the time, was his assistant. We had a great week together. We were an untried bunch, with only seventeen caps between us, but we won against an Irish side boasting more than 300 caps 17–13. Maybe Johnno got some good feedback from that.

In any case, it doesn't matter. The headline was that I was promoted straight into the England senior squad at the age of twenty.

Before the training camp, I assumed I was just along for the ride really, to learn from Danny Care and Paul Hodgson, the other scrum halves in the squad. And I do think that was the plan, certainly initially. I remember just trying to keep my head down in Portugal, work hard and earn the respect of the guys who had been there and done it.

Jonny Wilkinson was there. My first thought was whether he would even know my name. As it turns out, he did, and he couldn't have been a nicer, more welcoming bloke. A top man.

With that quality of player, the speed of everything in training with England was quicker, and the accuracy was noticeably different, even compared to a top club like Leicester. I was trying to learn all the new plays and it was complicated because England were quite structured then. They liked to have three phases planned out, like the Brumbies had been doing in Australia, which meant a lot of homework.

The whole thing had more layers to it than I was used to. We had meetings about things I had never even considered, like psychology and team dynamics. The set-up was all very high-end, as you would expect of an elite professional sporting organization, and yet at the same time it was also surprisingly shambolic.

While Johnno liked to dive into the mauling and sometimes get into the restarts – I remember one time him going up and beating Crofty in the air in the old pair of American football boots he had on – he wasn't a coach as such. He left a lot of that to Brian Smith and Mike Ford. Brian was an Australian who had played for the Wallabies and Ireland and had also had a spell in rugby league. He was the attack coach. Fordy, a Lancastrian whose playing background was in league, had coached with Ireland and the British Lions. He was the defence coach.

To a young guy like me, it was interesting to see how that relationship worked. Or didn't. Brian and Fordy would often go at each other in front of the squad in training.

Once, we were running through a defensive set-up drill and, because we were a few numbers down, Brian was filling in as number 8 for the attacking team. It wasn't a realistic match scenario, because the teams were a few forwards light, but the idea was to test the backline defence from an attacking scrum. Danny Care rolled the ball to Brian's feet at the base of the scrum but, instead of running the play for us to defend, he picked the ball up, sped down the blind side and scored, with everyone just looking on bewildered.

'What are you doing, Brian?' Fordy asked him.

'Someone's got to mark this space, mate,' replied Brian.

'Brian, there's going to be a flanker and a number 8 there in a game. You just ran straight through where they would be,' said Fordy.

'Someone's got to mark it, mate,' Smithy repeated.

They carried on at each other like this while all the players were standing around, waiting for them to wrap up. I looked across to Danny, who was wetting himself with laughter. But I was thinking: 'This is England. What is going on?'

The training facility at Browns Sports Resort in Vilamoura – a place I grew to know like my own back garden through the years – also had some tennis courts where the coaches and staff used to like to play football. Once, I was sitting outside watching the action – competitive but nothing crazy – and all of a sudden Brian came flying in from nowhere with a double-footer on Jon Callard, the kicking coach. And JC totally lost it. He booted the ball over the top of the fencing, went back at Brian and a scrap nearly erupted.

That trip was the first time I found my absolute trust in coaches slipping.

There was this Australian guy in the set-up, Gerard Murphy, who was a management-consultant-turned-psychologist. I was always puzzled about why he was there at all. He had skin like an old leather sofa and one of those noses that looked like, if you squeezed it, pure whisky would come out. He used to walk around and constantly tell us: 'See something, say something, mate.'

What the hell did that mean? We weren't on a train reporting a piece of unattended luggage, or some bloke being dodgy. It was ludicrous.

Gerard was into his team-building exercises. On one occasion, he put the squad into groups of five and asked one in each group to leave the room. The others had to write down all that person's weaknesses, all the things he needed to work on – everything negative about him essentially. Then the teammate would come back in, sit there, and four of us had to feed back to him. I wasn't sure whether it was supposed to be team-building or team-destroying. I remember sitting there with my notebook thinking it was bonkers. But I was a kid, so I just kept my pad blank and my mouth shut.

We had a friendly against Portugal at the end of the week, sup-posedly as a run-out ahead of the 2010 Six Nations, but it turned into a complete mess. We were trying to simulate a game, but there were loads of mistakes. The attacking shape was all over the place and we got nothing out of it.

It didn't bode well, but in fact England ended up beating Wales first up in the Six Nations, and then we won away in Italy, so we made a good start to the championship.

I was watching and learning. I would come along and train with the lads, then get sent back to Leicester when they trimmed the squad to the match-day lads on Tuesday afternoon. That was fine. I was just soaking it in, having fun with these top players and not really thinking about being selected. I would hang around with the other young Tigers lads – Crofty, Dan Cole, Toby Flood – happy just to be there.

But then we lost at home to Ireland in round three.

The following week was a fallow one, and it just so happened that Leicester were playing London Irish – which was me up against Paul Hodgson at scrum half – and we beat them well. With no Premiership game the week after, I signed up for a trip away to Tenerife with some of the Leicester boys. I mean, I wasn't likely to be doing anything else, was I?

Jordan Crane, who was in the England squad, but who like me was always surplus to requirements, found a flight that left on the Tuesday night to Tenerife. Perfect. The plan was to meet up with the lads who were already in the Canaries and enjoy some winter sun.

Anyway, we went back into England camp ahead of that week-end's Scotland game and got on with business. I was sitting in the bar area at Pennyhill Park, having a bite to eat, when Johnno asked if he could have a word.

Standing over me, with that perma-frown on his face, he came straight out with it: 'You'll be playing this weekend.'

I was confused. 'I'm not, Johnno. There's no Premiership games this weekend,' I said.

'No, no, you're playing,' he repeated. 'You're going to be involved.'

'No Johnno. I'm not playing. There's no Leicester game.' He was starting to get a bit impatient by this point.

'You need to listen to me,' he said. 'You're going to be playing for England against Scotland this weekend. You're going to be on the bench for us.'

'Oh right,' I said, the penny finally dropping.

I mean it sounds kind of dumb looking back on it now, but that whole conversation just shows where I was at mentally. I was enjoying being part of the squad, but actually playing for England was still not part of my thinking.

Obviously I was chuffed to bits at being selected, though – even if it meant I had to drop out of the lads' trip. I rang my dad and told him I was going to be following in his footsteps. He was so pleased for me, but I think he was as surprised as I was. He and Mum immediately booked to come up to Edinburgh for the game.

I floated through that week with my head in the clouds.

The day before the match, I was sitting in the team hotel in Edinburgh munching on a chocolate biscuit – there's a squad tradition of a pre-match treat when the preparation work for a game is done – when Steve Thompson came over.

'Lenny,' he said, 'how are you feeling about tomorrow? Are you OK?'

I confessed that I was feeling a bit tense.

'Don't worry about it, mate,' he said.

He then mentioned one of his Northampton teammates. 'He got capped twenty times for Scotland,' said Thommo. 'And he's absolutely dog shit. So you'll be fine.'

It was a sort of a compliment, I guess. I won't mention who he was talking about.

The game was billed as Scotland head coach Andy Robinson's revenge mission after being sacked by England four years before-hand, but we got out of Murrayfield with a 15–15 draw. The weather was filthy and the game was forgettable.

Because the scoreline was so tight, I thought Johnno would leave Danny on all the way through – and he did. But with twenty-five minutes left, Ugo Monye was involved in a nasty clash of heads with Kelly Brown. Toby Flood and Ben Foden, the other two backs on the bench, had already been brought on, so there was no one else to turn to.

Mike Ford put his arm around me and said: 'Right kid, you're going on t'wing for Ugo.' My heart skipped a beat. This was it. What a moment. But I was also wondering why Danny couldn't move to the wing? Then I could play scrum half, where I knew what I was doing. I had never played wing in my life before. The only upside was that the expectations surrounding a debutant playing out of position in horrible conditions would be pretty low, so I didn't actually feel that much pressure when I got on.

And so my first cap passed off without any major balls-ups, or even many touches. Had Mark Cueto given me the ball, with a two-on-one in attack and me in space, I might have scored a try, but he didn't and a draw it was.

I remember thinking after the final whistle: 'That was cool. Let's do it again', and it was lovely to meet up with my parents afterwards and see how proud they were, but I recall a lot of other games so much more fondly and with more emotion.

Everyone says that you always remember your first cap – and you do – but it wasn't my career highlight or anything like that. My first England shirt isn't framed. It's at my mum and dad's, I think. Underwhelming would be the wrong word – it was the culmination of a dream – but I intended it to be the first step on a journey to much bigger things.

It's funny how your outlook changes. Twenty-five minutes as an emergency wing one week, then when I didn't get off the bench in Paris in a narrow 12–10 defeat to France the following week, I was absolutely gutted. Not to be given a chance was very frustrating.

Throughout my career, I always felt that I could change a game. Put the ball in my hands and I would make things happen. That was my outlook. So being a spare part didn't sit well. I was angry and quite emotional in the dressing room after the France game. I wasn't just happy having won one cap. I wasn't envisaging I would get to 127, obviously, but I knew I wanted more. I wanted to push. I wanted to compete.

There was only so long I could sulk for, though.

There's a tradition with England whereby new caps have to sing a song on the bus after their first game, and have a drink with their teammates. I hadn't done it in Murrayfield, so for me the initiation was to come a week late in France.

Let me explain that a bit more clearly. New caps have a drink with *all* their teammates. One with the loose head, one with the hooker, one with the tight head, etc. And each teammate gets to choose the drink. It was Chris Ashton's first cap against France, so we both had to do it that evening in Paris.

We were lambs to the slaughter.

There was a post-match function in the city that night where the drink-off was to take place, but first we had to get through the bus journey and the song. I had to go first because I had got capped before Ashy. Nick Easter did the intro at the front of the bus and called me up to savage heckling.

Crofty had given me some words of advice. He told me to do a song that didn't last long and one that people were likely to join in with. All week I'd been mulling it over. Should I do 'Take Me Home, Country Roads', or 'You're the Voice'? Everyone would know those. Or maybe a Backstreet Boys song or a Take That number?

Then Crofty suggested 'Who the Fuck Is Alice?'

I wasn't convinced. I didn't really know it. But Crofty sold it to me as being really short and reckoned that because there was swearing, everyone would join in.

So I agreed to do it.

I think the lesson is that you should absolutely never listen to your mates.

From the moment that microphone touched my lips, I was doomed. Things were being thrown, there were demands for me to sit down, the abuse was pouring in from all parts. I stumbled my way through this awful version of a very poor Smokie song alone (except for some half-hearted help from Crofty, who obviously felt guilty for his terrible advice).

Destroyed, I handed the microphone to Ashy, who then sang 'Bananas in Pyjamas', bless him. And I thought I got heat.

After that, it was on to the function and the drinks ordeal. The French, having won the Grand Slam, were having a great time. Me? Not so much.

The seating plan had me next to Steve Thompson, Lewis Moody, Simon Shaw, Tim Payne, Nick Easter. It was like an invitation to hell. It was safe to say those five didn't mind a drink. They could all put it away. And those guys were cunning because they made sure, what with the buyer's choice my induction allowed them, that my drinks were being well and truly mixed.

Shot of vodka. Pint of Guinness. Glass of red wine. Pint of lager. Glass of champagne.

Before I knew it, I'd done five drinks in about ten minutes and was seeing ten of everyone. But there was more.

Along came the rest of the team . . . Shot of Pernod. Gin and tonic. Half a pint of white wine.

I want to be clear: this was a smart, black-tie function (even though the Rugby Football Union kitted us out in those off-the-shelf suits that never quite fitted anyone correctly). But the dress code was unravelling as fast as I was. The bow tie lasted twenty minutes, the jacket was off after about twenty-five, the shirt was untucked after thirty, the buttons were undone after forty.

And I was hugging the toilet after fifty.

I failed to complete the full team of players, of course. We ended up in a nightclub in Paris with me slumped in a booth coming in and out of consciousness, until someone scooped me up, chucked me on the bus and put me to bed. I woke up the next day with a monumental hangover, relieved that the England initiation was done and dusted – and, it's safe to say, significantly less bothered about the fact that I hadn't got off the bench. The squad flew back into London a few hours later, and I needed to pull myself together fast.

I had a lunch date waiting for me.

Growing up in Norfolk, I had known Charlotte Beardshaw from a distance. She was a couple of years older than me, but I'd often see her at family gatherings. Her sister Clare was dating my cousin Jake.

We had got chatting at a Christmas party. She was living in Richmond at the time, working as a nurse, so we left it so that if I happened to be in London at any time, we would meet up. Pennyhill Park, England's training base on the Berkshire/Surrey border, was near enough. We had met for dinner the previous week.

We had hit it off, so we had agreed to meet up again when I got back from Paris.

And despite the England initiation, that lunch together went well too. So well, in fact, that fifteen years on Char is my wife and we have been joined by Boris, Billie and Ettie.

My first England start came that summer of 2010 on a tour to Australia.

As a running scrum half with some pace, playing against Australia suited me. I enjoyed the climate, the dry ball and the fast grounds, and I had done OK when I had come off the bench for Danny in the last twenty minutes of the first Test. We had lost in Perth, though, so there was a lot of debate afterwards as to how the side might be changed for the second Test.

We were all enjoying some food in a surf-and-turf grill when Johnno broke the news that I would be in for the game in Sydney. We were watching the State of Origin rugby league on a big screen when Johnno asked to have a word in private. He took me round the corner, out of sight of everyone and told me: 'Look, you'll be starting this weekend.'

This time there was no need for any further explanation. I cottoned on immediately.

He added a few nice words about how well I had done coming off the bench, and how I was performing in training, and told me he was going to reward that and give me the opportunity.

Then he shook my hand with that giant mitt of his. I went back to my seat, not sure whether I was allowed to tell anyone, but Coley and Crofty had seen Johnno taking me aside and wanted to know what it was all about. They were chuffed to bits for me.

I was unbelievably excited. The only feeling I can compare it to was that Christmas morning anticipation as a six-year-old when you wake up and realize Santa has been. I had that same elation and energy inside me. Starting against the Wallabies in the Olympic Stadium? The same venue where England had beaten Australia after extra time to win the World Cup seven years earlier? This was going to be mega.

And, in fairness, it was.

From the moment I ran out onto the field as an England starter that evening, into the wall of noise, I was gripped by this overwhelming feeling of being so alive. I just felt so focused and so aware of my surroundings. There was an absolute clarity to everything. It was everything I'd ever wanted to do, and I felt like I belonged there.

I could have fallen flat on my face – my first action was a clearance kick to touch, which was very nearly charged down. Who knows how my international career might have turned out if it had been and Australia had scored? But from that sketchy launchpad, a rocket went up.

Seventeen minutes in, from a four-man lineout thirty metres out on the left side of the field, my good mate Crofty – one of the best lineout forwards England ever had – delivered the ball on a plate to me. As I caught the ball, already in motion, I saw Dean Mumm out of the corner of my eye rush out of the lineout, intending to intercept my pass to Toby Flood. I faked as if to throw it but held onto the ball and shot off through the hole he had left.

I hadn't planned it – the play was for the backline to hit it up the middle – but instinct took over when the picture in front of me changed. It was like I was on autopilot. It was the same dummy that I'd thrown in the garden against my cousin, in school games, and for Holt minis hundreds of times over – and suddenly I was in open space.

Drew Mitchell, Australia's wing, was covering across but I went in and out and took him on the outside. I think wingers are always surprised when opponents go for the outside because they usually aren't as quick as them.

But I was.

I burned around him and over the line before giving it the big Joe Rokocoko dive to touch down for my first England try.

A bit showy, maybe, but I firmly believe that you can ruin a great try with a bad dive. Brian O'Driscoll scored some crackers but his sideways slides were awful. I always loved watching Joe hover the air and fly in for his tries – it was proper cherry-on-the-top stuff.

Australia's scrum half Will Genia, who I had played against at youth level, came across as I dived in and gave my head a shove as if to say: 'You again? You're annoying.'

I guess that moment announced me to a wider audience. We rode our luck a little, with Matt Giteau missing a couple of penalties late on, but we won the game by a single point.

I was elated.

I did an interview with Sky Sports afterwards in which I said that I couldn't believe Giteau had missed a kick in front of the posts. I probably shouldn't have said that, but the filter was off. I was on cloud nine. It was almost overwhelming. What a feeling it was to be part of an England win for the first time, and to have played such a part in it. I'd helped create Ashy's first try as well, so things could not have gone better on my first Test start.

The expectation of me as a player changed off the back of that game. I was comfortable with that. After that game in Sydney, I swore to myself that it couldn't be a one-off. A lot of players can have a really good game once for their country and then never get to that level again. I didn't want to be one of those.

Luckily, there was another first to come that autumn of 2010 – a first England appearance at Twickenham. Against New Zealand.

England had lost to New Zealand on the previous eight occasions they had played them. The All Blacks had this aura about them, and they had some great players, but none greater than Dan Carter. Stop him and we stopped New Zealand, the management reckoned, so Mike Ford came up with a plan for how we would do so.

'I've watched hours and hours of footage on Carter and basically everyone sits off him. Why would you sit off him? We're not going to sit off him. We're going to pressure him,' said Mike, in this detailed presentation he had drawn up.

He wanted the scrum half to sprint out of our defensive line and try to get to Carter and spook him. Tackle him, charge him down or force him back inside where our big forwards would eat him up.

To train for this critical task, Danny and I would be given a dry run against our bench number 10, who would pretend to be Carter to test out the big idea. Because Floody was starting at stand-off, that was Jonny Wilkinson.

We couldn't get anywhere near him, obviously. We were racing out of the line and, before we even had the chance to get into his postcode, he would send a pass on its way or drill a kick somewhere into the distance. He was just too good.

Each time, Mike would tell us to start in a different position or take a different angle, but each time the outcome was the same. Jonny just waltzed off without batting an eyelid while we chased his shadow.

Fordy got Danny and I over after a while and he said: 'Right, boys, you've run it a few times. What do you reckon?' We looked at each other and Danny said: 'Well, Mike, it's not a bad idea. It's just that Wilko is bloody hard to get to. I reckon Carter might be too.'

The genius plan was scrapped on the spot.

Playing the All Blacks meant facing the haka.

I'd had a taste of doing that on the summer tour, when half the squad had stopped off in Napier on the way home to play New Zealand Māori in a game to celebrate their centenary.

We had flown into Napier Airport in a couple of separate groups, where we were all greeted by a welcome haka, which was a lovely touch. Diplomacy meant that someone was needed to say a few words of thanks on our behalf and, with none of the management on our flight, it fell to the team doctor, Mike Bundy, to do the honours.

He was a very well-spoken guy, but he wasn't used to this sort of thing and he did an excruciating job, stuttering through his speech and ending up thanking them for their incredible native welcome. It was honestly as though he was Captain Cook pitching up on some remote island that had never met civilization before.

There was another haka waiting for us on the pitch at McLean

Park before the game itself – in fact, there were hakas every-where we looked – so I reckoned I was tuned in to what to expect at Twickenham.

In the flesh, though, out there on the international stage, it was epic. Awesome and intense. It has a mystique all of its own, the haka. And I enjoyed it.

I made a point of fixing my opposite number, Alby Mathew-son, with my eyes, something I always did when I faced it in the future. My interpretation of the haka is that it is the laying down of a challenge, and locking eyes was my way of accepting it.

People talk about performing the haka giving the All Blacks an advantage, but facing it gives you a great surge of energy as well. It was a real privilege to face it and feel that. And before the game, you could just tell from the vibes that senior players were giving off, that the New Zealand game meant a lot to them. All those defeats had left some scars.

I took a quick tap early on, wanting to take them on, and the crowd responded, but I soon found out the harsh realities of playing the All Blacks when I went for a gap, only for Ma'a Nonu to shut it abruptly and knock the wind out of me with a ferocious tackle.

We gave it a pretty good go after a difficult start, but the All Blacks beat us in the end. Same old story.

The week after came the re-match with the Wallabies. I couldn't wait to go at them again.

I was sitting on the bus from Pennyhill Park to Twickenham with my headphones on, listening to music, and I looked down to see my leg jiggling up and down of its own accord. It wasn't the beat, it was the excitement. I knew I had a performance in me that day. The psychologists say that where your mind goes your body will take you, and I just had a strong feeling that it was going to be a good day.

In the end we didn't just beat them. We blew them away 35–18, with Ashy scoring one of the great Twickenham tries of my career.

We had built a decent first-half lead but Australia were hammering away at our line early in the second half, threatening a comeback, when Tom Palmer made a desperate tackle on Will Genia. Mike Tindall and Toby Flood got into the ruck and the ball squirted out on our side just short of our line.

When I picked it up, my first thought was to clear our lines. I was going to kick, but then I saw Quade Cooper coming round to charge me down, so I stepped him and suddenly I saw what was on.

One great thing about Johnno was that he absolutely backed you to play if it was on, and as a young guy that was music to my ears.

It was on. I gave the ball to Courtney Lawes, he fed it onto Ashy and, in a flash, he was off. I was trying to track him, chasing hard, but Ashy was away. He rounded Drew Mitchell, who was coming across to cover, and his pace did the rest.

Afterwards, it was dubbed England's try from the end of the earth.

To this day, I have never heard Twickenham like it. The crowd was beside itself. I reckon every hair on my body stood up on end as the noise reverberated around the place. I stood there drinking it in. I almost wanted to cry – that's how powerful the feeling was.

However high the highs of rugby, though, it always has a way of pulling you back down to earth. A few minutes later I was vomiting into the Twickenham grass. I had just been wasted by a thunderous full-frontal hit from the Wallaby prop Benn Robinson. He had almost snapped me in half.

Our physio Phil Pask came on and was asking me what was wrong, but I could not get enough breath to communicate with him. The only noise I could make was to retch. I was tackled hard plenty of times in my career but never as hard as that.

That was the end of my involvement in the game, which was a shame because I felt so in the groove, but that is the beauty and the brutality of rugby in a nutshell. One minute I was bathing in the afterglow of being involved in the try of the century, and the next I'm in the recovery position after being halved by some angry prop forward.

I just about got my breath back in time to say thank you for the Man-of-the-Match award – which, I'll admit, was a tough one for Ashy to miss out on.

If I was finding out how physical Test rugby was, then I had the ultimate lesson two weeks later against the Springboks. They were something else. They were so huge I felt like a little boy out there, playing against proper men.

We lost 21–11 and our team suffered a load of injuries – the worst of which was Crofty fracturing his shoulder. He let out this horrible yelp when it happened, like a dog when you stand on its tail. He was in a lot of discomfort.

It was an education in brutality, playing against guys like Bakkies Botha, Victor Matfield and the du Plessis brothers. Having been brought up at Leicester, it was probably the first time in my professional career that I'd ever played on the back foot. Like Leicester, England tended to have a power advantage against teams, and we'd gone well in the scrums against the All Blacks. But when you're going backwards and you're losing the collisions, the game suddenly becomes a lot harder.

The Springboks' personnel changed down the years, but their DNA never did. You knew exactly what was coming, but stopping it was another matter. Teams like Wales or Australia were probably more used to having to find ways to operate on the back foot, but as England we just weren't accustomed to being outmuscled.

We had a problem thinking our way around that, and I'm not sure we ever worked out a solution. We often seemed to struggle against them.

Despite the lesson South Africa taught us that day in autumn 2010, there was something of a feel-good factor developing around Johnno's England team.

From arriving in a squad that was stuttering ten months beforehand, there was suddenly a genuine buzz around the team, with some exciting young talent in Ashy, Crofty, Ben Foden, Floody, Coley, Dylan Hartley and myself. That positivity only grew through the 2011 Six Nations when we won our first four games to set up a Grand Slam shot against Ireland in Dublin.

Ireland had endured an in-and-out championship, and had nothing tangible to play for, but the experienced lads warned the rest of us that it would not matter when it came to playing us.

I'd never played in Dublin before but I thought, with the naivety of youth, how hard could it be? We were playing better than them. This was our Grand Slam for the taking. James Haskell had plastered on the fake tan the day before the game, ready for the celebration pictures. In short, we got miles ahead of ourselves.

As the wise heads had warned, Ireland turned up. They started hot and ran out into an early lead. Just before half-time, they were threatening again when David Wallace was tackled near the touchline by Floody. He threw the ball inside, I caught it and ran into touch, but as I did so I flipped the ball around my back and into the crowd so they couldn't take a quick throw-in. They were never going to take it quickly anyway, five metres from our line, so my chuck-away didn't make any difference at all – but Bryce Lawrence, the Kiwi referee, did not see it like that.

He blew his whistle and called me over. In his hand was a yellow card.

I honestly couldn't believe it. A sin-binning? For that? To me, it was an absolutely ridiculous decision. I couldn't think of another time that someone had been yellow-carded for something like that. I jogged off, stunned.

Johnny Sexton kicked the penalty to make me feel even worse.

I was determined to make amends when my ten minutes were up, to try to help England back into the game. But just as I was readying myself to get back out there, I was told I wouldn't be going back on and that Johnno had decided to replace me with Danny.

I watched on helplessly as Ireland closed out a 24–8 win and torpedoed our Grand Slam.

I didn't know what to say after the game. I kept replaying the yellow card over and over in my head. It was a bullshit call and I felt let down by the decision, but I was pissed off at not getting back on afterwards too.

I got slaughtered on social media afterwards. It felt like I was being made a scapegoat for the defeat and the lost Grand Slam. It was really upsetting, and I didn't know how to handle it. I just wasn't ready for that.

We had a few drinks that night to mark the end of the campaign – we had still won the championship, despite the defeat – but I was struggling. My head was spinning. I remember speaking to my dad and telling him that I didn't know what this meant for me. Would I never play again for England? Had I lost

Johnno's trust? Would he bin me off? I was overthinking things completely, but it was the first bit of real adversity I'd faced as an England player, and I found it very difficult.

In the middle of all this avalanche of self-doubt, Cockers sent me a text telling me to come up and see him in his office when I reported back in at the Leicester training ground on the Monday.

Not more grief. I could do without it.

Instead, when I got there, Cockers was strangely empathetic; I almost didn't recognize him. 'How are you doing, Lenny? Where are you at?' he asked. He must have known I would have been knocked sideways by what had happened, and he was reaching out.

'It's bollocks what they're saying about you, you've been brilliant. Don't worry about the noise, it's one incident. We value you here.' Cockers was being reassuring. Again, not like him at all. But, in another sense, it was.

The thing about Cockers was that while he felt he had the right, as Leicester coach, to call you a prick and tell you that you had let everyone down, he wouldn't let anyone else outside the group do the same. If they tried, the wagons would get circled. You were one of his Tigers and he had your back.

I appreciated his backing and immediately felt stronger for it.

We discussed whether I should play at the weekend against Bath and I said that I wanted to. It was just what I needed. We smashed Bath 37–6 at The Rec and I had a stormer. Cockers came out in the media afterwards and absolutely went to town singing my praises, making it clear in no uncertain terms how important I was to the club. That meant a lot to me. I needed an arm around me and – in my hour of need – he provided it.

Johnno never did explain his thinking and I never asked. I felt

I didn't have the right to at the time. I mean, who was I to question Martin Johnson? I was a kid not long into his Test career; he was a legend. But I could have done having the same sort of conversation that Cockers had with me with one of the England coaches after that Ireland game. The incident reinforced for me that, however exciting it was to play for England, it was important not to forget where home was.

Leicester was my safe space. And it would always remain so.

Spin-pass practice
on the farm.

Tiger cub –
celebrating
Leicester's 2002
Premiership title
at Welford Road.

Size isn't everything – on the move for Gresham's.

Waiting for a pass for Holt minis. I loved the ball in my hands.

Embraced by Geordan Murphy and Matt Smith after scoring in the 2010 Premiership final against Saracens.

All smiles in Sydney after scoring on my first England start.

Leaving Conrad Smith and Richie McCaw behind as England downed the All Blacks at Twickenham in 2012.

Celebration time after touching down against the Wallabies at Twickenham in 2016.

With England coach Eddie Jones after the third Test against
South Africa in Cape Town in 2018.

Running on fumes – making a break against the Springboks in the
thin air of Johannesburg in 2018.

Emotions get the better of me – but not my brother – as we prepare to play together for England for the first time against Fiji at Twickenham in 2012.

With Tom, celebrating the first Test win for the British & Irish Lions against the Wallabies in Brisbane in 2013.

Always great to beat the Aussies – with Fordy and the Cook Cup at Twickenham in 2016.

Over and out – sharing a beer with Owen Farrell after the World Cup bronze match at the Stade de France in 2023.

The try that never was – the disallowed score in the 2019 World Cup semi-final against New Zealand.

Pain in the rain – suffering at an England training session at Twickenham in 2020.

4

2011 WORLD CUP

'It was dysfunctional– that much was true – but we did care. We cared a lot. Which is why we all felt as empty as we did when we fell short.'

Dwarf-tossing, ferry-jumping, ball-tampering – England's 2011 World Cup campaign had it all. And, boy, did it leave me with regrets.

Sometimes, when I think back, I wonder if the biggest regret of my entire England career was our failure to go beyond the quarter-final stage of that tournament. It wasn't just our exit, but the repercussions with Johnno and the coaching staff that came afterwards.

To lose out to a France side that was in full mutiny mode against their coach, Marc Lièvremont, was a terrible waste. We had a good side, but it just didn't work out for us in that tournament, on or off the pitch.

Before we left, we had it spelled out to us by Johnno, by Richard Smith, the RFU lawyer, and by Will Chignell, our media guy, that we would be under the microscope out in New Zealand. It's a rugby-mad country anyway, but at a World Cup there would be no hiding place. Everyone had a mobile phone, so we needed to be on our guard – and on our best behaviour.

I think it is very easy for people to assume from the outside, in the light of what happened, that England was a totally dysfunctional set-up and that none of us cared, but that couldn't be more wrong. It was dysfunctional – that much was true – but we did care. We cared a lot. Which is why we all felt as empty as we did when we fell short.

The road to New Zealand began with a summer training camp at Pennyhill Park, where I almost lost the chance of going to the World Cup at all. Part of the preparation programme involved wrestling, with the idea being that we'd improve how we used our body weights in the contact areas. It became quite a big thing within the squad, with a load of competitive rugby players going at it full on in the dohyō every day. Scores would be posted in the team room and footage of the bouts played in the dining room. Like in sumo, you had to get your opponent out of the ring to win.

Matt Stevens, who had competed in Brazilian Jiu-Jitsu at the World Championship, fancied himself at it. When it came to his opening bout, Sos – as he was known – was down doing the splits, performing these special neck rolls and really looking the part. He was basically giving off the impression that he was the man. He was up against Nick Easter, who was a naturally strong bloke, but absolutely not interested in any of that warm-up stuff.

Sos bounded into the dohyō with all the confidence of a martial arts master – only for Nick to stride over, grab him in a bear hug, pick him up and toss him out of the ring like rubbish into a bin. Sos was left beating the ground with his fist in frustration, while those of us watching erupted with laughter.

The wrestling was divided into weight categories, so I was in with the backs. Taking on Toby Flood didn't seem like too bad a draw until he went to try to flip me over and my leg got caught. I heard this ominous pop. I lay there in the dohyō knowing I had done my knee. The physios rushed over looking worried.

I was on the ground thinking: 'Shit, this is the World Cup done for me.'

Floody just stood there feeling terrible. The session was abandoned.

It turned out I had injured my medial ligament and chipped some bone behind the knee, so I was booked in to see a knee surgeon called Andy Williams straight away. I was told I would need an operation and that the timeline for recovery was twelve weeks. I immediately did the mental calculation: twelve weeks took me to the week of our first game of the World Cup against Argentina.

Tight. Too tight, maybe. Johnno was going to have to take a risk if he wanted me on the plane. I wouldn't be able to play in any of the warm-up games, so I would be going in cold against the Pumas. And that was assuming there was no hitch in the rehab. I wasn't sure he would go for it.

I went straight in for surgery and woke up from it to a voice-mail from Johnno.

It could have gone either way, but he gave me just the message I wanted. He said that he knew it was a twelve-week injury, but that if I ran to schedule with my recovery, he would still take me to the World Cup. I wasn't to worry about that, I should just concentrate on my rehab. It was such a relief.

The RFU flew in Bill Knowles, an American reconditioning expert, and we were at the rehab process every day, building up the strength in my knee, doing fitness in the pool, basically everything possible to make sure I was ready. The importance of getting me fit in time increased when Danny Care hurt his ankle in one of the warm-up Tests against Wales and was ruled out of the tournament. It was a heartbreaker for Danny and a blow for the squad.

But, luckily, by the time the squad was announced, I was pretty much there. I was named along with Richard Wigglesworth and Joe Simpson as the scrum halves for the tournament.

Before we left for New Zealand, the RFU put on an eve-of-departure send-off party at Pennyhill Park for us. Lewis Moody, the captain, went to do the honours at the bar. As Moodos headed back to us with eight pints on a tray, Steve Thompson whacked him in the balls. In the inevitable carnage, the beer went all over our sodden skipper.

Start as you mean to go on, I suppose.

Our opening pool game was a tricky one, but Argentina were a team we were expected to beat. My Leicester teammate Horacio Agulla was in their side, and I ran into him pre-game. It felt very much like he didn't want to speak to me – or any of us Leicester lads. The gist of a very brief conversation was that Argentina had been building towards this one game for months and they had us in their sights. They were such an emotional bunch, and they were climbing the walls for this match.

Some bright spark at the RFU had decided our change strip for the World Cup would be all black, which we duly wore for the game. In New Zealand, there is only one team that gets to wear all black and it isn't England. Not only was the colour of the kit an own goal, but for some reason the numbers on the back weren't stuck on well enough and peeled off during the game.

Our performance was as scruffy as our appearance. By the time I got on the pitch with half an hour to go, we were in serious trouble. We were 9–3 down, Jonny was missing his kicks, and the Pumas were causing us no end of problems. It was a good time to make a difference. With thirteen minutes left, I split the

Argentina defence and sped through the hole to score the try that got us out of jail for a 13–9 win.

Those snipes were my trademark back then. The scrum halves I admired growing up like Matt Dawson and Justin Marshall were all good at that and it was one of my favourite parts of the game. I loved getting out to the first and second defenders around the ruck and challenging around the fringes.

Part of what made me dangerous was my acceleration, but there was also a strategic element. When I picked the ball up from a ruck, I would pull it to my hip and take one step away from the defence. It was a lateral movement but a backwards lateral movement.

The traditionalists did not like a scrum half taking a step. They thought number 9s should be just firing the ball to the number 10 all day, like scrum halves used to do back in the day, and certainly not wasting time by taking a step – but they were missing the point. That step opened up extra space to work in. It enabled me to arc outside the first defender and run at the inside shoulder of the second defender. That gave him a decision to make. He could either turn in on me and tackle me – which, nine times out of ten, would result in quick ruck ball for us – or he could turn outwards towards the other runners, in which case I would go through the hole. So that backward step was crucial.

Matt O'Connor, who had arrived at Leicester during Heyneke Meyer's short stay, was a key driver in developing it. He had worked with George Gregan, the great Australian scrum half, at the Brumbies, and that was what he did. To train the move, Matt would put a ball in a tyre for me to pull out time after time to build the muscle memory. Pull. Hip. Step. Pull. Hip. Step.

Repeat, repeat, repeat until, in the ultimate pressure situation of a World Cup game, I was able to do it without thinking. Through I went and scored.

There was a lot of pent-up emotion as I punched the ball away in celebration, both because of the match situation and my own personal feelings. It had been a long road back from the knee injury, and the last time I had worn an England shirt had been that grim day in Dublin. This felt a whole lot better.

We were happy we had won, but we knew we needed to be way better. Jonny had missed five kicks, which was totally unlike him, so he grabbed his tee and went back out onto the pitch for an hour to try to sort the gremlins out. This was his last World Cup and the end of his international career was beckoning, but his desire to improve was just as strong as ever.

The stadium was empty. Everyone had gone home. But there he was, grinding away, practising, even though he had just played a high-intensity Test match. That was the Jonny I had grown to know.

He was incredibly generous with his time and his advice, and so happy to facilitate my growth as a player. If I asked about any of the technical aspects of kicking, he would always share his deep knowledge. If I asked to pass him the balls while he was doing his drop goals, he would always say yes.

But that voice inside his head – driving him to do more and more and more – never seemed to go away.

He would be absolutely devoted to training with the team but, as soon as the session was done, he would spend maybe two hours just on him. That was often kicking but it could be passing, offloading, anything. It was an obsession.

His work ethic was astonishing. For most players doing 'extras' meant twenty minutes or so more out on the training pitch, but not Jonny. Being a young player, I would watch him and think:

'Blimey, if he's doing that much, I've got no right to go in and take my boots off.' But I did all the same. I just wasn't that person. I couldn't dedicate myself to that degree. I would sometimes do extra kicking after a session, but only if I felt like I needed to.

Jonny, who had earned the right to be the most confident in his skills of any of us, just couldn't let it go. He was never satisfied. He could have the best training session, kick for two hours and not miss a goal-kick, but there might be one kick that wasn't perfect and that would eat away at him. It would be an itch inside him that needed scratching.

I think if the physios had allowed it, he would have kicked for six hours a day. There was always a part of him battling the urge to do more. He had his list in his head that he needed to tick off before he could walk away from the training field feeling OK. It wasn't healthy.

That day, he wasn't happy with the match balls in Dunedin. He thought some of them were drawing from left to right for no reason, and it was killing him mentally. Johnno asked a few of us after the Argentina match if they were an issue. We all agreed that – although they were the same Gilbert brand as we had used in the Six Nations – this batch, which had come fresh out of the packet the day before the game, did feel a bit different.

Chignell advised Johnno not to mention the ball situation to the media afterwards. Johnno completely ignored him and went into the press conference and told the journalists straight out that the balls were different.

Ball-gate erupted.

Jonny didn't play in the next game – a stuttering but straight-forward win over Georgia – but he was back against Romania. He had worked out by now that it was just a few of the balls that were misbehaving. So his kicking coach, Dave Alred, and the team's strength and conditioning coach Paul 'Bobby' Stridgeon made sure Jonny got the balls he liked, by marking the ones that flew better and swapping out the balls he didn't. When it was discovered what they were up to, the pair of them were suspended by the RFU for a game.

Usually, Bobby was the bloke to bring Jonny's kicking tee onto the field when he had a shot at goal. He was a great character, and he had set himself the target at that World Cup of being the quickest tee delivery boy in world rugby. In training he would do his own timed sprints through the speed gates we used, carrying a tee and a water bottle – Jonny always wanted a drink before a kick – and trying to set his personal best. Then he would do another timed run with the team's water crates in each hand. They were pretty heavy by the time all the water bottles were filled – they weighed almost as much as Bobby – so he would be cramping up by the time he reached the gates.

He was a funny guy, great for morale.

We were involved in a running dispute with Bobby's S and C department throughout that World Cup. Crofty had managed to forge a link with a sweet sponsor, and he was milking it for all he was worth. They were flying in huge amounts of chocolate and sweets for us. In all, there was about 200 kg of the stuff – Dairy Milk, Boosts, Wispas, Double Deckers. It kept being delivered to the hotels where we were staying, and the S and C guys, who were not happy about it at all, would confiscate it and place it under lock and key.

There was a lot of stuff going on off the pitch. Some of the guys had gone wild pig hunting and managed to kill one that was then butchered to eat. Manu decided to keep the head, and it was put outside Ashy's room as a nice surprise for him when he opened the door.

It was all harmless really, just boys being boys, and it might all have stayed in-house but for Queenstown.

After the Argentina game, we had been given some down time in the South Island's adventure sports capital. It seemed like a good idea at the time. The other crunch match in the group against Scotland was three games along the road, the World Cup was a long grind and Queenstown was a great place to unwind. So Johnno told us to go and enjoy ourselves.

It started with a meal out on an RFU tab. Drinks were taken. Then a few more. If it had ended there, then there wouldn't have been a problem, but we were walking back to the hotel when a few of the lads announced they wanted to stay out a bit longer.

I'd had my fill and decided to go back. I was sharing a room with Crofty. When we woke up the next morning, I asked him if he'd had a good night after we had gone our separate ways.

He told me they'd ended up in this bar where there was a dwarf-chucking competition event on.

'Why didn't you give me a ring and get me there?' I said. 'That sounds like fun.' We had a laugh but didn't think too much more about it.

That day we were all heading off by helicopter for a wholesome day together in the beautiful New Zealand mountains. We took boats down the river and ate freshly caught fish and generally had a super-chilled time. It was quite remote, beyond the reach of phone signals, so we were totally oblivious to the storm brewing back at base.

We arrived back at the hotel and a few of the lads were asked to go catch up with Johnno and Chignell. The night out at the Altitude Bar at the Mad Midget Weekender had got out, and the papers were going to town on it. There were pictures; there was even talk of a video.

To be honest, at that stage it was still just a joke within the squad. We had been given permission to go out and no one had been harmed. It involved consenting adults – big ones and little ones. But the images of the lads worse for wear and the accompanying headlines had not gone down well with the RFU.

Johnno's advice on the team bus on the way to training was to keep quiet, not say anything about it and wait for everything to blow over.

Except it never did.

Because Mike Tindall was involved – who had just become a member of the royal family, having married Zara Phillips – there was more petrol poured on the fire. The media were all over it. Fortunately, none of the journalists ever found out that Crofty had done his back picking a dwarf up and was on the physio's couch for three days, or we'd have been given even more grief.

We had a team meeting to discuss the situation. In one corner, you had players who thought we needed to stop going out completely; in another you had players who felt that we needed to unwind from time to time for our sanity. I was in that camp. Test rugby is a high-pressure environment, and at a World Cup the stress is even greater – but we all agreed we needed to be more careful for the rest of the tournament.

Unfortunately, trouble just followed us around. There was more controversy, with Johnno having to reprimand three of the lads, after a complaint from one of the hotel staff who felt that they had disrespected her. They thought they were just being humorous, but it wasn't taken that way.

Then Manu was fined for wearing a sponsored mouthguard,

which meant more hassle for Johnno and a stressed Chignell, whose phone was blowing up from all the media calls he was having to deal with.

We were being depicted as the tournament's bad guys. The only way to change the narrative of our World Cup was to do something unforgettable on the field.

Having edged past Scotland in our last group game, we had a quarter-final against France – who we had beaten in the Six Nations a few months beforehand – ahead of us. It was a huge, huge match, and what we needed more than anything were some reassuring words from our coaches. It was left to Mike Ford to do the big scene-setter at the start of that week. We all listened intently.

'I can't help but think back to when I was coaching Ireland and we played France in the World Cup quarter-final eight years ago,' he began.

'I showed D'Arcy and O'Driscoll every move that Jauzion and David Marty had ever made. I showed them clips of Clément Poitrenaud and his footwork, Vincent Clerc and where he would pop up . . . I showed them move after move after move. I thought I had prepped them unbelievably well. No stone was left unturned. We had it all covered.

'Then they put forty points on us.'

We were staring at Mike, not really understanding where he was coming from.

'My point is,' he said, 'that I can show you every move that France have made in the past few matches, but the reality is I don't know what they're going to do. I have no idea. Nobody does.'

We were thinking: 'Is he fucking serious?'

Mike was one of my favourite coaches. He was very good. But

as an analysis of what was going to be coming from France, it was a bizarre take. Northern comedy gold.

France were unpredictable, it was true, but there was an expectation that England would win that quarter-final. We'd beaten them in the Six Nations eight months beforehand; they had just lost to Tonga and they were in disarray. But France, in typical French fashion, pulled something out of the bag from nowhere against us.

They scored two really quick tries in the first half and we let them get too far in front. We basically ran out of time to reel them in. We had our chances, but by the time we started to take them it was too late. We had the lead down to seven when Cueto finished off my quick tap with three minutes left, but France held out.

And that was it, our World Cup was over. I was just so gutted because, despite everything that had gone on, despite all the distractions and chaos, that was a good England team. There was a huge amount of belief within it that we could achieve something in New Zealand.

If we had won, we would have played Wales in the semis – a team we had just beaten in the Six Nations.

Ifs, buts and maybes. We were left with a horrible feeling of what might have been. We were out and we were going home – but we had a couple of days to kill before we flew back.

Just enough time for something else to go wrong.

I swear our intentions were good.

We wanted to go somewhere quiet and out of the way to drown our sorrows. After everything that had happened, we were just trying to keep a low profile. The England team had taken so much hammer that we wanted to bury our heads in the sand and hide. So a few of us Leicester guys decided to catch a ferry to Waiheke Island, to visit a vineyard for a *refined* lunch.

As inspired decisions go, that one turned out to be right up there with a couple of late ones at the Altitude Bar.

It started off OK – the ferry trip out there went without a hitch, and we found a nice spot to flush away some of the disappointment with a few nice glasses/bottles. We weren't bothering anyone, just minding our own business. Then we decided to head back.

On the way out to Waiheke, Manu had asked the rest of us if we thought he would be able to swim to the harbour if he jumped off the ferry. 'Probably not, mate,' we'd told him.

He clearly still had the idea in his head because, on the way back, with a few drinks inside him, Manu brought it up again, except this time he announced he was going to do it. So as the ferry neared Auckland Harbour, we went up to the top deck and Manu started stripping off.

This ferry was rammed with Argentinian fans because they were playing New Zealand that night in the other quarter-final in Auckland. They were going nuts, like they do, jumping up and down and chanting and generally being very raucous, and they were all egging him on. Cards on the table, we weren't discouraging him either.

It was pretty high up there – twenty feet maybe – but Manu, down to his underpants, was leaning over the edge, holding onto the bars like that scene from *Titanic*.

The Argentinians were going bananas. The boat was shaking.

We were standing there, holding his clothes, merrily pissed, not really thinking this through. Suddenly, there was this massive splash and a huge cheer, and Manu was in the water.

It was an all-out effort as he tried to swim away, though he seemed to be making very little progress, and the ferry started reversing, so for an alarming moment it looked like he might get run over.

Fortunately he kept on edging his way out of danger and slowly moving towards dry land and, as we disembarked with his clothes, we could see that he had made it safely to land.

We could also see the port police waiting for him. Uh-oh.

Crofty and Louis Deacon were dispatched to go to talk to the police and try to get Manu out of there with just a talking-to. 'Just a bit of fun, officers, no harm done . . .' but of course the police didn't see it like that.

Floody and I were in a taxi heading back to the hotel when my phone rang. It was Crofty telling me Manu had been arrested and was being taken to the station for questioning.

I told Floody. He couldn't believe it. 'That's ridiculous,' he said.

Coley had Manu's clothes, so he was sent around various Auckland police stations trying to find the one Manu was in so he could get dressed again. Meanwhile we headed back to the team hotel to pass on this latest bit of disastrous news to the England management.

We got back to the hotel and I took the lift up to the team floor.

The first person I saw as I stepped out was Will Chignell. He was looking absolutely exhausted, like one of Shackleton's men on Elephant Island. I reckon he'd lost fifteen kilos – and half his hair. He was a frazzled wreck of a man, just skin and bones.

He had taken a battering by this point. He had been knocked from pillar to post. All he wanted, I'm sure, was to get home with no further dramas.

'Hi Will,' I said. 'Have you got a sec? Manu's just been arrested.'

He didn't speak for a while.

Then he said: 'You're kidding me, right?'

'No,' I said. 'I'm not.'

'Arrested for what?' he asked.

'He jumped off a ferry.'

'*What?*'

'He jumped off a ferry.'

He just stared at me, with his mouth open, nodding dumbly. At that moment his phone rang and it was Johnno.

I could hear Johnno's voice.

'Manu's been arrested,' said Johnno. 'You need to come and see me.' Will walked off, like a condemned man.

I never saw Will again in my life. I hope he's all right.

There was a big management clearout when we got home. It was a shame because I thought there was enough in that coaching group for another World Cup cycle. Most of them, anyway.

I did think they would probably make a change with Brian Smith. I've no idea how he got an international coaching job in the first place.

He had us squirming in embarrassment at the captain's run the day before we played Romania.

We ran this move off the top of the lineout, which involved me feeding Nick Easter and then, after some midfield intricacy, Cuets taking the ball and going through the gap. It wasn't exactly rocket science, but we pulled it off smoothly enough.

Brian blew his whistle and screamed like a madman at the top of his voice: 'Who's gonna fucking stop us?' I looked around. We had just outfoxed a defence made up of Bobby, our forwards coach John Wells and Johnno holding a tackle shield.

Well, they weren't going to stop us, clearly, but it didn't exactly prove we were world-beaters.

I'd like to think the RFU wanted to keep Johnno after the

World Cup, but that he felt it was hard for him to stay when everyone else was going. Being a man of great honour and dignity, he quit too.

I was gutted. He was a manager, not a coach, but I thought he was a very good one. He knew rugby inside out, and rugby players inside out too. What he did really well was to control the emotion of Test week and make sure the mood was right and the messages were clear.

One of the great feelings I experienced as an England player was to have Johnno shake my hand as I stepped off the team bus before every game. He did it with all the players and it made you feel ten feet tall.

He was, and always will be, a legend of English rugby.

It's such a shame that, on the back of 2011, he hasn't been involved since. Such a loss for English rugby. He has so much knowledge.

Did we feel responsible when he went? I guess so, to a degree – but the truth is we just got on the wrong side of everything at that World Cup. If we'd gone all the way on the field, all the stuff off it would have been forgotten.

But we didn't. And it wasn't.

5

BROTHERS IN ARMS

*'It has always felt like we are on
the same team.'*

Lining up for the anthem in an England shirt before a Test match is a special moment every time, but sharing that moment with my brother at Twickenham took it to another level.

When Tom and I got to do that for the first time, against Fiji in 2012, it was a moment I knew I would treasure forever. The wave of emotion that swept over me as we sang the anthem together, arms around each other's shoulders, was so powerful. I couldn't stop the tears.

What made it even more fulfilling for me was that I knew how tough a journey he'd been on and what he'd had to overcome to be there.

While my career had been taking off, Tom's had taken a detour that had provided him with an incredible challenge. He had made his Premiership debut before me on Boxing Day 2006 at London Irish. It was a big day for him, and I had gone along to the Madejski Stadium to watch, excited for him, but it hadn't gone to plan. He broke a small bone in his leg after four minutes, somehow played on for another ten but eventually had to go off and was out for months. That was a knock-back to start with.

When he got back playing, he found himself at the back of a long queue of midfielders at the Tigers. He was a crash ball centre – direct and powerful but without too many airs and graces. He was good at what he did, but there were other players in the same position who had more strings to their bow.

When Heyneke Meyer arrived as head coach, he took one look at him and came up with a left-field suggestion. He thought Tom's physicality could be harnessed better as a hooker.

That must have been an interesting thing to hear – like a goal-keeper being told he should retrain as a central midfielder, or an opening batter being advised that he would be better off opening the bowling. Still, Heyneke was adamant Tom could make a success of the transition. Cockers, as forwards coach, was less convinced. He thought, at twenty-one years old, it was too late in the day for him to convert to such a specialist position.

Tom went away and thought about it and then decided he would go for it. That took a lot of balls because he was basically gambling his professional rugby career. But self-awareness is a huge asset in a player, and Tom realized that he was always going to hit a ceiling as a number 12.

If he'd stayed at centre, he would have resigned himself to being a club squad man who might start seven or eight games a season if there was an injury or an international player was away. If he switched, the future was wide open. There were no guarantees it would work out; in the time it would take him to learn the ropes at hooker, other centres would develop and knock him further down the pecking order.

What helped Tom roll the dice was his love of farming. He always knew he would head back to the farm after rugby. If this crazy idea blew up in his face then, worst-case scenario, he always had that as his safety net. He was sent on loan to Nottingham in the championship to learn his new trade under a Kiwi coach called Glenn Delaney.

Tom had always been the trailblazer, being the older brother, but pursuing this adventure turned the tables. Suddenly it was me who was forging ahead with my career while Tom effectively retrained as a rugby player. I gave him all the encouragement I could, but it was such a difficult transition. It was like starting again for him.

Scrummaging was one key area he had to pick up from scratch. He had that farmer strength, yes, but there was so much technically to pick up. He was still living with Crofty and me at the time, and he would come back to the house so battered and stiff he could hardly move. Slowly, though, his body adapted.

There was lineout throwing to master too. He played in plenty of games where that went wrong, but Glenn just played him and played him and played him until he got better.

There must have been plenty of times when Tom questioned whether he had made the right decision. Not many players would have possessed the tenacity and resilience to make a success of it, but then again there aren't many characters like Tom.

After two seasons at Nottingham, he returned to Leicester as a hooker, looking like he had never played anywhere else. He was picked by England for the 2012 summer tour to South Africa after one season in the Premiership, and featured in the midweek games on that trip.

I did an interview with a journalist while we were out there, predicting he would start for England in the autumn. The journalist didn't laugh, but he looked at me in a way that said: 'Yeah right. You're only saying that because it's your brother.'

But I wasn't. I knew what he could offer.

People might assume there was a sibling rivalry between us, but there never has been. It has always felt like we are on the same team.

Maybe the fact that we both did the same job had something

to do with that. We understood how much effort and commitment it took to have achieved what we did.

Standing next to him at Twickenham, red-eyed as the anthem boomed out that autumn, I was just so proud. To be together in an England shirt represented a shared moment of satisfaction and joy that all the money in the world could not buy.

For Mum and Dad too. For seven precious minutes, when I got on as a second half replacement before Tom was subbed off, they were able to enjoy watching their two boys playing for their country together at Twickenham. How many parents get to do that?

I say 'enjoy'. Dad knew there was no place we would rather be and, having been there himself, was able to watch our games and take pleasure from the experience. But Mum? Mum hated watching us play with a passion. She would be worried about us getting hurt, but also about things going wrong. She would live every throw-in of Tom's and every pass of mine, gripped by panic.

In the end, it got to the point where it became so agonizing for her that she didn't come to games any more, and didn't even watch them on TV. Instead, poor Elvis, the family's Shar-Pei basset hound, would have to endure a two-hour walk across Norfolk whenever we played. He would come home, tongue dragging across the ground, close to collapse. Only then, with the game over and the call from Dad to say everything was all right, could she relax.

When Johnno went in the middle of November 2011, thoughts had immediately turned to who his successor would be. To say I was surprised when Stuart Lancaster was appointed England head coach – at first in a caretaker capacity – was an understatement. I was staggered. I don't think Stuart's name had been mentioned by anyone, and it certainly didn't cross my mind for a second.

I knew him a little bit from that one game with the Saxons but, when I heard that he'd been put in place as an interim appointment, I figured that the person they really wanted couldn't have been available yet. Top coaches tend to have top jobs. There was a lot of talk about Nick Mallett, who had just stepped down as Italy coach and who'd previously had a lot of success with the Springboks.

So I thought that Stuart would be a stopgap for the 2012 Six Nations, and that would be it. I assumed that the real England coach would be appointed at the end of the season and that Stuart would be thanked for his contribution and go back to the day job.

Yet, when Stuart took over, he immediately put his own stamp on things.

We had been due to fly out to Portugal for a training week ahead of the Six Nations, but Stuart ripped up the flight tickets and took us to West Yorkshire instead. Being a northerner, he wanted to help the region in terms of the exposure they got to England rugby, so we went up to Leeds.

We trained at West Park Leeds – a level-eight club with a so-so pitch – as part of his idea to take us back to basics and change the culture around the England team. He felt that a lot of the credibility associated with England had gone after the World Cup in New Zealand, and that the players didn't value playing for the national team enough. Stuart had written to all our families to get them to spell out what it meant to them to see us play for England. He tried to tap into the idea of what it meant to play for England and why playing for England was so special.

A load of guest speakers were brought in. Gary Neville talked to us about how, for all his Manchester United medals, he'd never won anything with England; Jamie Peacock also spoke to us about how far he had been willing to go as a player to serve his team. Simon Brown, an Iraq veteran, talked about fighting for your comrades and your cause.

There had undoubtedly been mistakes made at the World Cup, so I could see where Stuart was coming from, but I think he misread how much it did actually mean to all of us to play for our country. We are extremely passionate, and care deeply, but the English way isn't to shout about it or celebrate it. One of English people's great strengths is their cynicism, and you won't find a more cynical group than a room full of English rugby players.

It didn't matter how many times we swept the changing rooms or coached kids in our free time, we would always still be the same cynical Englishmen. That should never be mistaken for a lack of passion when playing for England. It is just the way we are made.

Stuart had this massive obsession with All Blacks culture and their attachment to the jersey, and he was basically trying to create an English version of it, but I just think that's not us as a country. Forcing this great cultural shift never felt authentic.

He wanted to raise the standards in terms of off-field behaviour, too, so he imposed a ban on socializing anywhere other than the team hotel when we were together. I guess we had to win his trust after what had happened at the World Cup, but the upshot of the changes he brought in was that playing for England felt like being back at school.

It just felt so restrictive. Danny Care was left out of the squad because he had been convicted for drink-driving, and Stuart felt an example needed to be made.

I thought Stuart had that wrong. Danny had made a big error, obviously, but he had made it in his own time, not on England duty. He should have been included because he was a terrific scrum half. It's all right going on these moral crusades but this is professional sport. You shouldn't give away your advantages just so your halo shines a bit more brightly.

Danny had come through the West Park minis. It was ironic that, as we trained there, his England shirt was hanging up on the wall of their clubhouse – but there was no Danny.

That first squad from Lanny was a real turning of the page. He got rid of a lot of the old guard. There were a lot of young guys in it, and a lot of players who had played a number of games for the Saxons. But because we were a new squad with new coaches, we weren't all on the same page that first week. We were training against Leeds University and our backline was shredded by these uni lads who included an economics student called Alex Lozowski. (He was to go onto bigger things.)

Somehow we got it together sufficiently to win at Murrayfield in the opening game of the 2012 Six Nations.

That was a scrappy old game, which saw a twenty-year-old Owen Farrell make his debut at centre.

Owen's dad Andy – Big Faz – had come in as Stuart's assistant. I had been really struck by the energy and enthusiasm that Andy had brought with the Saxons, and he did a lot of the actual coaching – the defence and the backline attacking strike plays – while Stuart did the general attack shape.

Stuart favoured a rugby league attack set-up. He kept a close eye on league trends. He would show us clips of the NRL and how they ran certain moves.

A generic rugby league attack shape was all very well in theory, but it's not comparing like for like. In league there's no breakdown and there are fewer moving parts. The left-hand side just defend the left-hand side and the right-hand side just defend the right-hand side. There are no scrummaging props to try to isolate. It's different. I wasn't convinced.

With Wilko having retired from Test rugby, England's stand-off was Charlie Hodgson. He played well in our next game in Rome, an ugly win in snowy conditions that made sure we were two from two going into round three of the championship. Despite the victory, we hadn't really clicked as a team and, as the half backs, Charlie and I were under scrutiny.

When you're a totally new team under a new coach and you're the 9 and 10, you are probably in the most difficult positions, because you need time in the saddle in a new environment as the decision-makers. But in the dressing room afterwards, Charlie confessed that he thought we were up against it for selection for the next game against Wales. I disagreed. I thought Stuart would give us another go.

Charlie was right and I was wrong. Stuart dropped both of us. Owen took over from Charlie and Lee Dickson displaced me. I was really disappointed. If Stuart thought it was going to be brilliant from the start, that was naive of him, because that's just not how Test rugby works. It was always going to take time.

The game was in the balance when I came off the bench with twenty minutes to go. I was desperate to make a point, and I had a shocker trying to force things. I gave a penalty away, chucked the ball to no one trying to hit Crofty in a wide channel, and generally made a dog's dinner of everything. We lost and I was really frustrated with my contribution.

I was also frustrated with my treatment. As a half back, all you ever want is to be backed, and I hadn't been. As a number 9, you touch the ball more than anyone else, you call plays and there's a lot going on, so you need to be clear of doubts. Instead, I'd been left with a mind full of them.

Lee finished off the championship as the starting scrum half, which saw us win in Paris and then record a big win over Ireland at Twickenham after we smashed their scrum. I scored the last try off the bench in that game, but I remember thinking, 'Thank God that's over' at the end of that Six Nations. I hadn't enjoyed it under Stuart. It had felt like a long eight weeks.

I was expecting the Mallett head coach announcement – or whichever big hitter was in the RFU's sights – soon. It couldn't come soon enough as far as I was concerned.

The problem was that we had finished second in the table, behind only Wales who had won the Grand Slam. The perception from the outside was that it had been a decent championship for England. So the RFU gave Stuart the job full time.

'Oh shit,' I thought.

The situation was clear. I was just going to have to get on and make the best of it.

I was recalled as starting scrum half for the 2012 summer tour to South Africa.

Dad had lived and played in Durban briefly so, with the first Test being there, the tour was a good chance for him to come out and revisit some of his drinking holes with some old mates and see some rugby while he was at it.

I was warming up on the pitch before kick-off when I spotted him and his friend Jeff in the stands at Kings Park. They were obviously coming off a big night because they were making their way up to their seats – which were right at the top of the stadium – in instalments. Every ten rows or so they would have to stop, regather themselves and go again. Dad, perched on a chair pulling in air, Jeff bending over hands on knees – it was like they were climbing Everest. I was killing myself laughing at them.

We ran South Africa close, but they pulled away to win it.

While we were in Durban, we were given some daytime down-time and so we headed for the beach. Manu decided to hire a surfboard. We'd seen in Auckland that he wasn't exactly Michael Phelps in the water, but Coley and I assumed he would be a pretty good surfer given his Pacific Island upbringing, so we tagged along to watch.

He was looking the part until the moment he got in the sea. Then it all went wrong for him. He just couldn't get through the first break. Every time, he would paddle himself about ten metres out into the ocean, only for a wave to flip his board over and knock him off. In the end, after about half an hour, he gave up, exhausted, and crawled back out on his hands and knees while we looked on, chuckling.

The following week we were in Johannesburg, which was my first experience of playing at altitude. Five minutes in and I was feeling like my dad and Jeff had at sea level the week before. My head was pounding, my heart was pumping, and I felt so out of it. I was absolutely fucked.

Before we knew it we were a try down. I put the ball into a scrum near our own line, but there was so much pressure coming through from South Africa that Dylan Hartley was unable to strike for it. The ball just rolled straight out of the other side and Willem Alberts broke off the scrum, picked it up and touched it down.

It should have been a scrum reset because no one had touched the ball, but the referee Alain Rolland awarded the try. That was par for the course with Rolland. Some refs never seem to work out for you, and I always felt when he was reffing that England were ten points down before the game started.

We were actually nineteen points down after nineteen minutes that day. Although I scored a couple of second-half tries and we again ran them close, they clinched the series. Also, I injured my shoulder late on trying – and failing – to stop JP Pietersen from scoring, so I missed the draw in the final game of the tour in Port Elizabeth.

When we played the Springboks again that autumn at Twickenham, I found myself involved in what must have been the most unequal fight in rugby history.

Eben Etzebeth had made his South Africa debut against us in Durban, and it was pretty clear from the start that he fitted the mould of Springbok second row enforcer. I got to know Eben well as our careers went on and discovered what a nice guy he is off the pitch. On it, it's a different story. It probably wasn't the smartest move having a go at him at Twickenham after he kicked the ball away when I was trying to pick it up, but I wasn't really thinking in the heat of the moment.

The bear was prodded and suddenly this snarling 6-foot-8, 123-kilo monster was in my face.

He shoved my head backwards while I hung on for dear life. If I'd have let go, he could probably have flicked me into Row Z of Twickenham with his little finger. From close range it looked like he was about to eat me alive. Fortunately, the cavalry – my brother and company – arrived just as he was tucking in his napkin and getting his knife and fork out, so I got out of there in one piece.

Eben and his gang of bruisers beat us and, having lost to Australia as well, we went into the last game against New Zealand on a run of one win in six across the summer and autumn.

The pressure was building.

Stuart's set-up wasn't very player-led, and I wasn't a senior player, but the All Blacks game was going to be my twenty-eighth cap. I knew a few things about Test rugby by now.

We were doing a team review of the South Africa defeat at Pennyhill Park on the Monday and I asked: 'Do you mind if I say something?' Then I went on a rant.

'Boys, the same things are costing us games week after week, and we are going round in circles talking about them. The penny has to drop. We can't keep on making the same fucking mistakes. We have to take some responsibility. This has to be more important to us or we are going to be saying the same things after this game and staring down the fucking barrel . . .' Etc.

It was a bit of a risk putting myself out there, especially with a character like Stuart who took a headmasterly approach. He might have thought I was undermining him. But luckily it wasn't taken like that. When the meeting finished, Andy Farrell came up to me and complimented me.

'That was brilliant,' he said. 'It's just what we needed. We need you boys to own this.'

I didn't plan it, but it had come bubbling up inside and spilled out. I guess it was the moment I found my voice off the pitch with England.

The next day, Tuesday, was our main training day. We were sitting in the changing rooms at Pennyhill about to go out, and Andy did this ten-minute presentation. It was hairs-on-the-back-of-the-neck stuff. By the time he had finished telling us about the ferocity we were going to bring at the weekend, and how New Zealand were going to face defensive line speed the likes of which they had never encountered before, we could have played the game there and then. The emotion was simmering. It was a great training session and everything built from there.

New Zealand were unbeaten in twenty Tests and playing some brilliant rugby, and most people thought they just needed to turn up to win. Only it didn't turn out like that.

We played unbelievably well, putting Faz's words into practice. We put them under so much pressure flying off the line that they made uncharacteristic errors and allowed us to build a 15–0 lead. When the All Blacks scored two tries in the space of three minutes early in the second half, suddenly the lead was down to one and probably everyone in the stadium was thinking: 'Here we go . . .'

But what happened next was stop-the-clocks stuff. Manu turned New Zealand's midfield into a scrapyard.

First, Brad Barritt went over for a try after a slick exchange with him, and then four minutes later he put Ashy in after a devastating burst. I hit him with a pass off a lineout and he reeled off a rugby who's who of destruction, handing off Dan Carter to bust the line, leaving Richie McCaw in his wake and then brushing off Aaron Smith before feeding to Ashy who did the rest. When Manu scored off an intercept shortly afterwards, Twickenham went nuts.

It was a massive win – a record seventeen-point victory margin against New Zealand. Manu, that day, was just a wrecking ball, so incredibly powerful.

He went on to have a fantastic career for England but there's no doubt that, if it hadn't been for all the injuries he suffered, he could have grown into an even better player. There's nothing like playing for your development, and having all that time on the field taken away from him held him back. He was a phenomenal ball carrier and destructive tackler, but he was never able to layer on all the extra bits to his game, as a distributor and kicker, that a player like Ma'a Nonu was able to. Even so, he made such a difference to England when he was fit.

That win over the All Blacks stopped all the talk about Lanny's future and started a load of speculation about how many of that England side might make the 2013 Lions tour.

Suddenly, a lot of us were in the frame.

Lions selection is a strange thing because it is obviously individual, but team results affect how the individuals are judged. The team that wins the Six Nations in a Lions year invariably affects the balance of the tour party.

The New Zealand game had given the England team an injection of confidence, and we rolled through the first four games of the 2013 championship with four wins, only conceding four tries, to set up a Grand Slam shot against Wales in Cardiff in the final round. Wales could take the title themselves if they beat us by seven points or more, so it was all set up for a grandstand finish. There was a title on the line and more besides.

We knew the Millennium Stadium would be jumping for the game, so Lanny came up with the brainwave of playing Wales's anthem and Max Boyce's 'Hymns and Arias' at full blast in the indoor training centre at Pennyhill Park while we were going through our moves.

A few coaches tried similar stunts in my time, but they never worked. Nothing simulates the game atmosphere. That one didn't, anyway. The noise inside the stadium was off the charts. The volume was so loud during the warm-up, we were struggling to communicate with each other – we were calling plays the guy next to us couldn't hear.

It is one of the great joys in rugby to play at the Millennium Stadium – or the Principality, as it eventually became. It's a glorious cathedral of rugby, even as an Englishman, when it feels as if everyone inside is gunning for you.

We felt like we were in a great spot ahead of that match – the focus and the energy were there and we thought we were ready to go and do the job. Only we weren't. Not by a long chalk.

We actually started the game quite well. Manu had a great chance early on, with Wales's defence splintered, only to spill the ball. Had that stuck and he'd gone over, who knows where the game might have gone. But Wales had a lot of experience in their side and they were streetwise. They neutralized our scrum advantage by messing about with it and by half-time they were six points ahead.

Then, in the second half, in a pulsating atmosphere, they blew us away. The racket inside that incredible stadium as Alex Cuthbert went over for his second try from Justin Tipuric's pass was just indescribable. My ears were literally ringing.

We lost 30–3 and Wales took the championship.

The dressing room afterwards was a truly dark place. We were stunned. We were all sitting there silently thinking: 'What has just happened?'

It is a coach's job in those situations straight after a game to help players through it. It's a real skill and a hard thing to do so soon after something so painful, but as a player you need some guidance and reassurance. You need to be told why it has happened and where we all go as a team from here. It doesn't have to be sugar-coated. It should be honest, but the disaster needs to be placed into context.

'OK boys, you are right to feel like shit, we didn't get what we wanted today because of X, Y, Z, but this is what we are going to do about it when we next meet up.'

Lanny said nothing after that game. That was a dereliction of duty on his part.

The next day, the papers were, unsurprisingly, full of predicted Lions squads that were full of Welshmen, given their crushing win.

We had gone from being England's great white hopes to being labelled chokers who couldn't deal with the pressure. As head coach, Warren Gatland had stepped back for the Six Nations, to take an arm's-length view, but what he had seen in Cardiff had to affect his thinking. The squad was to be named six weeks later.

A Lions announcement is odd because, as a player, you find out when the rest of the world does. It is a TV reveal and no one tips you the wink beforehand.

There were quite a few of the Leicester lads nervously waiting to find out who had made the plane to Australia. It was a midweek day and Cockers, inevitably, scheduled Leicester training to coincide with the announcement. I'm sure he did it on purpose. The Lions might be the Lions, but to him nothing got in the way of Leicester business.

The forwards were still hard at it on the field as Andy Irvine, the tour manager, started reading the names out. Us backs had just finished and my heart was thudding away as I sat down in the training ground dining room and listened.

Andy worked his way through the full backs, the wings and the centres, and as each Lion was revealed, an image of them appeared on screen in a Lions jersey. Every home nations player involved in the Six Nations had taken part in a photoshoot during the championship, just in case.

Manu was the first Leicester player named. No surprise there.

He was through the fly halves by now. This was it – the scrum halves. 'Conor Murray, Munster and Ireland.'

Top player.

'Mike Phillips, Bayonne and Wales.' Bound to be in, Gatland favourite.

There would only be three 9s going – it was now or never. 'Ben Youngs. Leicester and England.'

I had made it. I was going to be a British and Irish Lion, a member of the most exclusive club in rugby.

The names kept on coming, with the props next. Coley was in too. Great. Then came the hookers – 'Dylan Hartley, Richard Hibbard and . . . Tom Youngs, Leicester and England.'

This was about as good as it could get. Two Youngs brothers on the tour? I wanted to rush out and give Tom a hug, but he was still out on the field, mauling away with the rest of them.

There were two other Tigers named as well – Geoff Parling and Crofty – so not only was I going to Australia with my brother, but also with my housemate.

Someone plucked up the courage to go out and tell Cockers that six of us Tigers were in the squad, and he pulled the forwards into a huddle and broke the news to the guys.

Ten Englishmen were picked for the tour in all. Sky Sports had rocked up at Harlequins, clearly expecting Chris Robshaw, Mike Brown and Danny Care to be selected, but none of them had been. Cockers interpreted that, as he would, as a Leicester snub, and was delighted their London-centric planning had backfired on them.

The *Leicester Mercury* filled its boots with Lions interviews that day.

All the other Lions players had been in camp for two weeks by the time the Tigers and Leinster contingents joined up, hungover to hell after our respective Premiership and Pro 12 victories.

I was so excited meeting up. The Lions had all that history, and everyone had told me how special a Lions tour was. I so wanted it to be everything that I'd been told it would be.

The first stop was Hong Kong on 1 June 2013, for a match against the Barbarians. It was a terrible venue for a game, because it was so humid, but the experience was a brilliant one in terms of bonding. Gats let us off the leash and the lads went berserk, whacking down shots like they were going out of fashion. I think we got back to the hotel about 5 a.m.

Gats had us up at 9 a.m. for a team meeting, and then straight out onto the training paddock in searing heat and extreme humidity. It was all we could do to get through it, honestly. Rala, the kit-man, was hosing us down with cold water to keep us going. Hibbard looked like he was about to pass out. The ball was slippery as hell, the lads were seeing two of them and we trained like rank amateurs. We were terrible.

So, having learned our lesson, of course we went out on the piss again that night.

Gats knew what the score was and was happy to let us carry on, even if it meant our training that week wasn't exactly razor-sharp. It was all about breaking down the national team barriers and getting to know each other.

There were fifteen Welshmen out of the thirty-seven players on the trip, including the captain Sam Warburton. I was rooming with Taulupe Faletau, the quietest man in rugby. You change roommates all the time on a Lions tour, so you get to know everyone, and as we worked our way around Australia, I got to know guys like Justin Tipuric and Rory Best really well.

I soon got to realize that rugby guys are just rugby guys, the world over. You might have preconceived ideas about someone, having played against them, but when you get to know them, whatever team they play for, whatever their accent, their outlooks are similar. They're just good blokes. Even Mike Phillips, who never passed a mirror without introducing himself. He loved himself to death, but in such an amusing way you couldn't help but like him.

The games came thick and fast in Australia, and so did the nights out. When I look back now, it was amazing how much drinking there was on the tour.

We would play on the Wednesday and then go out that night, then you'd be holding tackle shields on Thursday helping to prepare the Saturday team. Then we'd all go out together after the Saturday game, and so it would go on.

After we beat the Queensland Reds, a few of us decided to hit Brisbane's nightspots with Matt Stevens, our sociable prop, leading the charge. He was in a shirt and chinos, clearly ready for action. The rest of us were just in casual gear but Sos assured us we would be OK to get in somewhere decent.

'Just act confident, guys,' he said. 'I'll vouch for you and everything will be fine.'

He sped off, leaving the rest of us to try to keep up. He definitely had his clubbing head on. He powered on and soon he was half a street ahead of us. In the distance we saw him stop, point to his right and disappear through a door. We got to the spot about a minute later. There was no sign of Matt whatsoever. Just a couple of doormen.

'Sorry fellas, you can't come in, dress code.'

'But our mate has just gone in and he said he would . . .' Deaf ears.

Sos had just marched on in and left us high and dry. So we trekked back to the hotel while Sos had a great night out. On his own.

Christian Wade had flown in from England's tour to Argentina as injury cover, and he also fancied himself as a night-out fixer. He told the lads he had sorted a private booth for us at this club after one of the games, which sounded impressive, but when a gang of us turned up we found him sitting with a bottle of Grey Goose vodka in what turned out to be a booth for one. Rory Best tore into him, telling him what a waste of space he was.

'No, no, don't be like that Besty. I sorted a booth for the boys.'

'Smiling (Besty called him that because he was always smiling), there's ten of us and it's a one-seat booth.'

'It was the only one available, Besty.'

And they went on at each other like this with the rest of us giggling away.

Those two got on like a house on fire. They were like the odd couple – Wadey covered in bling with his Afro comb in his pocket, and Besty a County Down farmer – but they just really hit it off. I guess that's the magic of the Lions. Shared shirt, shared bond.

The tour games were effectively auditions for Test spots and we all wanted to be Test Lions. We were obviously all competitive individuals, internationals for our countries in our own right. It was a three-match Test series against the Wallabies and we knew it was winnable. Australia were a good side but they weren't a brilliant side. We thought we had their number.

I'd played well against the Queensland Reds, but I thought I was probably up against it for a starting spot for the first Test in Brisbane, because Gats knew Mike Phillips well and liked him. Phills had an outward confidence and Gats was big on that. I knew it would be me against Conor Murray for a bench place.

Gats revealed his Test teams in quite a low-key way. He just fished out a crumpled bit of paper and read the names off in the team room. And when he got to the bench, there I was. I felt really proud and honoured, and doubly chuffed because Tom was starting.

That first Test was a great game – George North scored a brilliant individual first-half try for us – and it went down to the wire. When I came on with twenty minutes to go, it just felt so tense and pressurized out there. The whole thing was so emotionally draining. I think part of it was the fact that I didn't want to let down any of these teammates who I had got to know over the previous few weeks.

Australia could have won it if Kurtley Beale hadn't slipped over as he took a late penalty but, as it was, we scraped home 23–21. It was such a feeling of relief at the final whistle. But there's no time to catch your breath on a Lions tour, and I was back on the bench for the midweek game against the Melbourne Rebels a few days later.

There was a funny incident when I came on. We were on the attack and Sos was over the ball protecting it at the ruck. I thought I'd spotted some space and gave him the call to pick and go. He went to pick the ball up and, as he did so, this Rebels guy appeared at full tilt from nowhere and absolutely splattered Sos. When he had recovered, he checked in with me.

'Lenny, Lenny,' he said, with grass sticking out of his scrum cap. 'Did you say to pick and go?'

'No Sos. I said to leave it for me,' I lied.

'I'm so sorry, mate. I misheard you.'

'Yeah Sos, listen more carefully next time.'

As I scored one of the tries in what was an easy win, I was tackled into the post protector and my shoulder went numb. I got it checked out the next day with Phil Pask, the physio. Pasky told me that it was important we got my shoulder right for the weekend. That was my first inkling that I might be promoted for the second Test.

I was able to train with it strapped up and I said I felt able to play if needed. It turned out I was. I was starting. Mike Phillips had a bit of a niggle and he had struggled a bit in that first Test.

After he had announced the team, Gats came up to me and asked if I had been expecting the call.

'No,' I answered. 'But it's a nice surprise.'

'You'll be fine,' he said.

And that was it from him. It was only about the second time he had spoken to me all tour. Bear in mind there were only two weeks left of it by this point.

There was this perception of Gats as some sort of coaching genius after all the success he had enjoyed with Wales, but if I'm honest I didn't see it. He didn't say much, he didn't get to know you – in all honesty I was left wondering what all the fuss was about. He cut quite a distant figure, less impressive than I'd hoped. There were no Jim Telfer-type speeches from him – it was Andy Farrell, the defence coach, who was the main motivational voice.

Still, I was grateful for the promotion.

For me, that second Test in Melbourne should have been a career highlight – I was starting the Test alongside Tom, which made us the first brothers to start a Lions Test together for twenty-four years – but it turned out to be an oddly flat experience.

Part of the problem was the venue. The design of Docklands Stadium, which was built for Aussie Rules, meant that the atmosphere was muted. Our support had been incredible on that trip, but I remember walking out onto the field and feeling that the sea of red in the stands was miles away.

Then there was the game itself. It was a half back's nightmare.

The scrums were messy, there wasn't much fluidity to the game and it was just a really stodgy, tense affair. I never felt like I could get into it. I was subbed for Conor after fifty-three minutes and we lost narrowly, with Adam Ashley-Cooper scoring the only try of the game late on. It was all a bit deflating.

The result meant it was all to play for in the deciding Test.

Our build-up was bizarre. There was no review of the second Test and what had gone wrong, nothing. We basically went on a two-day piss-up in Noosa. When we finally got back to training, Rob Howley, the attack coach, asked for a catch-up and questioned how I thought Melbourne had gone.

I was pretty honest about how difficult I'd found it to get into the game, and he said he thought that maybe I hadn't managed the referee well enough at the scrum. I disagreed, but the direction of that conversation made it pretty clear that I wouldn't be wearing the number 9 jersey in the third Test.

As it turned out, I wasn't going to be wearing any jersey. I hadn't made the bench either.

I was disappointed, obviously, but philosophical. You are keeping elite company on a Lions tour. Gats had decided to go Wales-heavy for the decider. There were ten Welshmen in the starting line-up.

And no Brian O'Driscoll! Dropping me paled into insignificance against that bombshell. The week before, Gats had got Brian to stand up in front of the group and tell everyone just how much this series meant to him. Seven days on and he had dumped him. Jonathan Davies, who was brought in, was a good player, but he was no Drico. As Gats read the team out in front of the whole squad, we were all thinking: 'This is mental. What is he doing?'

Gats told the rest of us who weren't involved that we were free to do what we liked in the evenings since our tour was effectively over, but we either had to come back to the hotel quietly, so we didn't disturb the Test lads, or not come back at all. Within ten seconds of him saying that, my phone vibrated. I pulled it out and there was a message from Besty, who was sitting about three rows behind me. It read: 'I'll take option two, Gats.'

The non-match-day twenty-three players still had a role to play in helping to prepare the Test team, though. When we ran as 'Australia' in training that day in Noosa, we scored one of the greatest tries I've ever seen in my life. It was incredible.

The starting fifteen were a few metres out from our line, running through a strike play off a lineout. But the ball was overthrown and bounced to Justin Tipuric, who flicked the ball on to Owen, who sent it down the line to Wadey on the edge of our 22. He stood up Alex Cuthbert, then fed it back inside to Tipuric. Drico got involved as well with this look left, pass right *work of art* before passing onto Wadey, who stepped another defender, chipped over the cover, regathered the ball and touched down.

It was a creation of total beauty, like that Baa-baas epic against the All Blacks from 1973 that gets replayed over and over.

The starters were fuming because they'd been absolutely skinned – Johnny Sexton and Richard Hibbard were really going at each other – but the one good thing for them was that, however well Australia played in the decider, the Lions would be unlikely to face anything so perfect.

That night, us leftovers were sitting in a bar feeling a bit sorry for ourselves that we wouldn't be involved, when Ian Evans, the Ospreys second row, arrived with a tray of lagers and plonked them down on the table. 'Cheer up, boys,' he said. 'Try being the only Welshman in the squad that's not made the twenty-three. How shit does Gats think I am?'

We just cracked up – and cracked on, Drico included. He took his dropping like a champ, even if the rest of the island of Ireland didn't.

The narrative of the whole week was that Australia had peaked emotionally in Melbourne and wouldn't be able to hit the same heights again. Andy Farrell articulated it perfectly during his famous 'Hurt Locker' speech. We were all in the room for that and, whether you were playing or not, the hairs on the back of your neck were standing up as he spoke.

Big Faz was right. The Wallabies couldn't hit the same heights. We smashed them in the scrum and won the decider pretty convincingly to clinch a series for the first time since 1997. We'd achieved what we had set out to do as a squad, and the changing room was a very happy place afterwards.

Those are the moments you treasure as a group of players, where everyone is congratulating each other and you are all part of a shared experience. The celebrations were full on that day. I was dressed in my Lions blazer and tie, but that didn't stop Crofty pouring a pint over my head.

The actor Daniel Craig came in at one point with some bottles of champagne to join in.

The victory party went on for a long time in there before we rolled on to the post-match function at the Sydney Opera House.

It was surreal really. The Youngs boys living it up at the opera house after swigging champagne with James Bond. We'd come a long way from the farm in Norfolk.

6

SHATTERED DREAMS

'To be honest it didn't really matter
to me either way, but I was up for it.
After all, who doesn't like a
bit of drama?'

The 2015 Rugby World Cup felt like a once-in-a-lifetime opportunity. It wasn't just a World Cup. It was a *home* World Cup.

This seemed to be English rugby's 1966 moment-in-waiting.
Unfortunately, it didn't turn out that way.

Lanny's England team had started to take shape, and all of us
had high hopes. We felt like we were moving forward rather than
stumbling about in the dark.

Instead, we became the first hosts to crash out at the pool
stages. With a game to spare.

It was as crushing an experience as I've had in rugby.

I had, by now, established myself as Stuart Lancaster's starting
scrum half, but it hadn't been a straightforward process.

After the Lions summer, two different factors meant that
I wasn't in the best shape: the injury I'd picked up ahead of the
second Test in Australia, and the fact that I had allowed myself
to fall so far out of condition after the tour. I only played two
internationals – both off the bench – in the 2013–14 season.

My shoulder was a problem. I had no power in it to pass
the ball. And I hadn't looked after myself at all in the four-week
break post-tour. I came back to training totally out of shape and
5 kg overweight. It's always an issue for international players
involved in post-season tours, trying to shoehorn in a pre-
season, but my unprofessionalism that summer compounded the

issue. My injury was having an impact on my running, so I could only really do bike work when we met up with England for the first time that season – when I really needed to be doing a lot more.

I think Lanny suspected I might be swinging the lead, getting too cocky after becoming a Lion, but I wasn't. I had gone to see a specialist in London, to try to figure out what was going on with the shoulder, and he did this weird test where a needle is inserted in your arm at various points and an electric current is passed through it, which makes your arm ping up into the air involuntarily. The test confirmed nerve damage, so I missed the start of the club season. On my return, I was still only operating at about 70 per cent and I certainly wasn't match sharp. I was struggling to make up the deficit.

That autumn was a bit of a washout personally. I got off the bench against Australia and New Zealand for a combined total of forty-one minutes, but I missed the Argentina game in between after being hurt in training by a monster tackle from Ben Morgan that folded me up and crunched my ribcage against my hip bone.

The 2014 Six Nations the following spring was even worse. I didn't play at all.

Throughout his time as coach, we players only got to find out what Lanny was thinking when we met up with the wider squad. One of the weird aspects of his time in charge was that between Six Nations, summer tours or autumn campaigns, there was no contact from him. Nothing. We all had to report individually for one-to-ones with him at his office at Pennyhill Park to find out the lie of the land.

We all had specified appointment times, so we would queue up for them like we were waiting outside a doctor's waiting room. He always used to make this big point when we had our first team meeting of the week of stressing how he had scheduled these five-minute sessions for us all, like he was doing us a favour. You wouldn't hear a peep between campaigns from him, but he thought he'd covered everything with these bloody one-to-ones.

Anyway, when Lanny had me in at the start of that Six Nations, he opened up with: 'How do you think you've been playing?'

When a coach asks that question, there is usually an ulterior motive behind it. He is basically inviting you to do his dirty work for him and admit you are playing crap. I told him that I was trying my best to make things happen at Leicester, but the team were a bit stuttery. Over to you, Stuart.

'OK, I don't think you're playing particularly well,' he said. 'I think the other two scrum halves are going better than you, so I'm going to start Danny and put Lee Dickson on the bench.'

'I don't agree that Lee can bring more off the bench than I can,' I replied.

It turned into a pretty heated discussion, which ended with him spinning his laptop around and showing me a series of clips of me in action. Not playing very well. He had evidence.

I was fit by then, but I had definitely lost form. I think the constant treadmill of rugby that I had been on since my career had started had finally caught up with me post-Lions, and I was experiencing burnout. I felt mentally flat. It was like I was running on empty.

I sought advice from Mike Catt, Lanny's attack coach, who I always found a really good sounding board in the England set-up because he had been through it all as a player. He advised me not to worry about getting picked, but just to try to get back to enjoying the game again.

I tried but nothing changed. It got to the middle of the championship, and I asked Stuart if I could talk to him again. We sat down together on the inflatable barrier by the side of the training pitch at Pennyhill Park and I opened up to him.

'You're right, Stuart, I haven't been playing well,' I said. 'I haven't been at the level that you want me at and, here's the big problem, I don't know how to get back there. There's no spark inside me. I feel a bit lost.'

He listened and he empathized with me. It was a proper heartfelt conversation, one of the few I had with him. At the end of it, I headed back home in the car. Lanny rang me on the journey back to the Midlands.

'I've just been reflecting on the conversation,' he said.

In fairness to Lanny, he was a very reflective coach. He thought deeply about stuff.

'Look, don't worry about coming into camp next week,' he said. 'I think you should probably try to get away, you know. It sounds like you need a reset.'

It was a fallow week – there wasn't a game to build towards – so the time off allowed me a clear week without any rugby. While it wasn't an instant reset, it did help.

By the time the summer tour to New Zealand came around, I felt in a better headspace.

I was still the number three scrum half in the England set-up, but events conspired in my favour. Danny went down in training and, because Lee had been playing in the Premiership final and had flown out late, he wasn't considered to start. So I ended up playing against the All Blacks at Eden Park in the first Test on 7 June 2014.

We had a scratch side, what with all the players who weren't available, but we should have won that game. It was almost like a free swing, and we played really well. No visiting side had won there for twenty years, but we were leading with fifteen minutes left and level with two minutes on the clock, only for the All Blacks to steal it at the end.

They went on to win the series 3–0 but that tour felt restorative for me. I started the third Test in Hamilton as well, and it felt as if Lanny was starting to believe in me and what I could offer again.

There is one particularly funny story from that summer.

It had been a tough tour at the end of a long season and, on the flight back home from New Zealand, Jonny May decided to get pickled. He didn't drink often but, when he did, he would get very silly. I remember Ben Morgan was minding his own business, not harming anyone, snoozing away flat out with his headphones on.

'Watch this. I'm going to go and wake Blobby up,' Jonny said.

He got a big cup of water and just hurled it over Ben, who shot bolt upright, suddenly very awake. Jonny ran off, then army-crawled his way along the floor back to his seat. Sitting back down, he was trying his best to look innocent. Ben marched down the aisle towards him, seriously enraged. 'I know it was you, Jon, you prick.'

Lanny, who was in another section, heard all this commotion and stormed down to ask what was going on.

'Nothing, Stuart,' said Jonny.

'Have you been drinking, Jonny?'

'No, Stuart,' said Jonny, who was seeing ten of him.

'Are you sure?'

'Yes, Stuart.' Lanny walked off.

As soon as he had gone, Jonny got straight back up and headed towards the business class snack area.

Lanny reappeared.

'Jonny, what are you doing?'

'I was just getting a snack, Stu.'

'Jonny, go back to your seat.'

It was like a headmaster telling off a naughty school kid.

We landed in Los Angeles not long afterwards, and were in the connecting flights area, but by then Jonny was really struggling. He was looking very pale. He announced that he was going to be sick and ran to the toilets, where he burst into the cubicle and closed the door. He lifted up the lid of the pan, about to redecorate the porcelain, when he spied out of the corner of his eye under the door some familiar shoes at the urinal just outside.

He recognized the awful retro white Nike trainers that Lanny always wore.

He desperately tried to hold the sick back, afraid the sound of him vomiting would give him away to Lanny. Instead he ended up being sick inside his own mouth.

The moment Lanny left the Gents, he unleashed.

As a team, we needed something concrete behind us going into the 2015 World Cup.

After a respectable autumn, when we had seen off one of our pool opponents, Australia, it felt like we had to deliver that season's Six Nations title. Three runners-up finishes in three seasons under Lanny made us look like plucky losers. That had to change.

Wales, first up in Cardiff on a Friday night, was a massive game. They were in our pool, too. You'll remember that, two years prior, we'd taken an absolute spanking there. We'd grown a lot since then, though. We weren't going to be pushed around this time.

Cardiff in the Six Nations regularly brought with it Welsh mind games, and one of their tricks was to send an opposition team out onto the field, and leave them there for ages with the strains of Tom Jones's 'Delilah', marching bands, goats and all sorts going off around them, before eventually coming out themselves. There was a laser show planned this time at the Millennium Stadium, and we decided that, rather than go out alone into the middle of it, we would stand our ground in the tunnel. The decision was made to only take the field when Wales did.

To be honest it didn't really matter to me either way, but I was up for it. After all, who doesn't like a bit of drama?

Chris Robshaw walked us out of the dressing room and into the tunnel. Not far behind him was Mike Brown, who was made for this sort of confrontational situation. The Welsh subs were already there, waiting for us, but – as we had expected – there was no sign of the starting team. When the broadcast people told us it was time to go out onto the pitch, it was the cue to activate our strategy.

Robbo said no. They tried again.

'Just chill out', Brownie told them, not chilled at all.

Then the ref Jérôme Garcès got involved, but he got told the same thing. I was chuckling away to myself near the back.

This went on for about five minutes, until eventually Robbo and Brownie, point made, relented. As we walked out, Brownie piped up to Jérôme: 'If they're not out in a minute, we'll come back in.'

To be honest, I still don't know if the stand-off made any difference, but 'Tunnelgate' set the scene for a great night for us.

There was a bit of an odd start. We had prepared a lineout attack play that we intended using at the first opportunity. All we needed was for the lineout caller, Dave Attwood, to call the correct five-man lineout code to launch it.

When we won an early penalty, George Ford booted it into touch. The forwards gathered together and waited for Dave. They were all looking at him. Nothing. They kept looking at him. Still nothing. Then he just let out this crazy scream – 'aaaaaaaaaagh' – and that was it. His mind had just gone totally blank.

That's what pressure can do. It didn't matter. The guys had practised the lineout so many times during the week, they just did it anyway without a call.

By half-time, Wales had opened up a 16–8 lead, but we came back strongly.

Wales's successes had been built on the blitz defence of Shaun Edwards. It was hard to penetrate, but I always felt playing against it there were chances to manipulate defenders close to the ruck. They would get really high on the outside, but around the ruck they would not advance as much, so playing off the number 9 was the way to get in behind them.

After Jonathan Joseph had scored a great try, I put James Haskell through a hole that gave him a clear run to the line. Somehow, he managed to run into the post protector, the absolute idiot, but fortunately we won a penalty, took the lead, and were never behind again. A late penalty from Fordy closed the game out.

It was a big feather in the cap for the squad and for the coaching team; in a way, a coming-of-age for us all after 2013. It also felt like a significant mental hurdle had been cleared on the path to the World Cup – especially with Wales and Australia being the big guns in our pool at the tournament.

That win in Wales should have set us up for the championship and maybe even a Grand Slam – we had it within our control – but we slipped up in Ireland in round three, losing a tight game, which sent the title race to the last weekend.

The way the results panned out on the final day, we had to beat France by twenty-six points in the last match of Super Saturday to win the title. We'd watched Wales pump Italy and then Ireland thump Scotland, and it looked a hopeless cause, but we just thought 'fuck it, let's just go for it.'

That attitude served up one of the most enjoyable matches I ever played for England – exhausting, crazy, but so much fun. I scored the game's first try after ninety-two seconds and they just kept on flowing from there. France would score one, we would score two, then they'd score again. It was absolutely bonkers. There was *some* defence – the tackle Courtney Lawes put in on Jules Plisson almost knocked him back across the Channel – but it was largely attack, attack, attack.

Twickenham was absolutely rocking and we were loving it too. We honestly felt like we could do it. One more converted try at the death would have given us the margin we needed, and we were almost at the France line when Nigel Owens, the ref, pulled us up for obstruction. Robbo was pleading with him but Nigel said: 'That's enough now, Christopher,' and blew for the end of the game.

We'd beaten France by twenty points but it was second place again.

After finding a small rugby-free window to marry Char on an unforgettable day in North Walsham, and squeezing in our honeymoon, my 2015 World Cup preparations began.

Lanny had brought on board Matt Parker, from British Cycling, as head of athletic performance, and he kicked off the build-up with a big presentation about what we were going to do to get us in the shape of our lives for the tournament of our lives.

The coaching staff thought there was going to be a high ball-in-play time at the tournament, so they wanted us to have an edge in aerobic fitness. As such, phase one of training was four draining weeks at Pennyhill where we ran and ran and ran.

They called it MAS running (maximum aerobic speed) and it was tough, especially when we were doing normal pre-season stuff – weights and the like – as well. We competed in groups to win this ceremonial dagger each week, doing tasks like flipping logs and carrying sandbags. One of the tasks involved pushing our kit-man's car up a hill.

A note on him. Dave Tennison, or Reg as he was known, was an ex-Royal Marines fitness instructor and he had been kit-man ever since I had first come on to the England scene. But, just before the World Cup camp, an email arrived in my inbox, supposedly from Reg, informing me that oil had been discovered in some Caribbean country and telling me that I needed to invest in this company called LGO Energy, which had the drilling rights. If I did so, it would make me loads of money. The company's stocks were ridiculously undervalued at the moment, apparently, but the value of them was about to go through the roof. At the bottom of the email was a request to keep the information contained in it strictly confidential.

I honestly thought someone had either hacked Reg's account or was holding him hostage and had demanded his password. It was obviously a scam. Wasn't it?

I checked the mailing list and saw it had been sent out to a lot of the squad. I just deleted it and didn't think anything else about it but, come the training camp, I discovered that quite a few of the other lads who had received the email had actually invested.

It turned out that Reg had indeed sent the email – and not at gunpoint either – and that instead of rising, the price of the shares was heading south fast.

The lads were having it out in the car park with Reg, asking what was going on. He was explaining about problems getting the drill or some such. I couldn't believe my ears. I was thinking: 'How the fuck have they been persuaded to invest in this by Reg?' I mean, he wasn't exactly Martin Lewis. He was a kit-man, for goodness' sake. If I wanted financial advice, I'd ask a financial adviser, not the bloke handing out socks and shorts. I'm not sure that oil drill ever arrived, because the boys ended up losing tens of thousands.

Reg was sacked for gross misconduct after the tournament.

That whole training camp was well-intentioned but ultimately misguided, to be honest. We had a series of motivational speakers come in – but they weren't motivational.

A security guy came in to chat to us about leadership. The theme of the talk was his involvement in a terrorist attack on a shopping mall in Kenya. As he started his talk, the first picture he put up on the screen was of his mum. We were thinking: 'Oh my God, did his mum get kidnapped? Or shot?' This was heavy-duty stuff. It turned out his mum hadn't been involved in the incident at all. He just wanted to put up a picture of her.

Anyway, he told us he'd received a call when he was in his car to tell him he needed to rush to the mall because an attack was taking place. He recounted how he pulled over on the way to make an action plan and then carried on to the mall. We were thinking: 'This is the bit where the story is going to go mental and this guy is going to turn out to be the action hero.'

So much for that. It transpired that all he did was set up an evacuation area and basically made a register of everyone who left the building. Like a teacher at a school fire-alarm drill. That was it.

I'm not sure that talk hit the mark.

Neither did our day pretending to be riot police. Yep, riot police.

Lanny wanted to do something different with us that would test our ability to work as a team under pressure but, by this point, it was week five of intense World Cup training and we were all pretty knackered.

We were taken to a police training centre and issued with all the gear – boots, helmets, riot shields, the lot. I was picked as one of the team leaders and we were told to go on a 2-km run with all this stuff. My team included Marland Yarde, who couldn't carry his shield – it was too heavy for him – and Kieran Brookes, who was gasping for oxygen pretty much from the start. We did not resemble an elite unit.

We had to pretend to be riot cops, checking for rioters, so every time we reached a junction we had to look left and right and then announce whether we could see anything. Joe Marler, who was also in my group, would announce: 'Junction clear' in this ridiculous, high-pitched voice, and then we would move on to the next one.

No one had a clue where they were going or what they were doing. We ran round one corner and straight into Robbo's group. This went on for ages, two hours maybe. When we finally located the rioters, a load of police people pretending to be a rowdy crowd, we were tasked with shepherding them into a specific area. Kieran charged out of formation and was wiped out in a hail of bottles by these fake hooligans.

We were hopeless. It was hopeless.

When we got back on the bus to go back to Pennyhill,

everyone was moaning like mad. It was an absolute waste of time. We didn't learn anything. And loads of the boys ended up with blisters from the boots.

Then Lanny put a cherry on top by telling us the police were going to review our performances and then give us a debrief about things that we could do better.

The next day was a Saturday, which was a big training day, and a lot of the lads were sore and pissed off. Haskell more than anyone. He was complaining his back hurt and that he was knackered, that the police trip had been a shambles and that there was no way we should be training on the back of it. He was pacing up and down, grumbling.

'If they want leadership, I'll show them leadership,' he said. 'I'll tell them we're not training.'

Andy Farrell appeared. He'd obviously caught wind of the dark mood. 'Look lads, I know that yesterday was challenging and different,' he said. 'I know you've all worked incredibly hard and you're tired, but we need to rip in for one more day. Do you think we can do that?'

He turned to Haskell. 'Hask, mate, can you do that? Can you manage it? How do you feel?'

This was Hask's cue, the moment for him to lead the rebellion.

Instead, he just caved in like a bad soufflé and said: 'I'm fan-dabi-dozi.'

The whole group just looked at him in disgust. Five minutes later we were running shuttles again and getting flogged.

The police guy came in after that training session to give his debrief, and I've never seen a room look so uninterested in feedback. We were trying to win a rugby tournament, not improve our riot control skills.

We went to Denver for a fortnight after that for altitude training, which in fairness was a much better experience. And by that stage, the boys thought they had earned a night out. The only problem was that Lanny was instinctively against it, living in constant fear (as he did) of a repeat of 2011.

At the end of a Six Nations, or an autumn together, under Johnno there would always be a place organized in London where we could wind down together with our partners at the end of a campaign.

There would be security there and we would always have a really good night before getting back on the bus and coming back to the team hotel.

Under Stuart, all that stopped. We just weren't allowed out. I could maybe understand that at first but, as time wore on, surely we should have earned his trust? It grated not being treated as adults, and by week six of the World Cup training camp, it had become an issue.

We knew he wouldn't be keen but, when we landed in the States, I told Robbo to ask him if we could go out that night in Denver. Predictably, Lanny said no. Surprisingly, he then relented and said we could go into the bar across the road from the hotel for a beer.

'Sweet,' we thought. 'Result.'

But when we got there, Lanny was there too. It felt as if he was spying on us.

So a few of us quickly got out of there and went out elsewhere in Denver, on the sly. We had a hell of a night, actually. Ashy ended up falling asleep on a park bench and a policeman woke him up and drove him back to the hotel in a police car.

It was a good job Lanny didn't see that. He'd have had kittens.

We also did some white-water rafting down the Colorado

River while we were over there, which involved an assault on the management's boat to chuck some of them overboard.

Lanny was on board, but we thought it might not be a good idea to go for him with selection not yet decided, so the two main targets were Nigel Jones, the team doctor, and our media guy Dave Barton – or Biscuit Barton, as we called him, because he was always eating the team's biscuits.

Biscuit was slung off the raft and the doctor got whacked in the chest with an oar, so he went in too. Every time they swam over to try to get on one of the boats, they'd be met with oars and splashing, so they ended up floating down the Colorado River for an hour.

We eventually pulled onto a bank for a refuel and, when Biscuit and Nigel came bobbing past, we threw out a big rope to haul them in. Bizarrely, five minutes later, Marland Yarde floated by. No one had any idea he'd gone overboard. Maybe someone threw him in as payback for having to carry all his stuff in the riot exercise.

We were doing lots of training as well, and the thin air at altitude was a killer in terms of the MAS running. For me, the only way to get through it was to remember that, however much I was suffering, I only had to look around and there was always someone worse off than me.

Mako Vunipola was that poor person. At 120 kg, he looked like he was about to expire.

What made it worse for Mako was that Lanny took to running next to him, trying to encourage him. It was well meant, I'm sure, but it was the last thing Mako needed. All he wanted was to be left alone to suffer in silence. He is a man of few words, but he only has to lift his eyebrow in a certain way to convey how pissed off he is. And the eyebrow angle as Lanny chivvied him along told me he was furious.

Despite the hard graft, it was rewarding, and we returned home feeling like we'd made some really good progress physically.

Back home, as the World Cup approached, the pressure built. You could sense it. As head coach, a lot of that fell on Stuart. I'll never truly understand the weight of expectation on his shoulders, but he seemed to change as the tournament approached.

In one of our warm-up games before the tournament in France, we came in behind at half-time and, instead of going through two or three key points as he usually would to help get us back on track, he just said: 'You boys have got yourselves into this mess, you can get yourselves out of it.'

That was maybe a sign of the stress he was under.

When we came back into camp at Pennyhill Park two days later, he pulled the leadership group into the gym and told us he had something to show us. In the room was a white robe covering up something pretty large – it looked a bit like a crap ghost with no eyes.

It turned out to be a bell – a massive one – which had come from a warship and had been gifted to the squad by the Navy. Lanny told us he wanted us to think about how we might best use this generous but unusual gift, as a squad. We brainstormed a few ideas before I came up with the suggestion of using the sound of it to signal a line being drawn under the last game and the start of moving towards the next one. Given we had just lost to the French, it seemed a timely suggestion, and it was taken up.

Lanny called the full squad in and gave this big speech about the bell, where it had come from, its significance, and how it was going to be an important part of us from now on. The tone was sombre and dignified. Robbo stood up and told the squad what we had decided to use the bell for.

Everyone looked on respectfully.

'I'm now going to ring the bell to signify that the France game is done, boys, and we're moving on to Ireland,' he said.

He pulled the robe off it and revealed it in all its glory. 'Here goes.'

Ding. Ding. Ding. Ding.

With perfect timing, Hask bawled out: 'Iceberg ahead!'

The whole room collapsed into fits of laughter. Except Lanny, of course. He was fuming.

Lanny and Hask always had a love/hate relationship. Hask was a big character in the squad – great for team morale – but Lanny really struggled with him. They were chalk and cheese as people.

As the bell meeting broke up and we headed down the stairs, we walked past Lanny giving Hask a dressing-down. Hask was grovelling like mad, telling Lanny he hadn't meant any disrespect and that he actively supported various naval charities – anything he could to get himself off the hook.

It was honestly all I could do to get out of there without exploding with laughter.

That afternoon, after a weights session, the bell provided some more amusement. Jamie George, who was still quite new to the squad at that stage, hit a personal best on the bench press.

'Awesome, Jamie,' I said. 'By the way, Robbo forgot to mention that you need to ring the bell when you hit a PB.'

'Are you serious, Len?' he said.

'I swear, Jamie. Dead serious. I don't know why Robbo didn't mention it.'

Jamie walked towards the massive bell, looking a bit embarrassed, and as he did so I pressed the pause button on the gym music so everybody automatically stopped what they were doing.

Just as the place went silent, Jamie rang the bell. Everyone turned to look at him.

'What did you do that for, Jamie?' he was asked.

'I got a PB so Lenny said I had to.'

'No, I didn't . . .'

He got so much stick.

With our opening game of the World Cup against Fiji only three weeks away, the final squad still hadn't been named and the uncertainty was stressful.

There were a handful of positions that Stuart was still thinking about. The big one was at centre, where it had boiled down to a head-to-head between Luther Burrell, who had been first choice for the previous couple of Six Nations, and Sam Burgess, Bath's big cross-code signing.

When Stuart had picked Sam for the wider training squad after barely a season of union and earmarked him for a position he did not play at his club, it caused a big stir in the squad. He was welcomed warmly enough, but there was some suspicion too, because we didn't know what he had been promised. For a player who was a genuine superstar in the NRL to switch codes was a massive decision, and you had to wonder what had been said in private in order to tempt him over from league. Had he been promised a World Cup spot on a plate, ahead of lads who had grafted to get the team to where it was? That was always the suspicion, the elephant in the room.

In saying that, you could immediately see what all the fuss was about. He was an inspirational guy and a natural leader. He trained bloody hard, too.

Stuart's plan was to stage an internal squad game the day before he announced the World Cup squad to finalize the thirty-one. It was a terrible idea. While it must be extremely difficult to pick that squad, he should really have known its make-up by then. He certainly shouldn't have needed an internal game to decide it.

The thing about these games – especially internal games so close to a big tournament – is that no one wants to get hurt, so they are all a bit cagey and messy. The other thing is that everyone knows every single call. So you call a move where you hit the middle of the field off a lineout and then come back on the short side and, hello, there's somehow twelve defenders waiting on that side. The games are unrealistic.

I was in the Pennyhill Park changing room ahead of this shootout match when in walked Hask and his roommate Tom Wood, wearing full England match-day attire. They didn't say a word, just walked to their lockers, headphones on, bobbing up and down to their music in full Test-match mode.

It released the tension of the situation and we had a good laugh about the situation.

But underneath, everyone knew what was on the line. Inevitably, Sam and Luther were selected on opposite teams. I felt really sorry for both of them. It all came down to this.

During the game there was an attacking lineout just outside the 22 for Sam's team, he hit a brilliant line, went past Luther and scored. He was picked and Luther wasn't.

Maybe Stuart had already made up his mind, maybe that just reinforced what he was thinking anyway, but it was almost as if that try decided it. I always suspected Lanny was trying to engineer a spot for Sam anyway but, even if he wasn't, to leave it as late as he did to make the final call was an error of judgement. Stuart got that so wrong.

The irony was that the whole Sam/Luther thing would probably never have been an issue had Manu been fit. He was the guy we really needed in our midfield, but injury conspired to rule him out – injury and off-field issues.

Before we met for the World Cup training camp, Lanny had rung me to tell me he wouldn't be picking Manu. I knew he had been struggling with a groin problem for ages so I wasn't surprised. But then Lanny said: 'I can't pick him after what's happened.'

'What do you mean?' I said. I had no idea what he was talking about.

'You don't know?' he said.

'No.'

'You seriously don't know?'

'No.'

'The incident with the police officer.'

It turned out Manu had got into some trouble a couple of weeks beforehand. The club knew about it, but they'd kept it under wraps. It was the first I'd heard of it. Anyway, Lanny decided he had to bring it out into the open and referenced it in a public statement explaining why Manu wouldn't be at the World Cup.

If you ask me, no one needed to know the details. He wasn't going to be fit anyway, but Lanny was so scared the story might come out mid-tournament that he felt he had to get ahead of it. I felt he had dealt with that the wrong way. So did a lot of the lads. They felt Manu had been hung out to dry. It's at a time like that you want a coach to back you, not expose you.

So there were a few things that were badly handled ahead of the tournament.

Another one was the Take That send-off concert for us at the O2 after our last warm-up game. That was massively over the top. O2 were amazing sponsors and they put on an awesome event, but it felt like the sort of thing that should have taken place had we won the World Cup, not before the tournament had even started. It was all too much. We hadn't earned the right and it felt really uncomfortable. I was pretty sure Lanny felt that too.

It was so out of sync with all the things that we'd done for the four-year build-up under him – all the stuff about being humble. It made us look entitled and it didn't feel right at all.

And, as things turned out, it was a hostage to fortune.

The opening game of the tournament against Fiji on 18 September 2015 happened to be my fiftieth cap. Ordinarily, I'd have led the side out for the game because of that but, with it being the big World Cup kick-off, Lanny decided he wanted the captain, Robbo, to do so instead. That was odd of Lanny. All through his time in charge, he'd put such an emphasis on the honour of the shirt and these landmarks, but it was as if he had been deflected by the scale of the home World Cup. With the big occasion so close, it felt like he was a little bit all over the place.

He tried to make it up to me by telling me I could lead the side out for the team run the day before (not quite the same in a deserted Twickenham), and by hosting a really awkward Ben Youngs quiz beforehand in the changing room. It was all about my England career – when I'd made my debut, and that sort of thing – but it had a back-of-fag-packet feel. Courtney, who I'd played with for England all the way back to the age groups, walked in on it halfway through because he'd been taking a shit. To be honest, I'd rather Lanny hadn't bothered at all.

The opening game itself passed off a little nervily for the team, but we got the bonus-point win we wanted.

I was a waste of space. I'd put all this extra burden on myself – because of the significance of the occasion, and the fiftieth cap – that I over-thought everything and I was miles off. From the first kick-off, which I didn't put my name on, I was awful. Of all the games I played for England, I reckon that could have been my worst.

Fortunately, the rest of the team bailed me out. We were up and running. Then came Wales.

Oh God. Just thinking about that game still sends me into a cold sweat.

Play that match ten times, and we would have won nine of them. But we lost and I have to live with that – and where it led to for us in our home World Cup – for the rest of my life.

All the time I was out there, I felt like we were in control. We'd scored the only try of the game after I had put Jonny May away down the short side in the first half, and we were on top in virtually every aspect. We had them up front, they were dropping like flies, and only Dan Biggar's boot was keeping them in it.

But Owen, who had been picked ahead of George, was kicking everything in sight too, and Sam Burgess was doing a good job of stopping Jamie Roberts, who they built everything off as a ball carrier. We had them where we wanted them. When Richard Wigglesworth replaced me with half an hour left, we were up by four points, 16–12, and I was convinced we would see the game out.

Somehow, we managed to lose.

When Wales broke away to score their try through Gareth Davies and level the game, you could almost sense the air being sucked out of the stadium. When you're on the pitch it's easier, because you know you can influence the game. When you're not, you feel so helpless. When Biggar, who just couldn't miss that day, kicked a penalty from halfway to put Wales in front, I could feel it all unravelling.

I was just thinking: 'This isn't right. This isn't how it's supposed to be.' And then we were awarded the penalty.

Everyone knows what happened next.

Were we right to go for the win by kicking to the corner?

It was bold, but pretty much every side in the world put in the same situation would have gone for the penalty and the draw, I think. There was no guarantee Faz would have kicked it from wide out on the right, of course, but I would have backed him to knock it over. I always backed him to knock kicks over. It's what he did.

Maybe the guys on the pitch felt like it was our destiny to kick to the corner, maul Wales over the line and win that game. But we were driven into touch and time ran out on us.

Perhaps that incident represented the chickens coming home to roost from our failure to actually take home a trophy as an England team under Stuart. Four times we had been Six Nations runners-up but, for all our good wins, we couldn't take that next step. So, when it came to that Wales mega-match, we just didn't have the knowhow and assurance to get a colossal call right with the game on the line.

We weren't mature enough as a side in the heat of that enormous battle to take the emotion out of it. Because we'd been in command and were suddenly on the brink of losing, we allowed hearts to overrule heads.

What that situation was crying out for was one of the coaches to run on with the kicking tee and provide some clarity. The message should have been sent: 'Take the shot.'

While it's extreme to demand that every possible scenario should be covered by the coaches beforehand, in that moment it was a mistake to leave it to the players. The stakes were just too high. Robbo was left to shoulder the burden, and afterwards the roof fell in on him.

I really felt for him, because he'd been a very good captain and an ideal front man for England. He's a great guy and he didn't deserve to be hammered like he was.

He was shell-shocked in the dressing room afterwards. We all were.

We were let down again afterwards by Lanny. He didn't address the team in the dressing room, when we really needed him to, or on the bus afterwards. There was nothing from him.

You are all over the place emotionally after a loss like that. It is a horrible space to be in. You feel so isolated and lonely. With no leadership from above, you naturally end up seeking out comfort from your support networks, and the squad splinters into its cliques. I could feel that happening after that Wales defeat.

Had it been Uruguay next, the weakest side in the group, I honestly think we could have taped everything back together and still given that tournament a shot. A soft game would have given us more time to process the Wales defeat and stop feeling sorry for ourselves. Bill Beswick, our psychologist at that tournament, always spoke about everyone having the choice about whether to be a victim or a fighter, and needing to get beyond that victim state.

It wasn't Uruguay, though. It was Australia.

I was struggling with an ankle I had rolled in the first half of the Wales game. I had landed on Dan Biggar's foot and turned my ankle competing for one of his kicks. It started to swell up instantly inside my boot. I played through it, but I had my foot in a bucket of ice in the dressing room afterwards.

It got worse in the days that followed, and it still hurt a lot as I prepared to do a fitness test on the Wednesday. I banged down the co-codamol and fought my way through it. I thought I could manage fifty minutes against the Wallabies with it strapped up and more painkillers inside me. Maybe the right thing to have done would have been to say I wasn't up to it and stand aside, but I was desperate to play. The home World Cup meant so much to me and I wanted to help keep us in it.

The next day was our last big preparation day and, before the session started, Lanny set out a semi-circle of chairs in the changing room at Pennyhill Park. We needed something inspirational to revive us after the Wales nightmare, so Lanny told us that he wanted to read us something.

'This is a great book and I'm going to read you this passage from it,' he said.

He picked the book up and we waited while he thumbed his way through it, looking for the motivational passage he was after. We waited some more. And some more. And some more. He was flicking through this book, backwards and forwards, licking his finger, trying more and more desperately to find the passage.

We were all looking at him. Prince Harry, a vice-patron of the RFU, was there too, and he was also poised, listening. The awkwardness was off the scale. There he was, the man charged with delivering the Webb Ellis Cup, hunched over a book containing the words he believed could put us back on course, but unable to find the right page.

It summed up our tournament, really.

In the end he slammed the book down and tried to tell the story off the top of his head. Basically, it was some tale about the dance of doom out in the wild between the lions and the buffalo. The lions wear the buffalo down during the dance – and you can guess the ending.

That was what we were going to do to Australia, apparently. Although, as things played out, we were the buffaloes.

Australia outplayed us that night. Bernard Foley scored a couple of great tries, David Pocock and Michael Hooper caused havoc at the breakdown and we ended up looking like a ragbag collection of misfits, well beaten.

If we had progressed, I wouldn't have been able to play in the rest of the tournament. My ankle was done. But that pain was nothing compared to the heartbreak inside.

In Lanny's defence, he tried to lift us with some comforting words in the dressing room afterwards, but it was like trying to raise a sunken ship from the foot of the Mariana Trench. We were beyond devastated. Lads were just staring into space, numb. We had put so much in for so little.

We were out, and it felt like we had let down the whole country.

It was easily the lowest I've felt in rugby.

We were given the option of going home for a couple of days before our last game against Uruguay up in Manchester, but I decided to stay on at the Pennyhill Park Hotel, as did a few of the others.

Robbo was really struggling; he had basically locked himself away in his room. Coley, Marler and I decided we needed to get him out of there and down to the bar. We kept texting him and finally he broke and came down to join us. No one needed to say too much. We just needed to be there for each other. We had a few quiet beers and tried to come to terms with what had happened. We couldn't.

When we travelled up to Manchester, Hask was asked to host a presentation event to thank all the staff for their efforts and try to lift the mood. He put together a PowerPoint with a series of slides, one of which was an image of Matt Parker's face on the body of someone standing outside a Job Centre. Matt – our head of athletic performance – was in the room. Everyone was laughing, including me, but it might have been a bit too soon.

Ian Ritchie, the RFU chief executive, came up to the hotel in Manchester and asked to see a good few of us to try to find out where our campaign had gone wrong, but at that point it was all too raw, really, to make sense of.

The leadership group did a debrief with Lanny after the Uruguay game, but we knew inside that he was finished. It's just top-level sport. He'd had a four-year cycle, and if you don't get to where you need to, then we all know what happens.

I remember going home after we had been eliminated and just trying to hide away.

The World Cup carried on without us for another three weeks. I still watched the games back at home, but I just didn't want to speak to anyone about England. When I did go out, people would ask me about it and what had gone wrong.

There was no escape. I remember going to my brother- and sister-in-law's house and having my nephew Alfie, who was four at the time, grill me about why I wasn't at the World Cup when it was still on the TV.

'I'm just not, Alfie.'

'But I thought you got picked.'

'I did get picked.'

'Well, why aren't you there then?'

'Because we lost.'

'Who did you lose to?'

'Wales and Australia.'

'Why did you lose to them . . .?'

And it went on and on like this, with my nephew giving me the third degree.

It's only now, with distance and with the experience of other England environments under my belt, that I can identify where we went wrong. It wasn't anything tactical, because I think by then we had a good game plan. We had a really good defence, and we could score tries. It wasn't the quality of the players – we had a good squad.

As I see it now, the problem was that we weren't really a team. We lacked cohesion and we lacked genuine team spirit. We weren't really mates; we were more like work colleagues thrown together. Ultimately, we just didn't have the deep-seated desire to achieve for each other. I think that was the biggest issue.

In English rugby there are intense club rivalries – Leicester/Northampton, Saracens/Harlequins, Bath/Gloucester – and that is one of the game's great strengths. But it can also be a problem for the national team. Before 2015, there was never any attempt to break all that down. So when the pressure came on (and it was pressure like never before at a home World Cup), we didn't have the cohesion and trust we needed to survive.

You have to work to create those deeper bonds. They have to be encouraged.

And the most straightforward way to do it in my experience is to let players off the leash a little bit to break down the barriers and get to know each other. Team socials are where you get to know each other on a deeper level, but Lanny just wouldn't go there.

I don't just blame the management. I think there should have been more effort from the players to deal with the cliques.

I'd been part of the squad for five years. I had become part of the leadership group and I should have addressed the issue head-on. But Lanny's England – like Johnno's – was always an environment where you stuck with your own group.

We had so many good aspects to us, but if you don't have that camaraderie and togetherness, you can't achieve what you hope to.

We didn't have it – and we failed spectacularly.

7

THE MIRACLE MAN

'When someone like Eddie tells you that you are smoking hot and the opposition won't be able to live with you, then you can't help but believe it.'

When I first heard Eddie Jones's name being linked with the England job, I was excited.

At that stage, I hadn't heard any of the horror stories of him pushing players beyond their breaking points, or of how tough he was on his assistants. All I knew about him was that he'd just coached Japan to victory over South Africa, and that his World Cup back-catalogue with Australia and the Springboks was mightily impressive. I couldn't have cared less that he would be England's first overseas head coach. All that mattered to me was that he might be able to help us.

We were shattered after the 2015 World Cup experience; we needed someone to put us back together.

My first contact with him was through a voicemail he left me at the start of January 2016, asking me to call him back. He had good news for me: I was in the Six Nations squad. Turning up at Pennyhill for the first time with Eddie as coach was an interesting feeling. I had by that point started to hear some of the stories. I was curious – and a little apprehensive – as to what England would be like under him.

We arrived to a WhatsApp message from the team manager, asking us all to pop in to see Eddie individually. I wasn't excited about the prospect of more Lanny-style one-to-ones, but I went along to his office and we got chatting about scrum halves. He wanted to know who I thought was the best in the world. I went for Aaron Smith and Will Genia.

He agreed they were sharp. 'But,' he said. 'I think you're really important to this team, and I think you can be really sharp too, mate.' He said he often spoke to Fourie du Preez, the former Springboks number 9, and that he apparently rated me highly. That was nice to hear, but then came the rub I was waiting for.

'I just want to see a small change in you, mate.'

'OK Eddie, what's that?'

'I want you to lose a bit of weight. I don't want you eating any more of these.' He took out a bag of sweets and shook them. This was different.

'Mate, what's your weight at the moment?'

'Ninety-two kilos, Eddie.'

'I reckon let's try to get to like maybe eighty-nine, eighty-eight, something like that. Let's aim for something like that and then I reckon you'll be a bit sharper as a running threat.'

He had pulled a figure out of thin air, but what he said made sense. 'OK,' I said.

'Go speak to the S and C guys and get a plan together,' he said. When I stood up to leave, he offered the bag of sweets to me. 'Mate, do you want to take these with you?'

'No thanks,' I said.

'That's a great start,' he said, and shook my hand.

What Eddie didn't know is that I don't like sweets. If he had offered me a bar of chocolate, that would have been a different story. I would probably have snatched his hand off, wolfed it down there and then in front of him, and that would have been that for my England career.

To lose the weight, I committed to doing extra conditioning stuff on a Monday afternoon and on a Wednesday when we were technically off. Because I just got on with it, I think Eddie didn't feel like he had to be on my case as much as he was with some of the boys.

My dealings with him from then on were pretty much always positive. That first evening we got together for a team meeting, at which Eddie proceeded to turn the narrative surrounding the side on its head. We were the 2015 World Cup flops, the team that had let down a nation, but you'd never have thought it from listening to him.

'Right boys,' he said. 'We've got an opportunity to win the World Cup in 2019 and we've got an opportunity to be the best team in the world. How good does that sound? Do you want to be a part of that?'

He spoke for a few minutes, setting out his vision of how we were going to do it and he hooked us all. It was unbelievable. He just had this way of selling a message. He commanded the room so well. At the end of his speech, the players who hadn't even been able to get out of their pool four months earlier were genuinely believing we could transform ourselves and become the best team in the world.

Unlike Lanny, Eddie didn't spend all his time talking about team culture. His take on it was that professional sport is about winning. That's the main thing. So keep the main thing the main thing and don't get distracted by sideshows. If you win, the culture takes care of itself.

He had done his homework and he knew there had been issues in the team with regards to our cohesiveness and he wanted them sorted. But by us, not him. 'If you need to have a fucking beer and thrash it out, go to the pub,' he said. 'I'm not here to babysit you. You're all adults, you do it.'

It was music to my ears – a coach who was willing to treat us like grown men and trust us. After the classroom environment that we'd been used to under Stuart, it was just what we needed. 'Thank God,' I thought. 'This is so refreshing.'

We knew we had responsibilities that went with the territory, and we didn't need reminding of that, but just the knowledge that the option was there if we needed it helped free everything up. It felt like a different environment instantly. We'd have a drink together in the changing room as a team after a game and, on a Sunday night during a campaign, we would sometimes go and have a beer after our team review as well.

Even midweek was judged OK. I remember one time I was in the bar at Pennyhill, sitting there having a beer on a Tuesday night. We'd just had our main training session of the week and I felt I'd earned it. Faz joined me for a glass of wine and Manu had one too. All of a sudden, a message pinged on my phone. It was from Eddie. I didn't even know that he was in the room.

'Good, mate,' it said. 'Get the team together. Make sure everyone has at least one.'

A drink together is part of rugby's tradition, and he was all for the social bonding it encouraged – even on a Tuesday. Whether that was the key that unlocked everything or not, it felt like we got close as a squad under Eddie pretty quickly.

He changed the captain, replacing Robbo with Dylan Hartley. He was a surprising choice to some, given his disciplinary scrapes, but he was brilliant. He is really good with people, and he was able to help knit the squad together and eliminate the cliques. He'd been captain at Northampton anyway, so it was a role that he was familiar with, and he was the on-field figurehead for the more abrasive, English style of rugby Eddie wanted.

When Eddie was confirmed as Lanny's successor, my assumption was that he would keep Andy Farrell on as his defence coach. Even though we had bombed out at the World Cup, that didn't change the fact that Big Faz was a very good coach.

There was a lot made from the outside about Andy and Owen being father and son – favouritism, and all that – but inside the squad it just wasn't an issue. The father–son thing was never even spoken about by the other players. You wouldn't have known they were related. Their relationship was really professional. Andy would challenge Owen as much as he challenged everyone else. So, as I say, I thought Eddie would retain Andy. But he didn't. He carried out a full-scale clearout, bringing in Paul Gustard instead, and calling in his old Japan assistant, Steve Borthwick, as forwards coach.

At the start, Eddie oversaw the attack. From the very first training session, he made it clear what he wanted. He watched us go through a couple of the old plays that we had been running where we went out of the back of the arrowhead. Then he stepped in.

'We're not playing fucking rugby league here, boys,' he said.

He wanted us to take the ball flat, hit the opposition hard and regenerate possession with lightning-quick rucks. It was a different approach to how we had been playing, but it suited the squad we had. Eddie was all about finding the best fit for the players he had, rather than trying to hammer square pegs into round holes. As backs, we used to spend hours with giant elastic bands wrapped around our waists in training to make sure we stayed square when we passed and ran straight. It was rugby basics, but it reinforced the muscle memory.

The game plan might have changed in its specifics from match to match, but it was always crystal clear. Eddie could watch an opposition team and instantly analyse how to beat them – he was the best I ever worked with at that. He would boil it down to three straightforward points that we needed to concentrate on. If we got those right, we'd win the game. For example, it might be:

1. Speed of ball
2. Turn them in three
3. Force them back on the inside

Speed of ball gave us a disorganized defence to attack. Turn them in three meant that if there was no momentum to our attack after the phases, we kicked. Force them back on the inside directed the opposition towards our heavy hitters.

The instructions were always simple and gave us clear direction on what we were going to do to win the game.

And we won games from the off under Eddie.

Before we knew it, we were going to France in the final round of the Six Nations, playing to win a Grand Slam. Honestly, who would have thought that was possible after what had happened at the World Cup?

I had been his starting scrum half for the first four matches but, for the Grand Slam game, Eddie said he was going to go with Danny.

There's always this perception that if you play in the same position as someone then there's bound to be this huge rivalry, but that was just never the case with Danny and me. I shook hands with Danny and congratulated him, just as he always did with me when I was picked ahead of him. We enjoyed each other's company – he's such a likeable bloke – and we genuinely always got on very well. I'm so thankful that was the case. And I'm sure

Danny was as well because, if it had been frosty between us for the length of time we were in the squad together, it would have been bloody awful.

When we played against each other at club level, we would always catch up in the warm-up for a chat and sometimes during the match as well. We'd have some banter at scrums, telling each other to stop cheating and the like. Because I respected Danny so much as a player, I enjoyed playing against him. I knew I had to be switched on because he was so good. We raised each other's standards and brought the best out of each other without doubt. We competed, but in a really healthy way.

And it was always about making the team better. Under Eddie, he made it clear when it came to scrum half selection that it was about getting the perfect eighty minutes out of that position. In his eyes, the perfect eighty minutes meant I set up the first fifty-five or sixty and Danny brought it home for twenty, because that played to both our strengths. I had to do certain things in the game to get us in a winning position, and he would come on to push us over the finish line.

Or, in the case of the 2016 Six Nations finale, the other way round.

Eddie wanted Danny out there early to exploit the space around the ruck that he had spotted in the France defence, then me on in the second half to do the same and close out the game.

In the twelfth minute, Danny burst away from a ruck through a hole and sped forty-five metres to score between the posts.

Three minutes into the second half, I replaced him. Soon after, Billy Vunipola hammered his way into French territory, I found some space around the ruck from fast breakdown ball and put a grubber kick in for Anthony Watson to score in the corner.

It was almost like Eddie could see into the future. We had the game won and, as I booted the ball off the pitch, the final whistle brought a glorious feeling of release.

England were Grand Slam champions for the first time since 2003.

After all the shit of the World Cup and the near-misses of the Lanny years, we had finally won something. It felt so good.

We had a trophy in our hands at last.

It was a wonderful moment – and it felt like the start of something too.

We headed Down Under that summer for what Eddie, who loved his cricket, dubbed the Bodyline Tour.

England had never won a series in Australia before. He talked to us about that cricket series in the 1930s, and how brilliant that Australia team featuring Don Bradman had been, and how England's way past them had been to beat them up. He told us he wanted us to do the same to the Wallabies. Australia had this pretty-pattern game, and he wanted us to disrupt and destroy it.

Sometimes summer tours felt like tag-ons at the end of a long season, but Eddie really bigged that trip up. For him it was personal, against his home country and his great rival Michael Cheika, the Wallabies coach. He referenced the Wallabies' threats in passing, but he mainly focused on us, emphasizing how our firepower would be too much for them.

In general, there are two types of coaches – those who concentrate on how their team nullifies the opposition, and those who are all about the damage their own team can do. Eddie belonged in the latter camp.

When someone like Eddie tells you that you are smoking hot and the opposition won't be able to live with you, then you can't help but believe it, especially when he puts the evidence forward to back up his claims. It wasn't just hot air and bluster with Eddie – he would show us the clips and data to prove what he was saying.

Eddie's old schoolmate, Glen Ella, was going to be joining us for the tour to help out with the attack. As one of the famous three Ella brothers who had lit up the game in the 1980s, I was looking forward to meeting him. I had a surprise when he walked into the Gold Coast hotel lobby with his suitcase, sweating heavily and looking like he'd eaten the other two of them.

I knew looks could be deceiving, though, and I was willing to give Glen the benefit of the doubt. That night, we had our first meeting, and Eddie showed us a few video clips. The first one was of a five-man lineout. Glen was at the back of the room.

'Hold it there,' he said. The clip was frozen.

'David Pocock is standing at first defender,' he pointed out, with emphasis.

We were puzzled. A back row would pretty much always stand at first defender off a shortened lineout. It was like stopping the clip to show that I was wearing the number 9 jersey. There was an awkward moment while everyone waited for Glen to add something more profound, but that was it.

He didn't have much of a clue on the training field either. Thank God we had Owen and George there to sort everything out. He was a great bloke, but we learned pretty early on that Glen, who would miss meetings while he went for afternoon siestas, was basically best at drinking wine with Eddie and playing cards with the lads.

Another Australian joined the squad at our Surfers Paradise training base ahead of the first Test in Brisbane. We'd noticed him in his grey suit and tie, taking notes on the sideline as we trained. But then when we went into our team huddles, he would come over and crane his neck into them and listen in attentively. It was odd, but we just assumed he must be another of Eddie's mates.

Anyway, we'd finished training, and Danny and I were walking off towards the outdoor swimming pool to cool off when this guy appeared again.

'G'day boys,' he said. 'Ready for the weekend?'

We politely said something along the lines that we were hoping it would go well. Then, out of nowhere, he came steaming in, eyeballs popping.

'Hope?' he said. 'Hope? Hope is what you put on the lottery. You're gonna smash them, you're gonna grind them into the dirt . . .'

All this fire and fury came pouring out of his mouth. We'd never even spoken to this guy before, and had no idea who he was. 'Fellas, you're gonna terrify them.'

This was Danny and me he was talking to – two of the least intimidating rugby players to have ever pulled on an England shirt. On and on he went, venting about how we were going to break their bones. He was the most aggressive bloke I think I've ever met. He told us he was going to go along to Cheika's press conference the next day and was going to stare him out. Then he was going to get into the tunnel on game day and do the same to the Wallabies team.

Danny was looking at me, trying not to laugh. I had to pick up a towel from the sun lounger and put it in my mouth. I was going. I didn't want to be disrespectful or rude, but this guy was nuts. Danny kept on teeing him up for more.

'What else should we do on Saturday, do you think?'

The outbursts got more and more outlandish. My shoulders

were going up and down as he ranted and raved. When he eventually finished and walked off, Danny and I were howling.

We were desperate to find out who the hell this guy was. I went to ask Dylan and he rolled his eyes.

It turns out he was a sort of self-made psychologist called Bradley Charles Stubbs who had created a role for himself as a 'coach whisperer'. He had got in touch with Eddie during the Six Nations and offered his services. Eddie had told him he could come along and observe what we did.

Safe to say, we didn't see him again.

England had never beaten the Wallabies in Brisbane before, but you could see the new-found confidence in the side from the way we came back from a shaky start to make history.

Eddie hooked Luther Burrell after just twenty-eight minutes and went to a 10 and 12 combination of George and Owen instead. It was rough on Luther, but it worked for the team, with Jack Nowell scoring right at the end to win it. That victory was the springboard for the rest of the tour.

We won the second Test in Melbourne to clinch the series with a real backs-to-the-wall triumph. It was all hands to the pump, but wins like that are often the most satisfying.

Australia liked to play phase after phase, but we just refused to break. Just before half-time we completed this incredible defensive set to keep the Aussies out.

There had been plenty of chat before the game in the tunnel and on the pitch from the Wallabies, reminding us that we'd been the only World Cup hosts ever to go out before the knockout stages – 'fucking hopeless Pommies', that sort of thing – so we gave them some back. 'You boys have got nothing. You've shot your load. We could have defended for another ten minutes . . . blah blah.'

Tempers were fraying. The back and forth carried on as we left the pitch and headed down the tunnel. Nick Phipps, Australia's scrum half, was carrying it on, and by that point I'd just had enough of the sound of his voice. He was just in front of me, so I grabbed his collar and yanked him – but I yanked him harder than I meant to and, as there wasn't much of him to begin with, he went flying over the top of a table.

The whole thing escalated. Guys were flying in, there was a big commotion, it was all going off. Having started it all, I scuttled off towards the safety of the changing room, leaving mayhem behind me. Eddie was standing there looking like the cat that had got the cream. He loved it. This was Bodyline made real.

It was a great win, but we weren't done. We wanted the series whitewash in Sydney.

We were staying at Coogee Beach ahead of the third Test, and Eddie decided that, instead of doing our recovery session in the pool, we would do it in the sea.

There was one problem with that – Maro Itoje couldn't swim. Eddie had that covered, though.

'Maro, mate, there's no need to worry,' he said. 'We'll put a rope around you and strap you to Glen on the beach because he ain't moving anywhere. He can be your anchor.'

Poor Glen. It was his birthday during the tour and, instead of a cake, the boys presented him with an iceberg lettuce with a candle in it – which Eddie just loved. He was copping it left, right and centre about his weight, but he was loving it. He was on the holiday of a lifetime.

We went on to take the third Test 44–40 – after Eddie had

done another of his ruthless first-half substitution jobs on Teimana Harrison – to complete a 3–0 win.

Before the game Hask, who was injured, had been given the job of presenting Teimana with his shirt for the match. Hask gave this speech that was supposed to be all about Teimana but, after about ten seconds, diverted into five minutes all about himself. He had played really well in the first two Tests, and he was determined to milk his moment, as he always felt he never got the credit he deserved. He described himself as the unflushable turd of English rugby because he kept on popping back up despite no coach ever rating him.

At the end of that tour, he unilaterally created a Man-of-the-Series award, which he awarded to himself!

It was a great tour – one of the best I've been on – and we let our hair down at the end of it with a big celebration in Sydney.

By the time we reached the departure lounge for the flight home the next day, the party animals had slowly fallen away so it was just Jamie George and me left in the game. We were on the gin and lemon bitters by then, knocking them back with abandon. We boarded the Emirates flight to Dubai for the first leg, determined to carry on the party, and rolled up to the bar after take-off to down some more. I remember blurrily looking at the flight map on the TV at one point, thinking we must be nearly in UAE airspace, and being horrified to find we hadn't even got to Perth. Australia really is huge.

We carried on gamely but, in the end, we were beaten somewhere over the Indian Ocean and sloped off for a kip. I was woken up by the sound of Jamie throwing up. All over his T-shirt.

He took off the offending item and washed it out, but no one would give him a spare, so he flew the rest of the way to Dubai with his gut out. When we disembarked in the UAE he bought a shiny darts-style 'I love Dubai' shirt to cover it up for the rest of the journey home.

We had a re-match with Australia that autumn. We carried on where we had left off on tour, winning 37–21 to complete an unbeaten November and perfect 2016 calendar year.

Our four tries against the Wallabies that autumn included a tap-and-go touchdown from me.

The tap and go was one of my favourite parts of being a scrum half. It is all about instinct. You don't have enough time to scan the field. You take an instant picture and go off that image. Can you see a hole? Can you see a space? Are there a lot of bodies in the ruck who are out of the game?

Analysis fed into it. I would look at tapes of opponents when penalties were given and make a mental note of which players would switch off when the whistle was blown. Who would use it as a chance to take a quick rest? Who would be out of the game feeling sorry for themselves? There would always be a few in a team.

But, in the end, it would all come down to the moment.

The key thing was that you had to be all-in. If you were even fractionally unsure then you would be better off pulling out. You had to be committed. The second you hesitated, the opportunity would be gone. Often, it was about getting in behind the opposition defence and giving the side something inviting to attack on the next phase.

Against the Aussies, when I got the ball, I was off and over the line in a flash myself. Nick Phipps – my old mate from the tunnel spat – was in my sightline when I set off. But at that point you just read the situation unfolding in front of you. You check your opponent's body angle and make a call on what to do next from that. I gave the dummy and he bought it all ends up, and finished somewhere in the hospitality suites while I went over to score without a finger laid on me.

I was named Man of the Match and Player of the Series – a genuine award, as opposed to Haskell's creation from the summer tour.

Usually, when the time comes to disperse and go back to your clubs at the end of a campaign, you're ready for it. And playing for England means quite a long time away from home and family, and the pressures of Test rugby are draining – but I never wanted that autumn series to end.

I remember wishing there was another game.

We were riding the crest of a wave. Everything we were doing with England was far more advanced than anything I'd done before. The way we trained, the speed we were working at, the tactical framework – everything. There was always a step up with England from club rugby, but under Eddie it had become a giant leap.

The detail was forensic. On a Sunday, we would always have a tactical meeting, a team meeting and separate forwards' and backs' units meetings. We would also have a leadership group meeting. The way Eddie was, you had to be switched on and well-prepared for those meetings because you were only seconds away from being asked a question to which he would expect an answer.

On Monday morning, the leadership group would come together again for an alignment meeting ahead of training, after which there would be a units meeting to review how it had gone that day. On Tuesday after training, we would have another debrief meeting in the evening. On Wednesday evening, there was a scenarios meeting, to run through how we proposed to handle situations that might come up at the weekend.

Thursday would be our final big training day, followed by a team comms meeting, which was a forum in which any issues the players had could be raised. The psychologist and Neil Craig, Eddie's performance guy who had come from AFL, sat in on this. Friday would be the last run-through, followed by a players' meeting in the evening when we would talk through what was on our minds ahead of the time and mark any milestones.

Then there was a game of rugby on the Saturday.

There was a lot more off-feet planning stuff than I had been used to. It was pretty full-on. But it helped us feel as if we were leaving no stone unturned, and that we were as prepared as we possibly could be for going into Tests.

At the same time, Eddie was trying to get us to own the game plan to a much greater degree. He might call a walk-through session for 6.30 in the morning, when we'd turn up and there'd be no coaches there, so it would be up to us to run the training session ourselves. That sort of responsibility was helping to build our self-reliance.

This was a high-performance environment in every sense, and we were beginning to feel unbeatable. We rolled on through the 2017 Six Nations, extending our run.

Beating Wales at the death in Cardiff in the second round was a narrow squeak. Jonathan Davies probably still regrets not going for touch with his clearance kick late on, but our response to set up the match-winning try for Elliot Daly in the corner just showed how we had evolved. George Ford had fielded Jon Davies's kick near halfway and set off, firing the ball right to left to Owen, who charged towards the fractured Wales defence.

When Faz's dad was with England, Owen used to do this drill with him where they would whip these passes to each other. They were like missiles. There wasn't even an arc on them, they were just so flat. Owen pulled one of those out of his repertoire and fizzed this bullet pass out to Elliot, which was so perfect he didn't even have to break stride. He just swallowed it up at full speed and flew over in the corner for the try.

It was so simple but so beautiful. Not this time, Wales.

We put sixty points on Scotland and wrapped up another championship on the penultimate weekend. We made all the right noises afterwards about finishing the job in Ireland on the final weekend and clinching another Slam.

But I think winning the title early conspired against us.

We wanted another clean sweep and, if we completed it at the Aviva, then we knew we would also beat New Zealand's eighteen-game world-record-winning run in top-level Test rugby. We weren't short on motivation. But maybe we did rest on our laurels with the title secured. Subconsciously it's hard not to. It's human nature.

And Ireland beat us fair and square.

They were so competitive at the breakdown that they disrupted our system.

Tactically, we got that game in Dublin all wrong. We had been using pods of two forwards off the number 9 to either hit the ball up or act as decoys to go out the back. It had worked well for us but, seeing the success Ireland were having, we should have adapted.

If we had switched to a pod of three – which is what a lot of teams do off the number 9 – we would have been better placed to withstand Ireland's breakdown threat. The extra man would have given us another body to clean out with. Instead, we stuck stubbornly with the two and Ireland jackalled the hell out of us. As the rain came down, things went from bad to worse for us, and the Grand Slam slipped through our fingers.

It was a lesson for everyone, Eddie included. He would always be the first to criticize himself, and I think he fell off his unbelievably high standards in allowing what happened to happen. It's fine going in with one game plan, but you need to be flexible if it's not working.

Nevertheless, we had won another championship – the first time England had gone back-to-back since 2001. We had our self-respect back and were a team to be feared again.

A lot of the players who won those back-to-back championships were basically the same ones who had failed at the World Cup, but the injection of belief we'd been given had transformed us.

He might not have been everyone's cup of tea, but it was incredible the turnaround Eddie had engineered. I'm not going to sit here and say that everyone had good feelings towards Eddie, because he certainly challenged some lads in ways that were sometimes extremely to the point, and people aren't used to that.

I can only give a verdict from my viewpoint; he just pressed the right buttons inside me.

Maybe I was at an age where I was naturally maturing into the best version of myself, anyway, but playing under Eddie empowered me. He really believed in what I could bring. He made me feel valued and, if you feel valued in any job, you perform better.

He would tend to be critical at the start of the week, breaking you down with areas you needed to improve for the game ahead. But as it approached, he would build you back up again with praise, so by the time game day came around you would be feeling like a million dollars. And his communication when we were away from England was outstanding. Eddie was always in touch with a text message here or there after a club game – sometimes during a game. It was so refreshing after the silence from Lanny.

Sometimes the content of the message was motivational. 'Will be your best ever Six Nations mate. I'm sure of it.'

'Keep pushing.'

'We're stepping up mate.'

Sometimes it was technical. 'Great break 62 minutes, Benny. Loved it mate. Can I see more of it?'

'Really loved the tempo you brought.'

'Better awareness to run mate.'

He would send me infographics with metrics like my passing accuracy off both hands and compare them to other top scrum halves. It was just constant feedback.

I still have all his messages on my phone. There is one that simply reads: 'Best number 9 in the world. Trademark.'

David Priestley once said to me that, with coaches, the thing that you'll remember most after you have finished is how they made you feel. That will determine whether you probably have a good association with them or a bad association with them.

For me, that period from when Eddie took over until 2020 coincided with the best rugby I played in my career.

Eddie made me feel like a world-beater.

8

TIFF

*'We sat there and talked and it was
very emotional. They were upset and
frightened. We were shell-shocked
and devastated.'*

People sometimes ask me, even now, if I regret turning down the Lions in 2017.

I don't. Not for a second. I mean, how could I, when the decision was set against the heart-rending context in which it was made? Rugby is important to me, but insignificant in comparison to my family.

When I came to write this chapter, there was no way I could put everything into words by myself. I needed Tom by my side. It felt only right that, even in a memoir about me, this particular period of my life is something that we should speak about as brothers – because it affected us both in different ways, and I wouldn't trust myself to be able to tell the story alone. So the following is taken from a conversation with Tom: the best man I've ever met. Tom's words are *italicized*.

Tom's wife, Tiff, was first diagnosed with Hodgkin's lymphoma, a type of blood cancer, in 2014. It's the reason Tom didn't tour New Zealand with me and the rest of the England squad that summer. Now, the success rate in treating lymphoma is quite high so, while it had been a shock to find out about her diagnosis in the first place, I had genuinely assumed she was going to be all right. She was such a strong, determined woman – of course she was going to get better, and the horrible nightmare she'd been living would be over.

Hodgkin's lymphoma wasn't a really aggressive form of blood cancer. If you were going to get one, it was almost the one that you'd want to get. It was meant to be a six-month chemotherapy course when we started the treatment, but it just turned to shit, really.

It went from 'This is going to be OK', to the first scan, three months into Tiff's treatment, when we found out the cancer was still there, growing. The consultant told us that the problem with blood cancer is that you've got it on a defined road, but that it can just turn right and then turn left, and you have to constantly try to work out which way it's going to go.

Tiff had a transplant of her own stem cells, which worked for a time, but she fell ill again during the 2015 World Cup. The scans weren't good – again – so we had to find a new treatment. Off we went with that. We kept on changing tactics, hoping something would work. In the end we got to a situation where she had a donor's stem cell transplant.

As the 2017 Six Nations was ending, Tiff was waiting to find out whether her donor transplant had worked or not. We knew that if her body had taken to it, then she was on the road to recovery. If it hadn't, though, the prognosis wasn't good.

We had the scan three months on from the transplant and they found some lymph nodes on her liver. It was at that point that they said there was nothing they could do, and they told her she had about six weeks to live.

I remember being sat in that room in the hospital in Leicester when we were told. I looked out of the window at this cloud and thought: 'Holy shit, this is actually genuinely going to happen.'

My brother rang me from the hospital to tell me that it hadn't worked, and that the cancer had spread to her liver. That was it, he said.

I couldn't process the information.

I asked Tom what I could do, and whether he wanted me to come over. They said they would come to ours. They came in and it was just awful. Beyond awful.

We sat there and talked and it was very emotional. They were upset and frightened. We were shell-shocked and devastated.

Tom and Tiff had a three-year-old daughter, Maisie. It was a horrendous situation.

The next day, Tom came into the club and spoke to all the Tigers, to tell them the news. Somehow, he held it together. I really don't know how he did it, but he stood up in front of the whole group and told them he needed a couple of days off – but that he wanted to carry on training and playing. It was his way of dealing with it.

By then, Tom was Leicester captain. After the World Cup in 2015, Eddie had rung him up and told him he wasn't part of his England plans. That was so tough on Tom, for his last experience with England to be that traumatic tournament. To go from starting hooker at a World Cup – and starting hooker on a Lions tour two years prior to that – to being overlooked for even a squad place was tough to work out. I still felt he had a lot to give in an England shirt. I never really understood Eddie's decision. Selection is so subjective.

But Tom being Tom, he didn't mope, he threw himself into the club stuff. He was respected and liked by all the players at Leicester, and a lot of them in that room were very upset by what he had told them. At that stage, no one on the outside knew and no one on the outside needed to know. It was a deeply private matter.

Selection for the summer Lions tour to New Zealand, which had been front and centre in my thoughts, was suddenly irrelevant. All I could think about was Tiff, Tom and Maisie.

When squad announcement day came, I was waiting to find out whether I had been picked with very mixed feelings. The situation had changed everything. I wasn't sure if I wanted to go now. I was in the car with Char when the names were read out on the radio, and the thought struck me that it would be easier if I just wasn't picked. There would be no decision to make then.

But I was.

'Fucking hell,' I thought. I turned to Char and told her that I couldn't leave. Not with the way things were. I wasn't going to tour. I was going to say no to the Lions.

She was fully supportive. She thought I was making the right call. I knew I was.

I went to see Geordan Murphy, Leicester's director of rugby at the time, and told him I wasn't going. I said to him that I hadn't discussed it with Tom or Tiff because they would have been mortified if they felt like they had swayed my decision, but that I had made up my mind. I was comfortable with the call – the problem then was how was I going to drop out without making Tiff's condition public?

I suggested to Geordie that he put out a statement saying that I needed an operation in the summer, or that I had mental burnout and needed a rest. He said that I needed to talk to Tom.

So I did. I told him I needed to stay here with him in whatever capacity he needed me.

'Are you sure?' he asked.

'Yes,' I said.

I couldn't believe it when he told me. I said: 'What do you mean?' He said he didn't want us to ever feel guilty about it because it was his decision. He wanted to stay back here and have some decent family time. You can never repay that sort of loyalty.

I was pretty emotional. I just thought he was an incredible brother at that moment. To decide to stay back home to support me was big. It's not like he was missing an England tour. The Lions is the Lions. The Lions was the best thing I ever did in rugby. It was massive for me. I loved it. They could have won in New Zealand and had a fantastic time.

Sometimes, you let opportunities go by and you regret it, don't you? I was worried that might be the case for him. But we had a real tough, sad family situation.

And, being honest . . . I didn't want him to go. I wanted him to stay, because I was in a bloody pickle and I wanted help. But I would never have said it to him, because it wasn't my decision and it's not the kind of person I am.

We've always been very tight, but you never know how tight you are until it's tested. It was unbelievable of him to do that. I suppose it's a reflection of how we are as a family that we tend to look out for each other and do the right thing when we need to.

I'd always like to think that I'd have done the same. It's a very easy thing to say. But you never really know unless you're in the situation.

Tiff was extremely touched by it. She felt a bit guilty that he'd done it, but I told her not to because it was his decision and it was what he wanted to do for us.

I never spoke to Tiff about my decision not to tour. Let's be honest – it was so insignificant, compared to what she was facing.

We still had to break the news that I was withdrawing from the squad. I went to Simon Cohen, who by now was Leicester's chief executive, and asked his advice. 'Can't we just say that I need an operation?' I said.

He knew how delicate the situation was, but he was worried

that if I pulled out of the tour citing an injury, a journalist would check on the story and potentially find out it wasn't true. Then the real reason would come out and we wouldn't even have a chance to influence it. He felt that we were better off controlling the narrative as best we could.

We checked with Tiff to see if she was all right about it and we drew up a statement to release. I'm still very uncomfortable about it, even now. Simply because of what I did for a living, a totally private matter was going to become a matter of public record. But what else could we do?

We did find that hard. It was hard for her family too. But we understood it wasn't a normal situation we were in. We also looked at it in terms of the fact that we weren't the only ones out there dealing with something like this.

No one's invincible, and sometimes it's a good thing to be honest about that. It's OK not to be OK, you know.

If I could turn back time, maybe I would have called Gats and asked him not to pick me in the first place. That way, no one would ever have needed to find out – but then, I suppose he would have been asked why he hadn't selected me.

It did mean that I still had to call him to explain to him that I was pulling out, though. He was totally understanding. It wasn't a long conversation. He was totally supportive; his view was that my family was the only thing that mattered.

Greig Laidlaw was called up to replace me.

Once the statement was announced, Tom and I were bombarded with kind messages.

Rugby is like a giant family, and at times like those it really pulls together. The support was amazing. It wasn't just teammates who got in touch, but opponents I didn't even really know particularly well. Yann Maestri, the French second row, was one.

I got a phone call from my sponsors, Adidas. They were due to pay me a big bonus for getting picked for the Lions tour. They told me they were going to honour the payment regardless. They said it was obviously down to me what I did with the money, but that maybe I could use it to take Tom, Tiff and Maisie away on holiday.

We couldn't go abroad because Tiff's immune system was so up and down, but we managed to get away to Center Parcs and create some special memories.

When they do a stem cell transplant, to try to stop the two immune systems fighting, they put you on some drugs. But at that point, the doctors took Tiff off all of that and just said: 'Look, get some living done now. Enjoy some life.'

We had such a nice time at Center Parcs. It was lovely, and special. I can't tell you how often I think about the fun and the laughter we had there together.

I watched quite a lot of the Lions games on that New Zealand tour on television, some of them with Tom at our parents' house back in Norfolk. Never once did I think I should have been with them. I was exactly where I was supposed to be.

Six weeks after the terminal diagnosis, Tom rang to tell me Tiff had been admitted to hospital and that things weren't looking great.

I was thinking: 'Oh, my God, this is it.'

She had gone downhill and she had sepsis. It didn't look good. I thought it was going to happen.

But it didn't happen.

Tiff's condition improved. She was discharged from hospital. As the weeks went on, she slowly began to look a little better.

By the time it got to Maisie's birthday in November, she was actually looking well. It was a bit baffling.

It was genuinely like she reached the lowest point possible and then just gradually started to crawl her way back.

She fell ill again in February 2018, with a chest infection, but she was looking really well. She went for a scan and, when they got the results back, they told her that the cancer was gone.

She was in remission.

They couldn't believe it. It was like her body had rebooted itself. Scientifically, they spoke about whether it was perhaps because they were frozen stem cells that were transplanted into her, that they were late to kick in or something. No one really knew for sure why. It was unbelievable.

It was a miracle.

We had these bonus years and off we went. We lived it and we loved it and we had a great time as a family, with Maisie, making the most of every day.

Tiff was with us for another five precious years until the cancer came back very aggressively.

It just snuck in out of the blue again.

It turned out this time she had acute myeloid leukaemia. Not the one you'd want – let's put it that way. They gave her three to six months. She died nine months later.

We'd been together since we were teenagers. To lose her absolutely broke me.

Tiff lost her fight in the end, but my God, she gave it plenty. She was such a strong woman. I feel blessed to have known her; I just wish I could have known her for longer.

The memories we have of Tiff, and of being with Tiff, will always be precious.

9

HEAVEN AND HELL

'Benny's mega-log had gone up spectacularly and the fire was out of control. It was chaos out there. And no one got a wink of sleep all night.'

There is only one game in my entire career that still gives me flashbacks: the 2019 World Cup final.

I will have moments when I am alone with my thoughts, driving along in the car maybe, when suddenly an image from that evening in Yokohama will randomly pop into my head. I don't have that with any other game. I've lost Grand Slam deciders, I've lost Premiership finals, I've lost plenty of other big matches, but that one stands apart. I suppose World Cup finals tend to do that to a person.

We played such great rugby in Japan. We really did. We had beaten the All Blacks a week before, with one of the great England performances, and then when it came to the biggest game of our careers, we didn't fire a shot. When that match repeats itself in my mind, I always end up asking myself: why?

I've spoken to other England players who were involved and it's the same for them. It's like it's an itch we cannot scratch. If only we could have that eighty minutes again.

From the very beginning of Eddie's time in charge, everything had been aimed at the 2019 World Cup final. We had all been given a countdown clock, ticking down to the day of the final. There was another one at Pennyhill Park. We were in no doubt as to what everything was building towards.

We were going hard at what was in front of us, of course, but Eddie always had Japan at the back of his mind, and he was willing to push us to extremes to try to get us there as the best team in the world. Eighteen months out, he went into full-on mad professor mode, ramping things up into the red zone in training to try to squeeze more out of us.

We lost three games – to Scotland, France and Ireland – in the 2018 Six Nations, largely because Eddie was pushing us so hard in training that we were knackered on game day. He had the boys going at it like it was pre-season, only during the season. The lads were in pieces. There was nothing left in the tank come Saturday.

It genuinely felt like we were the lab rats in an experiment.

Maybe it was a physical test. Maybe it was a mental test. Maybe it was both. But regardless, it was an unsustainable intensity. I was lucky to miss most of that flogging; I was injured in the opening game against Italy in Rome and didn't play in the rest of the championship.

I was bending down to get the ball away when Dylan was counter-rucked backwards and landed on my knee. I felt a pop and immediate pain. You can tell in a situation like that how bad the physios think an injury is by the way they look at each other as they are attending to you. At that moment they looked properly concerned.

I was carted off into the medical room, where the England doctor and the independent doctor both took a look. They thought I'd done my ACL (anterior cruciate ligament), which carried a nine-month injury prognosis. All sorts of dark thoughts filled my head when I heard that.

I went to see Andy Williams, the knee specialist, in London the next day. He examined the scans, moved my leg around a little bit and, with God-like assurance, told me that it wasn't an ACL injury after all. I was so relieved.

It turned out to be the less-serious MCL (medial collateral ligament) injury, which still put me out of the tournament but meant that, after a course of painful blood-spinning injections, I was fit for the 2018 summer tour to South Africa – where, in another of his experiments, Eddie decided he would base us at sea level near Durban for the entire three-week trip. Even though we were playing the first two Tests in Johannesburg and Bloemfontein. At altitude. It went against all the usual thinking.

The base was great in one sense – the five-star Beverly Hills Hotel at Umhlanga Rocks was lapped by the Indian Ocean, and we were looked after like kings. The general manager was all over us like a rash, checking everything was just so. How we'd slept, whether we needed anything, making sure everything was perfect in our worlds. He would go crazy with the staff if anything wasn't.

'Can I get you a coffee?' he'd ask.

'I've actually got a coffee coming, thanks.'

'Is it not here yet?'

'No, no, but I only just ordered it.'

'One minute, sir.'

Then he would storm off through these swing doors into the kitchen where you could overhear him ranting.

'Where the fuck's the coffee? They want coffee. Where is it? WHERE IS IT?' he would scream. Then he would come back, all smiles, with the coffee.

He was like a South African Basil Fawlty. Every time our team bus left for training, he'd be at the front to wave us off. He had all the staff outside *singing* for us. God knows what happened to them if they hit a duff note.

It was all happening at the Beverly Hills. We were divided up into groups and each group was given a little bit of money, tasked with providing an entertainment night for the rest of the squad. I thought it would be a good idea to bring a reptile guy in to show us some snakes and spiders. I didn't do much research, but it looked pretty good online. I reckoned the boys would love it.

When he turned up with a leg missing, though, I was a bit wary. Had he lost it from a bite? If so, just how reliable was he? He had brought his daughter with him to help. They carried these large plastic boxes into the room, where all the boys were waiting expectantly. Inside were some sacks that held the snakes. So he slams his boxes down on the table, and evidently the snakes didn't care much for that gesture, because when the guy flicked the lid off one box and hauled a king cobra out from its sack, it looked seriously revved up.

The room was quite small and the whole squad was in there, so when the guy wafted this cobra around, it got pretty close to us. He didn't exactly seem to be in control of it. Some of the lads didn't fancy the entertainment quite so much by this point, and management were looking on from outside through glass doors, enjoying our discomfort a lot.

The reptile guy put the cobra away and, after a debate with his daughter, decided to pull out a green mamba. He told us it was so poisonous that we'd be dead in ten minutes if its venom got into us. He added that the nearest antidote to its venom was a two-hour flight away in Johannesburg. The boys were just getting more and more uncomfortable with this whole arrangement, as you can imagine.

He fished out this killer snake from its bag and it looked even more annoyed than its friend had done. It was whipping its head about, back-and-forth, clearly trying to get away. When he let go of its tail and it threatened to slither off, there were some boys fully up on their chairs, yelping. Fortunately, his daughter managed to grab the snake and they stuffed it back into the bag and snapped the box lid shut on it.

So – yeah, it was all, um, *fun and games* at the Beverly Hills – but staying at sea level made for a massive shock to the system when we flew up for the Test matches.

We raced into early leads at both Johannesburg and Bloemfontein, but then we just ran into a brick wall physiologically. We were gasping. We hung on in there for as long as we could but, in the end, we just ran out of air and went down to two defeats. The second Test in particular gave us a real taste of the Springbok forward power. We conceded a penalty try from a scrum pushover, which was unheard of for an England pack.

In any case, it was suddenly five Test defeats on the bounce for us, including the Six Nations. From being a side that had forgotten how to lose, we had very quickly become one that had forgotten how to win. The pressure was on to salvage something from the tour in the last Test – at sea level this time – in Cape Town.

When Jesse Kriel put the Springboks ahead early in the second half with a converted try, it wasn't looking good. That one was my fault. I was the one out of position as defensive sweeper. But Owen's goal-kicking nudged us ahead and Danny Cipriani, whom Eddie had picked at number 10, won us the game with a nice chip through for Jonny May to score. So at least we got something positive out of the trip.

As we were packing up to fly home, I saw Eddie with this huge bottle of wine – almost as big as him. I asked him where he'd got it from and he told me that Rassie Erasmus, South Africa's coach, had presented it to him after the game.

'Here Benny, you have it, mate,' he said. 'Something to remember a famous win at Cape Town by.'

To be fair, he wasn't short on stocks. After the first Test, he'd been involved in an argument with an aggressive Springbok fan (is there any other type?) in the tunnel. Later, to the media, he explained the row away as a conversation with one of the locals about where he could get a decent bottle of Pinotage. It was genius product placement from Eddie. In the days that followed, crates of the stuff turned up at our hotel. You would go to see Eddie for a meeting and you could hardly get through the door for bottles.

He basically had his own private wine lake.

That South Africa trip saw Scott Wisemantel come on board as attack coach. He was a very energetic, excitable Aussie with lots of ideas. Then, in the autumn, John Mitchell – who had been the All Blacks' head coach – came in to replace Paul Gustard as defence coach.

What with Steve Borthwick's detail around the lineout and forward play in general, and Neil Hatley's scrum expertise, it felt like we had hit upon the ideal blend of personalities and skill sets in the coaching set-up by that point. And I really warmed to Mad Mitch, as we came to call John.

He had all the experience of having coached at the highest level, but as an assistant coach he seemed able to enjoy himself more, without the pressure of being the top guy. He took empowering the players to a whole new level, almost to the point where we wondered what he was there for. In terms of planning, Mitch's approach was very much a case of: 'Boys, how do you want to approach this?'

We would be thinking: 'Well, shouldn't you tell us, Mitch?'

'It's always better when you own the plan,' he'd say.

'We need a plan first, Mitch!'

When defence sessions were going on, he would sometimes be chucking NFL balls around in the background, not even paying attention. And he was very rogue in terms of some of his presentations. Once he brought this bucket into a meeting and pulled out two huge racks of ribs from them. 'Should we go get some of these this weekend, boys?' he asked us.

We got the message – brief though it was – but Eddie was nonplussed. 'Err, anything else, Mitch?' he asked. No. That was the extent of it.

Mitch's responsibilities also extended to the breakdown, where he doubled up with Steve. He introduced a forfeit whereby – for every breakdown turnover we conceded in a match – he would have to scull a bottle of Corona in the changing room afterwards. One game, against France, we coughed up seven turnovers. He was halfway through his fourth Corona before he had to come up for air.

Mitch was such a brilliant bloke to be around that, for all the lack of detail he provided, everyone went the extra mile to do a great job defensively for him just on a personal level.

We ended up doing OK that autumn, beating the Springboks and Australia but just losing out to New Zealand. We came off the field knowing we should have beaten them. If the TMO hadn't spotted Courtney being fractionally offside when Sam Underhill went over late on, we would have done. We were pissed off afterwards but, in another way, we were emboldened. We were convinced we would get them next time.

As the World Cup year arrived, it felt like everything was coming together.

We kicked it off with a massive team piss-up. Granted, not the usual way to launch a Six Nations campaign, but bear with me. We decided to get together as a squad a day earlier than scheduled. It was still a couple of weeks out from the game, so where was the harm in sharing a couple of mid-afternoon beers?

We booked a bus to take us into central London and absolutely went for it. After the last stop, Luke Cowan-Dickie threw Jack Nowell into a pile of bins outside the bar and wouldn't let him out. He kept pushing him back into them so, when he eventually emerged, he stank something rotten for the journey back. We were all hanging the next day, but Eddie loved it.

We started the 2019 Six Nations with a fantastic win in Dublin against Ireland – one of the best performances in my time with England. Everyone was talking Ireland up. They were Grand Slam champions and they had beaten New Zealand in the autumn.

They were a good team, but the way some of the Irish pundits were talking before the match was really arrogant. It was like we were just the support act for them. At the team meeting the night before the game, I stood up and told the team that I felt like we had been disrespected and overlooked. We knew how good we were, even if Ireland didn't. They would find out first hand at the Aviva.

They did. We played so well. We were so clear and efficient and so physical. We would have beaten pretty much any side in the world that day.

We trounced France at Twickenham in our second game, and I honestly thought we were on for a Grand Slam, but Wales did a number on us in Cardiff, exploiting our indiscipline, and went on to complete the Slam themselves.

Then, our championship ended with the maddest game ever at Twickenham, when Scotland almost came back to beat us from 31–0 down, only for us to 'rescue' a 38–38 draw.

Eddie was not best pleased with how we had let the lead slip. There was an awkward postscript to that game for us as a leadership group. At the end of a tournament his rule was go out, have fun, and look after each other. He would never set a curfew; he would leave it up to us to decide.

So, after the Calcutta Cup game, we went out in London and set a 3 a.m. cut-off, which you might have thought was late enough. Billy Vunipola and Ben Te'o didn't think so. They went the distance. It might not have been an issue, except for the fact that they overslept and missed the medicals we all had to undergo before we split up.

At the end of every campaign, we'd always had a leadership group meeting. And at that one, Eddie added a pressing item to the agenda: what to do about Billy and Benny.

'You guys need to decide what happens next,' he said, and left.

The leadership group was made up of Owen, who had by now taken over from Dylan as captain, Fordy, Jamie George, Tom Curry, Elliot Daly and myself. Maro was on it too, but he was injured at the time. A few of the group were clubmates of Billy's at Saracens, and you could tell they really didn't want to be a part of the discussion at all.

Neil Craig, who had stayed in the room, told us it was a great test for us. 'In itself this isn't major, but just think about if this happened at the World Cup in Tokyo and the press got hold of it. Things spiral,' he said. 'A small thing can end up being a big distraction.'

I thought back to the 2011 World Cup and how a few boys going out having a good time had completely blown up. He had a point, but it was uncomfortable sitting in judgement on your own teammates.

The pair of them came in and sat down. They gave their version of events. Billy was very apologetic, but Benny was still pretty pissed and defensive and said he didn't see what the problem was. In many ways, none of us had much of a problem with what they had done either, but we put the World Cup scenario to them, emphasizing the importance of putting the team first at all times.

The suggestion at the end of the discussion was that they go to see Eddie and apologize, and then check in with the medics, which I'm pretty sure they did.

While it was disappointing to have finished second in the Six Nations after the start we'd made, I still felt we were in good shape heading into the World Cup.

Eddie was good at World Cups. He knew that and we knew that. So we had real confidence in the programme he devised for us in the build-up. He had rowed back from the craziness of 2018 and, although training was tough, it no longer felt like it was designed to break us.

Because of the humidity that was expected in rugby's first Asian World Cup, we all had to do a sweat test to see how comfortable we would be with the conditions. We went up to Liverpool to work out in a heat chamber on bikes, and our fingers were pricked for blood samples as we exercised. The idea was to find out how well our bodies naturally coped and to try to help those who struggled. The 'help' involved being made to sit in forty-degree hot tubs for ten minutes after training sessions, to try to get our bodies better attuned. Given it was summer, and we were all dripping with sweat after intense training sessions anyway, the overheating was seriously unpleasant.

We would train at 6.30 a.m. before breakfast – we used to call that session bacon and eggs – then it would be gym stuff before lunch and a team rugby session. I'd been involved in plenty of pre-seasons where you never got to see a ball, so it was reassuring that Eddie wanted to use the fitness sessions to an end – playing under fatigue – which was how it would be for us in Japan. We also did team physical challenges in smaller groups, with each one assigned a coach to mark us.

It was great if you were on Mitch's team. He would do absolutely anything to win, which meant he was happy for us to cut corners left, right and centre. At the other end of the scale was Steve, who wanted everything done totally by the book. If something wasn't done perfectly during the exercise, he would have his team repeat it until they did. The coaches would get arsey with each other because the officiating was so inconsistent, but the end result was always that if you were on Mitch's team you'd win, and if you were on Steve's team you were last.

One of the challenges was the worm. The worm was a long bag full of sand that weighed about 160 kg and was incredibly awkward to lift. Each group had to carry it 200 metres.

I remember being part of the winning team in one of these worm races – Team Mitch, of course – and being flat out on the ground recovering afterwards. I looked up to see Team Steve fully 100 metres behind. I don't know how many repeats Steve had demanded, but the poor guys were really going through it. Kyle Sinckler looked like he wasn't much longer for this world.

It seemed to be mandatory ahead of a World Cup to go on a

team-building trip. Where Stuart had gone with his disastrous police training idea, Eddie decided to bring in the marines.

We had to hand in our phones before being flown by military plane to a mystery location somewhere in the south-west, where we were put into groups for a survival night. We were given some basic equipment, sent out into the woods, and told to go make a camp for the night with a shelter and a fire.

On my team, Fordy, Mark Wilson and Anthony Watson were charged with putting up the accommodation, and they did a truly terrible job – the word 'shelter' was completely redefined that night. In the meantime, Ben Te'o and I were in charge of getting the fire going – which, surprisingly, we managed successfully. The only problem was that neither of us had thought to check the wind direction, so all the smoke blew straight into the shelter.

The marine who was with us suggested we move the fire. Benny really got into the axe work and hacked off this enormous piece of wood, which he dragged over and put on the new fire. We were on a rotation where two or three people watched the fire while the others were supposed to rest. At the end of our fire shift, we got our heads down in the shelter only to be stirred by a huge commotion outside.

Benny's mega-log had gone up spectacularly and the fire was out of control. It was chaos out there. And no one got a wink of sleep all night.

The next morning, naturally, we were sent to take on an assault course. Something was bound to go wrong for someone, and that someone just happened to be the angriest man in the squad, Mike Brown.

We all had to work together to help each other under and over all the obstacles, and Ollie Thorley was charged with holding a rope in place for Browny to make his way across a ropeway. I don't know what happened inside Ollie's head, but it was like he momentarily forgot Browny was there and he suddenly let go of the rope.

As the rope went slack, Browny fell to the ground and landed in a pile of bark. The chippings flew everywhere and Browny eventually got to his feet with bark in his mouth, up his nose and hanging off his orange helmet. He was fuming. He tore into Ollie, telling him what a knob he was, while Jonny May and I watched on, giggling away.

The instructor, who was called Foxy but I renamed Bingo after the online gambling site, blew his whistle and brought everyone in. He got quite fired up, ranting that we couldn't allow things like this to happen. 'Bingo needs to just chill out,' whispered Jonny.

That sent me over the edge. I completely lost it.

Fordy, Mr Sensible, was kicking me, trying to get me to shut up, but I couldn't. I was crying with laughter. I had officially lost it. Maybe it was the sleep deprivation. The moment we were back on the military plane for the flight back, everyone was asleep.

The team leadership group also spent a weekend together at an RAF base.

As far as these things went, it was a worthwhile couple of days, where we looked at communication, clarity, messaging – that sort of thing. Towards the end of it, we did this exercise where we had to work as a group to get to a rendezvous point at a specific time to intercept a helicopter.

Faz, as captain, was team leader. Everyone else had a support role. Mine was as a timekeeper. Walking along towards the intercept point, Faz asked me: 'How long is left on the time?' I checked the watch. 'Thirty-threeeeeeee minutes,' I said, making the three go on for ever. Just being silly. Mako Vunipola started sniggering.

Faz didn't catch what I had said, so he checked again: 'Len, what was the time?'

'A minute less than what I just said.'

Faz, knowing me like he did, laughed. But the RAF guy who was with us, observing, didn't see the funny side at all. 'What did you just say to him?' he asked me.

'A minute less than what I just said it was,' I replied.

'Would you speak to him like that on the field if he's asking for the time on the clock?' he snapped back at me.

'Well, no mate, because if he wanted to know the time on the clock, he'd just look at the big screen.'

'Owen, are you going to take that?' demanded this guy.

'Mate. It's just Lenny,' said Faz. 'He's just pissing about.'

The guy carried this on. 'In the heat of the battle, you can't be doing that . . .'

'Obviously, if it's a Test match, I'm not going to turn around to Owen and go: "There's thirty-threeeeeeee minutes left" . . .'

Anyway, we went into the debrief afterwards and this guy was at it again in the feedback session, saying I had been totally disrespectful to my captain. Owen was looking at me as if to say: 'What's this bloke's problem?' He couldn't let it go.

If rugby hadn't worked out for me, I don't think I'd have made much of a success in the military. What with the survival camp and the leadership training and my own tendency to laugh at inappropriate moments, I didn't seem to have the right mentality for it.

The final leg of our preparation camp ahead of the 2019 World Cup was a heat camp in Treviso. Northern Italy was supposed to mimic Japan's conditions – which it did in terms of the temperature, but with the added bonus of thousands of insects to swallow as we trained.

Those conditions were draining. Charlie Ewels went down with such bad cramp during one session that the physios couldn't peel him off the ground for almost an hour. So it was a joy when midway through the camp we were given a day off for a squad social in Venice.

Somehow, Mitch managed to get himself on the trip. We were on a boat playing a drinking game called flood where, if anyone shouted: 'Flood!', you had to try to get your feet off the ground, and there were some predictably chaotic scenes. At one point I looked over at Mitch and he had a lifebuoy ring around his neck, his glasses were all over the place and he was hollering 'FLOOD' like a madman. He was loving it.

I swear some of the other coaches must have been thinking: how does Mitch get away with it? He was literally living his best life.

Then it was back to serious training again. Eddie had brought the dreaded sandbag worms out to Treviso, but they mysteriously just sat on the side of the pitch at every training session, unused. He could have just been playing with our heads, but it must have cost the RFU a bomb to get them out there.

On the last day, we trained at Treviso's home stadium, and then went for an end-of-camp drink together. After Eddie had cleared it, I had asked Charlotte Gibbons, the team manager, if she would be able to sort out a beach bar where we could relax and wind down together after a tough ten days. The squad's two security guys would be there, so what could possibly go wrong?

Everything. Everything that could possibly go wrong, that's what.

I only had a couple of drinks, but a few of the lads really went for it – and that had unfortunate consequences. Browny and Benny ended up scrapping on the walk back to the team bus.

When the punches stopped, the verbals carried on between them on the bus.

As if that wasn't bad enough, the edgy atmosphere between them seemed to set other people off as well. Before you knew it, there were a few others arguing. Maybe we had been in camp together too long by that point. We'd trained hard, we were knackered, and a few drinks brought some underlying issues to a head. The disputes were about nothing important, just petty stuff, but there was tension all the same. Maybe we weren't as tight a group as we had thought we were.

I'd seen lots of scraps in training between teammates – I'd been brought up at Leicester, after all – and I'd seen overspill at team socials before, so I didn't see the Browny v. Benny business as the end of the world. But it wasn't a great look, and when we got on the bus to the airport the next day, Eddie gave it to us straight.

'Some of you fucked up last night, didn't you?' he said.

He told us this story about the Australia team he had coached, and a similar incident ahead of the 2003 World Cup, which, he said, had ended up bringing them closer together when it had washed through. He said what had happened would either gal-vanize us for the tournament or it would break us apart. It was up to us to decide.

He made his own call on that by deciding to leave both Browny and Benny out of the final squad. How much of that was down to the fight and how much down to form, only he will ever know – I suspect it was more the latter.

But the funny thing was, I was never part of a more connected England squad than the one that went to Japan.

After blowing away Ireland in a morale-boosting warm-up game, we took down Tonga in our opening game in Sapporo.

Proud dad with his boys – after Tom and I played our first game together
for England at Twickenham in 2012.

Sharing a beer with Tom and Dad in the Tigers' dressing room
after my 250th appearance for the club.

Lifting the Premiership trophy with Tom in 2010 after Leicester
went back-to-back at Twickenham.

Tom Croft misjudges where the Tom Richards Trophy is after
the Lions win the series against the Wallabies in 2013.

A champagne shower from Dan Cole after England clinch their first Grand Slam for thirteen years with victory in Paris in 2016.

Tom is persuaded to come onto the Twickenham pitch to share in Leicester's 2022 Premiership triumph.

Soaking up one of England's best performances during the Eddie Jones era, with (left to right) Jonny May, Ellis Genge, Manu Tuilagi and George Ford, in the Aviva Stadium changing rooms after our win against Ireland in the 2019 Six Nations.

Holding the triple crown after our victory over Wales at Twickenham in 2020, flanked by George Ford and Owen Farrell I loved playing with those two.

Relaxing in the Stade de France dressing room with George Ford and Dan Cole after I called time on my England career.

Extra running sessions with George Ford at Leicester University's pitches to get in shape for the 2019 World Cup.

Left: Sealed with a kiss – on the England team bus with Fordy and the Six Nations trophy in 2017.

Right: A day to remember, after England's victory in Rome in 2020 – the Six Nations trophy in one hand and a golden cap from the RFU to mark my 100th match in the other.

Below: Guardian angels – Coley and Joe Marler with me before my final England game in Paris in 2023.

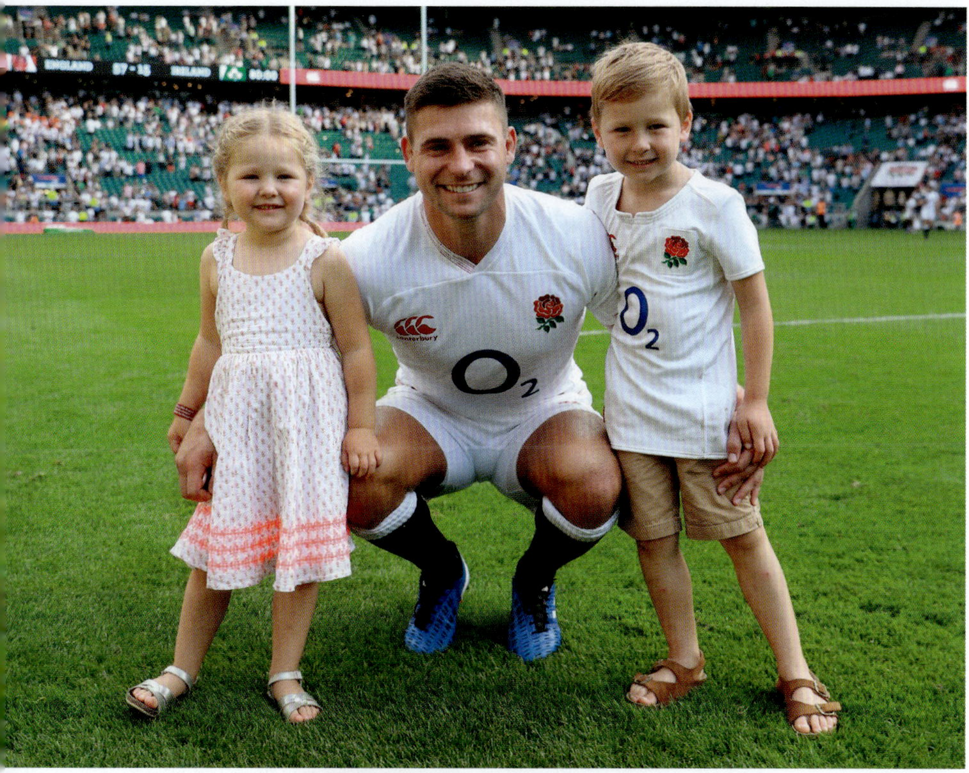

bove: Summer
ugby – Boris and
illie join me on
he Twickenham
itch after England's
omprehensive 57–15
vin over Ireland in
he 2019 World Cup
varm-up match.

Right: With Char, our little Ettie and a large Premiership trophy at Welford Road after Leicester's 2022 triumph.

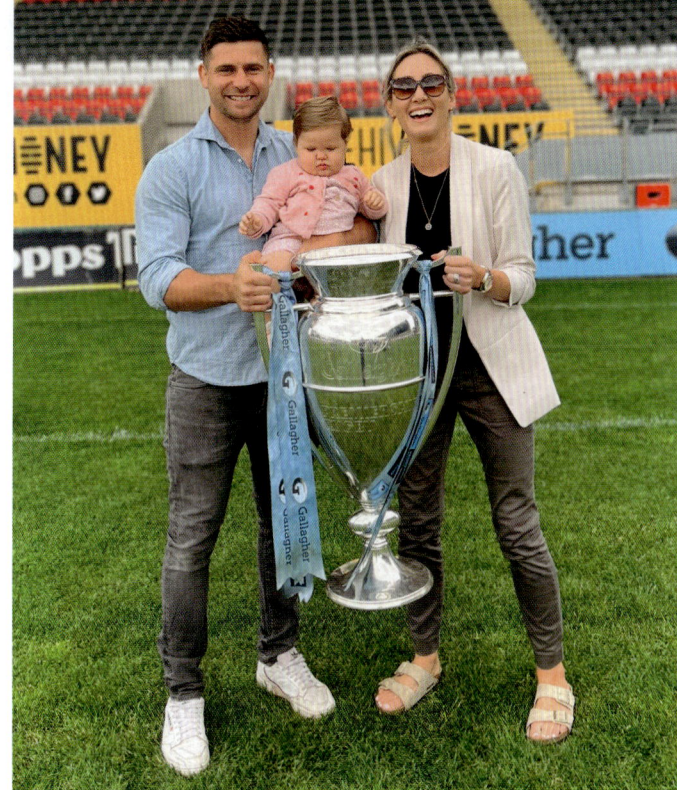

All smiles with Char, Boris and Billie after Leicester's Premiership final win at Twickenham in 2022.

On the Stade de France pitch with Boris and Billie after my final game for England in 2023.

Joy among the despair – sharing Leicester's Premiership win with Tom and Maisie, as well as Boris, Billie, my nephew Alfie and my cousin's son Charlie (hidden).

We didn't play our best rugby but, as Eddie had stressed beforehand, you don't need to play your best rugby first up. You just need to win.

Game two in Kobe against the USA was played in a greenhouse. It was absolutely roasting with a roof on – guys lost 5 kg in eighty minutes – and we had some trouble with the sweaty ball. It was a different sort of slipperiness to a rainy day at home – much worse – and it took some getting used to, but we put them away 45–7.

The big pool game was Argentina in Tokyo and, by then, we were moving into our stride. The 39–10 win took us into the quarter-final with a game to spare. They lost Tomás Lavanini to a red card, which helped, but we would have beaten them anyway.

We still had France left to play to decide who topped the pool, but that game would never be played. Typhoon Hagibis saw to that. We escaped to Miyazaki while it did its worst.

The storm gave us a fourteen-day mid-tournament break, which I thought we'd use to catch our breath and relax. Instead, we were hammered in training.

That was our first big mistake of the World Cup. It wasn't just the fact that we trained hard in Miyazaki. In isolation that wouldn't have been such a problem. It was the fact that we had trained hard from the moment we had joined up.

The thing with cumulative load is that at some point there is going to be a price to pay. And we were to pay it down the track.

Wales's win over Australia in the pool stages meant it was the Wallabies for us in the quarter-final in Oita. We had beaten them on the previous six occasions we'd met, but at the back of our minds was the thought that it would be just like the Aussies to pull a big performance out against England at a World Cup. That worry made for an emotionally draining week. It felt like the fear of losing was becoming bigger than the joy of winning.

Eddie made a big call for the game by leaving Fordy out and playing Owen at number 10.

They are both outstanding players and I feel really lucky to have played with both of them. It's almost impossible to separate them, but if I absolutely had to express a preference about who should be outside me, it would be George.

That was because I knew him inside out. I instinctively knew where he would be and what he needed from me, whereas I had to work a little bit more at it with Owen. Because we'd never played together at club level, we didn't have quite the same number of minutes in the bank together. Owen and I would have conversations after training to talk things through, but all those conversations had already happened with George.

Anyway, my real preference was to have them both in the team.

The beauty of having George and Owen next to each other was that it gave us two playmakers. Off first phase, I would be hitting George with my passes, but once we got into multi-phase it might be George or Owen. It became much more fluid. They were two equally good distributors and equally good kickers, so having them both there kept opponents guessing and gave us a much greater attacking range.

For me, England's best midfield combination was George at 10, Owen at 12 and Manu at 13. We played some brilliant rugby with those three together.

But Eddie went with Manu and Henry Slade in the centre for that game. It came good when Sladey intercepted a pass from David Pocock to put Jonny May in for his second try of the first half. The Aussies weren't done though, and Marika Koroibete scored a brilliant try early in the second half to pull them back to within a point.

They had their tails right up and it was game on. But we came up with the perfect response, with Kyle Sinckler taking a great line off Faz to score his first international try. From there we ran away with it, although the score – 40–16 – didn't reflect how tense it had been and how much pressure they had put us under.

We were pretty relieved afterwards. We ended up watching the All Blacks versus Ireland quarter-final together in the hotel afterwards, knowing we would be playing the winners.

There had been a banner up in the Pennyhill Park gym with our likely route to the World Cup final on it. New Zealand were down as our semi-final opponents.

And now, after they had swept aside the Irish, here they were in front of us.

They were hot favourites – they had beaten South Africa in their opening group game and strolled through the tournament from there – but we fancied this. We knew we had a huge game in us.

Eddie was right on it, straight away, in the team meeting, before we flew up to Tokyo for the game.

'Boys, there's no one in the world who thinks we can win this weekend. How good is that?' he said.

'The people in this room know we can. And the only people we need are in this room. They talk about walking towards pressure, but we're going to chase them down the streets towards it, boys. They're going to be looking around every junction because they're going to know that we're coming for them. The All Blacks psychologist is going to be the busiest man in New Zealand; their wives are going to be on the phone all night with them because they'll be shitting themselves . . . Take them the distance, boys, and they will panic. The burden of expectation will become too much. And we will win the game.'

At the end of the meeting, he clapped his hands, as he always did, and said: 'Right boys. So are you ready? Of course you are. Let's go.'

This was all on Sunday morning. The game was still six days away.

We didn't train particularly well that week – until the warm-up on the day of the match, when we were fizzing – but what we did do was get our minds right. Our mentality that week was that it was the All Blacks who would have to deal with us in the semi-final, not the other way around. We were going to impose ourselves on New Zealand.

That all started with Eddie – he played a blinder ahead of that match, he really did. He was chucking curve balls out left, right and centre to the press, ramping up the pressure on New Zealand and putting them on the back foot. Steve Hansen, their coach, was having to put out fires all over the place.

Eddie even claimed they were spying on us at one point, because he spotted someone on the balcony of one of the apartments that overlooked our training ground in Tokyo. It was just some bloke on his balcony, wringing out his flannel probably, but Eddie was up to all sorts of tricks.

The day before the game, he called a team meeting at our hotel in Tokyo's Disneyland and showed up with an actual samurai sword. He was swinging this thing around as he talked about the game, the blade glinting as it slashed through the air.

To round off his speech in style, he brought the sword slamming down onto a kiwi fruit and split it in half.

'This, boys, is what we're going to do to the Kiwis,' he said.

The night before the game, Eddie told us he wanted us to think about the haka and how we would respond to it. He wanted us to dream something up that would make them think twice, something to change the picture for them. So we met as a leadership group and that was where the V idea was hatched. It was Faz's idea.

It wasn't actually supposed to be a V. It was meant to be a semi-circle, but we hadn't practised it beforehand, so we didn't quite get the shape right. As we explained it to the rest of the squad pre-match, I drew up the positions we would take on a flipchart. There were Xs and Os where we should stand in relation to the All Blacks.

It just wasn't going in for Luke Cowan-Dickie. 'Luke, just stand where you're put when we get out there, mate, and eyeball the All Blacks,' I told him in the end. He was all over that.

World Rugby ended up fining the RFU £2,000 because Joe Marler strayed over the halfway line – opposition teams have to stay in their own half for the haka – but it was worth it for the spectacle. The iconic image was of Faz, who was in the middle, smirking at the Kiwis.

It wasn't meant to be disrespectful. It was intended to let the All Blacks know they weren't going to have everything on their terms.

There is a risk attached to doing something like we did. It can blow up in your face. When Wales refused to move after the haka in 2008, it created a spellbinding moment of theatre in Cardiff, but it just stoked the All Blacks up. If you put something out there, you have to back it up. We knew that. If the semi-final had gone wrong and we'd lost, we would have had everybody asking: 'What were you thinking?'

But it didn't go wrong.

There aren't many times in my career when I've been involved in something approaching the perfect game of rugby, but that was one of them. There was just something about us that day.

One of the big things we always spoke about, especially as senior players, was to give off an air to your teammates that you were ready on game day. That presence and positive energy becomes infectious. We were ready.

Walking around the hotel, I could just sense the sparking electricity inside everyone. In the changing room in Yokohama, we were primed – a pack of England attack dogs.

Tom Curry was walking up and down with his headphones on in his own world, Maro was standing, firing guys up, Sinks was in the toilet retching, as he always did before a game. I was just sitting down quietly, thinking about my job. Whatever other thoughts you have in your head, they've got to go at that moment. Whatever the chimp in your head is saying, that is the point at which you have to shut him up and clear the mind.

I had visualized what I was going to do, how my game was going to unfold, selling myself an inspiring, team-leading performance. Now I had to deliver it. We all did.

Eddie's last message, as he circled the changing room, was the same one he had been drumming into us all week.

'There's a storm coming for them. We're going at them, boys, right from the fucking start. They won't have experienced anything like it . . .'

It was right on the edge in there. There was no need for a last call to arms from Faz.

'Let's go,' he said, simply. He led us on the long walk from the dressing room, up the steps and out onto the pitch and into the noise.

Everything we had planned was designed to throw the All Blacks out of their rhythm – from the haka response to the trick play kick-off we had up our sleeves. We set up for George, who was back in the side at number 10, to kick to the right, but at the last moment changed it so Owen took over and went left. Then, at the first lineout, we switched things up again. New Zealand would have expected us to maul it because we had troubled them in that area at Twickenham the year before, but instead we went off the top.

Seven phases later, ninety-seven seconds into the game, Manu forced his way over for the opening try.

It was the dream start.

The pace of that game was faster than anything I'd ever known. It was like there was no air in the stadium. But it felt invigorating too. We were on top, we were dominating. Coming up to half-time, we'd been in their 22 a few more times – Sam Underhill had a try disallowed – but we had come away with nothing. Everything I'd learned about playing New Zealand down the years had taught me that you have got to take your chances – because if you don't, they will get you in the end. So I kept telling George to drop a goal.

'We've got to convert something,' I told him. He wouldn't.

'We've nearly got them,' he insisted.

By the interval we had stretched the lead to 10–0 with a penalty. The boys were feeling good. The messages at the break were all positive. But we knew New Zealand still posed a huge threat. What was stressed at half-time was that we had to be really hot on finding our shape if there was a turnover, because New Zealand were so lethal in that situation. Even if it meant giving space on the touchline, it was so important not to let them flood through the middle. If that happened, we were in trouble.

The main thing was to keep doing what we were doing. We had the All Blacks on the ropes. As we made our way out for the second half, I looked up to see Faz at the top of the steps turning round with a smile on his face. 'It's raining boys,' he said.

We backed our defence big time, and even a side as skilful as New Zealand would be handicapped playing catch-up rugby in the rain. It was like the stars were aligning for us.

We thought we had scored again when I sniped over from a driving maul, only for the TMO to bring play back for a knock-on and cross off the try. When Ardie Savea brought the All Blacks back into it with a try from a lineout overthrow, a lot of people watching must have thought: 'here they come', but we never allowed them to build on the momentum.

Fordy put us out of range with a couple of penalties and, this time, they weren't coming back.

The final whistle brought a 19–7 victory. We had beaten New Zealand.

The instinctive feeling was one of elation but, with the final still to come, the job wasn't done, so it was a strange in-between kind of emotion when it came to celebrating.

We could at least allow ourselves the satisfaction of having taken England to number one in the world rankings for the first time in fifteen years. Steve Hansen came into our dressing room and gave a lovely speech, congratulating us on our win and wishing us luck for the final. What a class act. He said it was one of the best performances he'd come up against in his time as All Blacks coach.

Rugby is so messy and it has so many moving parts, it's impossible to achieve true perfection, but the synergy and cohesion was just beautiful that day. Everything just clicked.

It was the most complete team performance I played in during my career. Ireland away in that year's Six Nations ran it close, but

I think because of the opposition, and what was at stake, that display edged it.

If only we could have bottled that performance and reproduced it in the final.

The day after the semi-final, Eddie was in a press conference, when one journalist quoted Warren Gatland's observation that teams don't always turn up in a final after hitting the heights we had.

'You just send my best wishes to Warren to make sure he enjoys the third and fourth place play-off,' said Eddie.

Unfortunately, it turned out that Gats was right.

Maybe we did play our final against New Zealand, but the thing was that we had to. If we hadn't played so well, we wouldn't have beaten them. They were that good.

There was a huge come-down after that All Blacks game, and we had to find a way of managing that and making sure we got right back up to the peak for the final. We didn't get that right. Underplaying the fact that we were in a World Cup final was our second big mistake of that tournament.

The tone of the team meeting on the Sunday was very different to how it had been ahead of the New Zealand game. The positive, aggressive message from Eddie had been watered down. It was a lot more measured. As a leadership group, we echoed that. It was almost as though we were approaching it as just a normal game. But it wasn't just another game.

I understand why we took that route – because we didn't want everyone's heads to be clouded by the scale of the occasion, and we didn't want everyone to be over-hyped, but I think we made a big error with our mentality ahead of that final. If you watch South Africa's *Chasing the Sun* documentary, you can see how

Rassie was really driving into the motivational aspect. They were representatives of South Africa playing for something much bigger than themselves, they were being told.

While they were stoking the fires, we were putting them out.

Rugby, as a physical contact game, is built on emotion, and a World Cup final of all games needs emotion. They got the temperature right; we didn't.

Perhaps they just had more left in their batteries anyway. Our knockout route – Australia and New Zealand back-to-back – had been much harder than theirs; they had faced Japan and Wales. After being flogged in Miyazaki, maybe we just didn't have enough left to win that final.

The thing is, you can ask yourself why until you are blue in the face. There are many possible answers. But the one about the team bus being late? That's a red herring. That was most definitely not why we lost.

We had moved hotels from Tokyo Bay to the centre of the Japanese capital for the final. Yokohama was twenty miles away. On the train, the journey would take half an hour. By coach it takes longer, given how busy Tokyo is, but we had a police escort, so it shouldn't have been an issue.

We set off in good time. The problem was that the Japanese – and I can't tell you how much I love Japan – are so polite and respectful that even their police won't jump a queue. So when the traffic started clogging up, the two police cars in front – which had been assigned to make sure that we got to the stadium safely – just sat there.

At one set of lights, it felt like we were held there for about twenty minutes. Maybe Rassie had hacked into the control system! The team started to become aware that time was ticking by. Some players put their strapping on inside the bus, but no one panicked or lost the plot; we just rolled with it. When we finally arrived, we were half an hour late, but there was still an hour until kick-off.

Some of our routines went out of the window, sure. I would have loved to have gone out into an empty stadium, had a walk around and done a bit of visualization, but that wasn't an option in the circumstances. It did feel a bit rushed – it was pretty much a case of coin toss, warm-up, whistle – but to blame that for losing a World Cup final would be an absolute cop-out.

The fact is we just didn't perform.

We started loosely and that set the tone.

Billy sent across a loose ball in our own 22 which left Faz, who had already thrown a stray one himself, exposed, and South Africa took the lead with a penalty. Then I tried to go over the top with a pass to the wing as Faf de Klerk raced out of the Springbok defensive line, but there was no one there. I said to Ant Watson: 'Where were you?', and he apologized because he'd forgotten the call, but the lads were looking at me as one of the senior players thinking: 'Why has he just done that?'

When a few players start like that, it spreads. There were countless examples in the first fifteen minutes: we were just doing uncharacteristic things. Even when we could hold onto the ball, it seemed like everything we tried, they'd prepared for. We had an obsession with coming back to the middle and then using the short side to get inside their high defensive press, but the Springboks were all over that.

And we were losing the arm wrestle up front. I had been rooming with Fordy that week and I confided in him that I was worried about our forwards.

'George,' I said, 'I'm not sure our pack can deal with them. If we're getting beaten up and not on the front foot, we need a way of counter-punching somehow.'

I was thinking back to 2018 and Bloemfontein. History was repeating itself.

Losing Kyle Sinckler when he was knocked out three minutes in didn't help – he'd had a great tournament, and it left Coley having to go seventy-seven minutes at tight head. That's exactly what the Springboks wanted. For us to match their powerful scrum, it would have needed near enough a half each from our six front-rowers to bring parity. As it was, they just ground us down. Every time there was a scrum, they seemed to get a penalty, and Handre Pollard knocked them over.

They were playing their game perfectly – kick-heavy, with an aggressive defence and going hard at the breakdown – and getting the grind on. And once South Africa get grinding, they are just so hard to stop. They just squeeze the life out of you.

We had glimmers of opportunities. We put some pressure on their line just before half-time, and Courtney almost wriggled out of a tackle as we pounded away. If we could have managed a pick-and-drive score then, the tide might have been turned. It might have settled us down and given us a window to draw breath at half-time.

But the one part of our game that we never, ever practised was goal-line attack. It just wasn't something Eddie valued – we never spent any time on it, we never talked about it – and that came back to bite us in the backside in that final. Instead of keeping at it, we went out the back, got smashed twenty metres behind the gain line, and the chance was gone.

It had been a horrible half where everything that could have gone wrong had gone wrong, but even then, we were only 12–6 down.

Our second moment came early in the second half when Tom Curry won a breakdown penalty. Faz had the chance to cut the deficit to three points from forty-five metres but missed. That was fine – it happens, and Faz's boot had kept us in touch up to that point – but almost immediately we were penalized for sacking a maul and Handre banged over another one. What could have been a three-point game was suddenly a nine-point game.

From there, South Africa pulled away.

Watching Siya Kolisi lift the trophy, we were just numb. I was trying to process what had just happened and failing. We all were. After all the work we had put in, we had ended up with nothing. We had saved our worst game for the biggest stage. It felt like I had blinked and the World Cup final had gone. It was almost like it had passed us by.

Eddie got us in a huddle in the changing room afterwards to thank us for our efforts. 'We didn't bring our best and we'll have to live with that. It's going to be very difficult,' he said. 'But you've made a lot of people proud, don't forget that. Whatever happens next, I want to wish you all the best.' I don't think he knew at the time if he was staying or going.

I just sat there and wept.

When I eventually left the changing room, I sought out Char and my dad. At times like that, you need to be with people who you know care for you unconditionally. I needed them so much at that moment.

In all honesty, I loved that World Cup. I loved Japan, I loved the teammates I shared it with, I loved the rugby we played, I loved the way we represented England. I loved everything about that whole experience.

Except for those eighty bloody minutes . . .

10

THE END OF EDDIE

'He didn't shout or bang the table or anything like that. His rage was controlled, but he was angry and he made sure we knew that.'

Post-Japan, Eddie couldn't simply reset the countdown clock to target the 2023 World Cup, so he went for a new aspiration: aiming to make England the best side in the history of the game. It was a lofty goal, and we never came close – he ended up being sacked.

I always felt that, as a team, we were swimming upstream after Tokyo. It felt like the mood had changed. We went from being the flavour of the month to something that seemed to leave a sour taste. In the end, it felt like the English public was tired of Eddie and tired of us.

Moving on after the World Cup final disappointment wasn't easy for any of us. Eddie spoke to us at Pennyhill Park ahead of the 2020 Six Nations, where he tried to turn the page, but the experience was still raw. It had only been two months. At one point, I honestly thought he was going to cry. He just about held it together, but he was clearly very emotional. I knew where he was coming from, and it was reassuring, in a way, to know that he was still hurting as much as I was.

We lost to France in the opening game of that Six Nations. That was the game in which I joined the Antoine Dupont fan club. I had played against him a couple of times before that and was aware that he was a very good scrum half, but I remember coming off the pitch that day thinking: 'Shit, this guy's on a different planet to me.'

What separated Dupont was the range of his skill set. The try he set up for Charles Ollivon in the second half of that game was like a magician's trick. He took a pass just inside our half and – in the same blurring movement – stepped Sam Underhill, then burned outside Maro, Sinks and me to rip our defence apart and put Ollivon away.

You would think you had scragged him in a tackle, then he would just hand you off like you were a little kid, before bumping some back-row forward out of the way and accelerating off. He was phenomenally strong, and as much a threat over the ball on the turnover as he was an open-field runner.

What a kicker, too. You would try to put pressure on his right foot, because he would be banging fifty-metre clearances away with it, and then he would go and do the exact same off his left foot.

And the vision he had for the game was exceptional. My God, he was good. I had played against Will Genia, Aaron Smith and all these guys, but I had never come off feeling like I did that day. It was his twentieth cap and my ninety-sixth but I felt like asking for his autograph after that game. Antoine came into our changing room and we swapped jerseys. I said to him: 'Mate, you're going to be a superstar.'

And, of course, that's exactly how it turned out. He's the best number 9 I ever played against; maybe the best rugby player, full stop.

That said – even with Dupont, the French weren't invincible, and their loss to Scotland at Murrayfield in round four put us back in the title race. We had bounced back from the loss in Paris with three wins on the bounce, including an eventful one against the Welsh at Twickenham. There was a lot of speculation ahead of that Wales game over whether it might be cancelled or played behind closed doors because of the Covid outbreak, but it went ahead as normal.

At our team comms meeting ahead of the game, we had addressed the issue of what our response should be if Alun Wyn Jones targeted Sinks. He had made a point of getting under Sinks's skin the year before, and Sinks had given away a lot of penalties. Joe Marler stood up and announced: 'Boys, don't worry about Alun Wyn. I'll take care of him. I'm going to out-Alun Wyn Alun Wyn.' Then he sat back down again.

Nobody knew what he meant and he didn't say another word about it. We found out – as Alun Wyn did – just before half-time, when he grabbed the Wales captain's nuts and gave them a squeeze. The TV cameras caught the incident and Joe ended up getting a ten-week ban.

That was Joe all over – he was just a wind-up merchant. When I played against him at club level, I'd be at the bottom of a ruck and he would lie on me so I couldn't move and then try to undo my laces. He would work his way around the sides of mauls and deliberately stand on my foot. I reckon he was more bothered about that than stopping the maul.

He made life entertaining, at least.

There was one more thing of note from that game, I guess. I was sitting down pulling my boots off in the Twickenham changing room after the match – it was my ninety-ninth cap – when this short bloke with wild blond hair appeared next to me. It was Boris Johnson. The prime minister spent about thirty seconds in the room, during which time he shook hands with every single one of us. So much for Covid prevention, eh?

The virus wreaked havoc, and the climax to the Six Nations,

like most of the rest of life, was put on hold. By the time we travelled to Italy for the final game of the championship, a full seven months had passed.

I will say that, with Eddie, you could never be comfortable enough to assume anything, so to be picked for cap number one hundred for England was a relief – as well as an honour. The guys had a whip-round and bought me a watch and a massive bottle of champagne and put together a video that was shown the night before the game at the team hotel in Rome. There were a lot of nice messages on there from family, rugby players, people from other sports, even comedians (Jack Whitehall sent one). Videos were a regular thing for cap landmarks, but they usually lasted for two or three minutes. Mine went on for about ten minutes – which made me feel a bit awkward, but was lovely all the same.

The Covid restrictions meant the game was played in a deserted stadium. I had a laugh with Jamie George – who was winning his fiftieth cap – as we ran out onto the field. The applause for us rang out from a grand total of two people: our team managers, Charlotte and Richard Hill. The Olympic Stadium is a cavernous place anyway but, with no one inside, it was a total echo chamber.

It was a pity that my family couldn't be there to share the moment, but it was just the way of things at that awful time. A lot of other people had to put up with a lot worse. At least we were still able to carry on playing.

I'd learned my lesson from my fiftieth cap game and made sure I didn't overthink things, and it went like a dream. I scored a try early on, tracking a break from Faz, and then went over for another one later in the game. A ruck guard had left a gap that I went through and, although I had Faz outside calling for the pass, I ignored him and stepped the full back instead to score myself.

A Man-of-the-Match award to go with the mounted golden cap the RFU presented me with was a nice way to celebrate the one hundred caps.

And, best of all, we ended up winning the Six Nations title on points difference.

With teams from the southern hemisphere unable to travel because of the pandemic, the European nations quickly cobbled together an Autumn Nations Cup.

Those games felt strange. It was a privilege to be able to do our jobs during Covid but, at the same time, running out in front of an empty stadium made the games feel flat. They lacked intensity and buzz.

It didn't help that Eddie shut down our rugby completely. The game plan was turgid. It was kick after kick after kick. Don't get me wrong, it worked – we won the tournament – but it was so dull. The group game against Wales at Parc y Scarlets was particularly diabolical. With no fans in the stadiums, it was the perfect time to roll the dice and try a few things – to play a brand of rugby that would really get us and the people watching at home excited. Instead, we were playing the worst rugby imaginable.

It required me to suppress all my natural instincts. You want to express yourself as a player and, for me, that means taking people on and moving the ball, not endlessly kicking it into the sky. There are obviously times in a game where you need to be pragmatic, but if the whole eighty minutes is dry as dust, it ends up being as boring for a player as it is for the fans watching on TV at home.

Eddie thought that the way the laws were being interpreted

during that period meant a team was better off without the ball than with it, and he took that to an extreme. Steve Borthwick must have liked Eddie's tactics, though, because when he left England after the 2021 Six Nations to take charge at Leicester, he brought the same rigid approach with him.

That was not a good period of my career. Having to play that sort of anti-rugby for club and country, I could feel my passion for the game slowly draining away. From a break-making scrum half, I suddenly became the box-kick king. That's not a title I ever wanted. I had no choice but to fall in line, but I couldn't stand how restrictive it was. Steve loved his data and the data was telling him that the more kick metres you made in a game, the more likely you were to win.

If you went off-grid and used some initiative, you would get pulled up for it. I remember taking a quick tap for Leicester in one game because the opposition defence wasn't set, and receiving a video clip of it the following morning from Steve, with a message asking why we hadn't kicked for the corner instead. It was by-the-numbers rugby, and it felt so uninspiring that it was painful to play.

It wasn't just the style that was a problem for me, it was Steve's rotation policy too. His way of doing things was that each of the three frontline scrum halves would, in turn, start a game, then miss a game, then be on the bench. When you did start, you'd be taken off just after half-time. It meant that you couldn't get any continuity going at all. Steve's view was that Richard Wigglesworth and Jack van Poortvliet, the other two scrum halves at Leicester, were very good too, and that we should all be treated equally. And don't get me wrong, both are exceptional rugby players – but I was England's starting number 9.

What particularly pissed me off was that the rotation policy never seemed to apply across the board. I didn't see Fordy or Coley get rotated out. I didn't need people to treat me differently just because I was an England international. All my career at Leicester, the squad had been full of those. I didn't need people to pump up my tyres either; that wasn't part of the culture at Leicester. But what I could have done with was some recognition of the added value that I brought, and I never got that with Steve.

I have to admit I found it difficult playing at Leicester under him.

By 2021, we were approaching the halfway point in the World Cup cycle, and I had a big decision to make. If I wanted to try to push on to a fourth World Cup, by which time I would be thirty-four years old, I knew something had to give.

There was a Lions tour coming up that summer. I knew how much the Lions tour had taken out of me after 2013 – I just wasn't the same player the following season, and that was as a young pup, not as a thirty-something. If I was going to make the World Cup with England two years on, I needed to prioritize. In late April, like fifty-six other players, I received an email from the Lions asking whether I would be available for the tour of South Africa. I don't know if I would have made the final cut or not, but I took the call out of Warren Gatland's hands. I ticked the box that said 'no'. I decided I wasn't going.

When I had toured with the Lions eight years earlier, I had gone with my brother, Crofty, Coley and Manu – four really good mates. The tour had been to Australia, one of my favourite countries, and my whole family had been out there following us. We had won the series. There couldn't have been a better blueprint for the perfect Lions experience, yet while it had been good (amazing, even, in some moments), the truth was that touring with the Lions still hadn't felt like the 'ultimate'. The whole mythology of the Lions makes it almost shameful to admit that, but that's just how I felt about it.

The Lions is special and unique and it has a mystique all of its own. To tour with them is recognition that you're deemed to be one of the best of the best. Every rugby fan in Britain and Ireland dreams of wearing that jersey. I had done too, when I was younger. But for me, the reality just didn't match the dream. Maybe my expectations had been set too high, but I could never, hand on heart, look back and say that it was the best experience of my career.

I was proud of being a Lion and I had unbelievable memories of the tour, but playing for England at a World Cup was bigger, in my eyes. And if I was to maximize my chances of doing that again, I could not tour that summer of 2021.

I rang up Eddie and told him what I was thinking. 'So 2023 is my big goal and I need the summer off to give myself the best chance of making it,' I told him.

'Good for you, Benny, you're making the right call,' he said. 'We won't take you to Argentina either this summer. Get yourself right, come back, and hit the season running ready for the autumn.' He supported me completely.

Then I rang Steve. The difference in the conversation was striking. I sensed down the phone that he was totally flabbergasted that I would say no to the Lions. Steve had been the forwards coach on the previous New Zealand tour, and he couldn't comprehend it.

I knew my decision was unlikely to sit well with a lot of people, but I was comfortable with it. Maybe my 2017 Lions experience offered a deeper perspective. I knew I could pass up a Lions tour and my world would still turn. I'd done it before. Rugby was just rugby when it came down to it.

As far as I was concerned, that email in April was the end of it. When the squad came out, I wouldn't be in it and that would be that. But somehow the press got hold of the fact that I'd turned the tour down. Tim Percival, the England media guy, rang me to tip me off that there was a story about to run on it. I was really pissed off. Who had leaked that?

Another journalist – Gavin Mairs from *The Daily Telegraph* – rang my agent. We decided it would be best to get the story out there ourselves while we still had some control of the narrative. It was agreed that I'd do an interview with Gavin. The line we came up with was that I wasn't available to tour because Char was expecting our third child – which she was – although in reality Ettie didn't arrive until September, two months after the tour had finished.

That was a smokescreen. The overriding factor was that playing in the 2023 World Cup with England meant more to me.

The Lions tour squad was duly picked – Gats took Gareth Davies, Conor Murray and Ali Price as his scrum halves – but I had no regrets.

Much more important things were happening that made any grand career plan of mine irrelevant.

The morning the Lions were due to meet up, my brother-in-law Jake passed away after a three-year fight with motor neurone disease.

Four months later, Tiff's cancer returned. They were hammer blows.

Through the autumn, as Jason Leonard's England cap record came closer and closer, there was a lot of chat surrounding it and me. But it was growing harder and harder to justify being away, what with Tiff getting more poorly by the day.

Char was going back to Norfolk every weekend, trying to be there for Tom, Tiff and Maisie, while spending as much time as she could with her sister, Clare, who was grieving the loss of Jake. Char had our three kids to look after, too. Life was manic, and I wasn't there to play my part. I was away, playing rugby.

I knew all the people I cared about didn't want me to stop – exactly the opposite, actually. My rugby gave them fleeting windows of enjoyment during a nightmare time, and helped them to temporarily block out how awful reality was. It was a place to escape to.

But playing on as if nothing was wrong plagued me with guilt. I felt stuck between a rock and a hard place.

By early 2022, Tiff's brave fight was nearing its end. When I finally broke Jason's record with cap number 115, in the win over Wales in the Six Nations, I tried my best to enjoy the moment. I appreciated the ovation at Twickenham, and I said a few words in the dressing room afterwards.

Cockers was England forwards coach by this point, and I thanked him for the part he had played in my journey. 'It's weird how rugby goes full circle,' I said. Jason himself sent me a message congratulating me, and the RFU commissioned a mural of me that was sprayed onto the side of the clubhouse at Holt Rugby Club.

From the outside, it must have looked like life had never been better for me, but the reality was that it was falling apart.

The smile I was wearing was a mask.

I felt like the walls were closing in all around me.

I remember coming back home from England camp and saying to Char in the kitchen: 'I'm not sure I can do this any more.' I felt selfish even saying it – she was the one juggling all the balls – but the whole thing was just too much.

Char was incredibly supportive, as always; so was Eddie. A month from the end of the season, I met him for a coffee. He wanted to talk about how things were for Tiff and Tom and whether he could do anything to help. He wanted to know how I was doing emotionally.

It was strange that my club coach, who I saw every day, never asked the same question. Unbelievable, actually. What sort of man management was that? What sort of basic human decency, even? I guess if it wasn't written on a data sheet, Steve didn't compute.

Eddie and I chatted about the upcoming tour to Australia that summer. He told me it didn't matter. 'There's no pressure from me to come on the tour at all,' he said. 'If I was you, I'd take the summer off to be there for the family and look after the body, and then when the autumn comes, we'll get you back involved.' For him to give me that reassurance was priceless. I decided not to go.

Tiff died in June 2022. Char and I were there at her bedside in the hospital at the end in Norwich. I was broken. We all were.

I played in the Premiership semi-final against Northampton three days later and, on auto-pilot, helped get the side to Twickenham. My reward was to be dropped by Steve for the final. He picked Wiggy, his thirty-nine-year-old assistant, to start at scrum half ahead of me.

In the circumstances, when he told me I was on the bench, I did well to keep my head.

The scenario with Wiggy was bizarre because he was a player-coach, so I was competing with him for a place in the team he was helping to pick. It was ultimately Steve's call though, and I felt badly let down by him. I was brought on for the last fifteen minutes of the game – just in time to pass Freddie Burns the ball

.rop goal that ended Leicester's nine-year wait for a
..iership trophy.

Winning the league was fantastic for the club, and for so many
of the lads, but I was in a totally different headspace. It almost felt
wrong to celebrate with everything that was going on. I was all
over the place.

Tom came to the final – the game that should have been his
last rugby match. It was meant to be his final season as a Leicester player before he retired to concentrate on the farm, but he
hadn't played since the autumn when he had taken indefinite
leave to care for Tiff. I went over to him at the final whistle and
told him to come onto the pitch and join us. He wouldn't – he
didn't want any of the limelight – so I asked Ellis Genge, who had
taken over as captain from Tom, if he would try to persuade him.
He managed to twist his arm.

Tom got to lift the trophy with Gengey. He had played more
than 200 Premiership games for the club and had given his heart
and soul to the Tigers. He deserved that moment so much.

For me, the joy of playing rugby had gone, though.

While Eddie was as good as his word, getting me back involved
in the autumn, one game in – a bad loss to Argentina – I hit
another wall.

I was checking in with Tom most days to see how he was
doing. It was so hard for him. He'd got through the summer by
throwing himself into the farm work back in Norfolk in typical
Tom style, but when the nights had drawn in, he'd been struggling with loneliness. Once Maisie was tucked up at 7 p.m., it was
just Tom and the dog.

The support network he'd once had at the club was no longer
there, and that included me. We'd spent our whole lives together,
but at the point he really needed me, I wasn't beside him. I rang

as often as I could. Sometimes we wouldn't have a great deal to talk about – it was just about being on the line – but the day after the defeat to the Pumas, we did.

I rang him as usual. I told him I thought I was done. 'I don't know what I'm doing this for any more,' I told him. 'What's the point if I'm not enjoying it?'

I was so emotionally spent after all the trauma of first Jake and then Tiff passing, I was unhappy playing under Steve at Leicester, and I just felt like I had to get off the treadmill. I wanted out. Tom heard me out then he talked me down, reassuring me that I would work through this and pointing out I was less than a year away from the 2023 World Cup.

'The decisions you've made have been about getting to 2023, so why throw it away now?' he said. 'I understand why you feel like this and I get it, but if you fast forward twelve months you probably will be thinking, "Why did I do that?" when the World Cup comes around.'

As usual, he was full of common sense. I had been so close to knocking on Eddie's door and saying I was finished but, after that conversation, I decided to stick it out. If I was to have another World Cup in me, he was the guy to bring out the best in me there.

Only it turned out he wouldn't be there with England. He was about to lose his job.

After two successive seasons in which we had lost more games than we had won in the Six Nations, Eddie was under pressure. The Argentina loss had increased it and, while we fought back for a draw against the All Blacks, a heavy defeat by South Africa in the final game of the autumn was the final straw for the RFU.

The team leadership meeting felt very different the next day.

Eddie basically said the ball was in our court now. He clearly knew he was gone.

With the World Cup in mind, Eddie had tried to experiment and had brought in some young guys in key positions, but when you're playing against the best teams, you get found out very quickly. You're either ready for it or you're not. Ultimately some of those guys weren't. He picked Marcus Smith and Jack van Poortvliet at half back against South Africa, who were so early on in their careers at that point, it wasn't really surprising we came unstuck. Eddie was doing what he thought was best for the team long term, but there was to be no long term for him.

He departed as the most successful coach in England history in statistical terms, winning fifty-nine out of eighty-one Tests.

I touched base with him after his sacking to thank him for giving me one of the most enjoyable periods of my career and some of my most memorable rugby experiences.

He always divided opinion, but I can categorically sit here today and say that he is the best coach I've had, without a doubt. Some of the things he came out with used to wind people up. Some thought he was disrespectful or downright rude – the 'scummy Irish' line didn't land too well, nor did his description of Wales as a 'shit little place' at one sponsors' event.

But he was a straight talker and I respected him for that.

During his first Six Nations, there was an outcry over remarks he made before the Ireland match over his fears for Johnny Sexton's safety – he put a media ban on himself ahead of the Wales game after that – but he loved to engage with the media and he was quite prepared to go toe to toe with them. He didn't mind crossing swords with the press. That was different to Stuart Lancaster, who I always felt was intimidated by the media and was trying his best to please them as a result.

Eddie was fully aware that the English media could be difficult, but he was quite happy to draw the heat. He was very clever at making the build-up to a game about him. What that did was pull all the attention onto himself, and away from us, so all we had to worry about was training and preparing for the match.

He was portrayed as this monster by some people, but I never saw that side of him.

The most intimidating version of Eddie I encountered was ahead of the 2019 World Cup at the Treviso camp, when he really let the leadership group have it. We'd had a training week in Bristol the week before that had finished with an inter-squad game littered with squabbles. Everyone was moaning at each other. Eddie had blown his whistle and stepped in.

'You haven't got time for this, boys,' he had warned us. That had clearly been eating away at him because, after getting us together at the hotel where we were staying, he told us exactly what he thought of us.

'The leadership of this team is poor,' he said. 'You blow a lead against Scotland when you're up by thirty points. You can't allow that. In Bristol it's the same shit. It's everyone else's fucking fault. You're too mentally weak. When it got tough in training, I stepped in, but I can't step in during a game or at a World Cup. It's on you. You need to fucking sort this out.'

He didn't shout or bang the table or anything like that. His rage was controlled, but he was angry and he made sure we knew that.

He was driven to make England as good as we could possibly be. To that end, he had no issue calling guys out. Often in public. On that same trip to Treviso, I was walking through the hotel lobby with Jack Singleton when Eddie spotted us. Jack was a young hooker who was making his way in the squad at the time.

He was a good player, but clearly third choice behind Jamie George and Luke Cowan-Dickie.

'Singo. How are you, mate? Are you happy?' Eddie called across the lobby. 'Yes, Eddie, I'm happy,' he replied.

'There's your fucking problem, mate,' barked Eddie, out of nowhere. 'You're just happy to be here.'

Jack was stopped in his tracks. I had the awkward choice of whether to stop too, or leave Jack to it and get the hell out of there. I fled to the lift and pressed the 'Up' button repeatedly. Behind me, Eddie was giving it to Jack across the lobby.

'You're just happy to be here, mate. You've got Jamie and Luke, two of the best hookers in the world here, and you're not competing with them, you're not trying to learn off them. You just want to be fucking third fiddle. Have you ever thought about trying to be better than them?'

As this tirade went on and on, the blood was slowly draining away from Jack's face. The thing was that Eddie had a point. He was trying to push Jack on – he just had an unorthodox way of doing it sometimes. Some people might have taken this as bullying, but he would take a crack at anyone if he felt like it, regardless of their status.

Prince Harry often used to be on the receiving end of Eddie's banter when he came into camp. At one point, when Harry was promoting environmental causes, the papers had also shown him hanging out with Elton John.

Eddie said to him: 'Harry, mate, how's the saving the planet going? How's the eco stuff?'

'Good, thanks Eddie,' said Harry.

'And how's Elton's private jet going, Harry?'

Harry would try to give him some back, but there was only one winner there. Eddie was far too sharp. He would just tie him in knots.

There was a warm and caring side to him as well, though. You should have seen him fussing his little papillon dog Annie at training. Eddie and his wife Hiroko lived at Pennyhill Park for quite a while when he came over, and Hiroko would walk the dog around the pitch while we were hard at it. When we finished, Annie would race onto the pitch and play with Eddie while I did my kicking extras.

I was always worried in case I landed a spiral bomb on Annie and splatted her.

As a coach, he was never happy to stand still. He once had this bright idea of arranging two training blocks with Georgia – the world's most ferocious scrummagers.

The first was in 2018 during the Six Nations. We'd been having a lovely time in the fallow week in Kensington, and then the Georgians turned up. They stepped off the bus at Latymer Upper School, where we were training, looking like something out of *Con Air*.

Eddie claimed the Georgians were born with beards and wrestled their dads when they were in nappies. I can't say with any confidence that he was wrong.

The pitch wasn't the best and the heavy going suited the Georgians down to the ground. Those boys didn't mind a maul, it is safe to say that. They scored two tries from mauls that we just couldn't defend. They were mauling the England pack back twenty metres. Eddie, who had been rubbing his hands at the opportunity for us to mix it with these tough guys, was bawling at the forwards: 'What's going on? Why is no one stopping it?'

The scrum was going backwards. They were basically killing us up front. We were going nowhere in attack against them either.

It got so bad that Fordy put over a drop goal. That was all we had. We ended up losing the twenty-five-minute 'friendly' to Georgia 10–3.

The following year, Georgia came over again, this time for a two-day session. We were training at St Edward's School in Oxford and, although it was a closed session, some of the pupils were watching. The backline plan was for Georgia to run some attack plays against us and then we would run some attacks at them.

Georgia went first. They set up, and their backline was so flat it was hard to work out if they were attacking or defending. I looked at John Mitchell and asked: 'They're attacking, right?'

'I think so, mate,' he said.

From nowhere Georgia, who were hardly renowned for their back play, executed the slickest double miss move I've ever seen in my life. No one in their backline moved forward. It was just catch, miss one, catch, miss two, score in the corner. They went nuts; we didn't know what had hit us. Browny was the last defender and he didn't take kindly to being done on the outside. He was fuming.

Meanwhile, across the field, the forwards were getting down to some heavy-duty scrummaging. Our pack had been stewing on their humiliation against the Georgians for a year and they were mad for it. They had lost a part of their souls the year before, and they were ready for revenge.

The next minute, there was this almighty eruption and a mass brawl broke out. Haymakers were going in, all sorts. In a flash, the entire Georgian backline was in. The England backline was just standing there watching, gobsmacked.

'Oh Christ,' I was thinking, 'we have to get involved now.'

So we ran over there – Browny led the charge – and we

pretended to throw a few but thankfully everyone got separated and it all died down. The backs went back to their places and carried on with some moves, but within a few minutes it was going off again among the forwards. Eddie was absolutely loving it.

'Who wants it, mate? WHO WANTS IT?' he was shouting.

I guess he felt he was finding out who had that mongrel in them that he loved. He was a street-fighter himself.

He was a demanding guy to work for, and maybe that caught up with him in the end. He would ride his staff hard with his 4 a.m. emails, the stick he would give them and the standards he constantly drove. Basically, Steve was the only person who could take the punishment – and even he left in the end.

Because Eddie was such a hard taskmaster, some of the best people wouldn't have wanted to work with him. Those who did had a tendency to leave pretty quickly. The turnover became a talking point among the players. After having such a strong set of coaches in 2019, Eddie was never able to put together a group of the same quality afterwards.

I think part of the reason we abandoned the plan to play the world-beating rugby he had talked about was that the coaches Eddie had around him weren't good enough to implement the style he thought we might be capable of. He simplified the game plan because he knew that he didn't have a good enough attack coach to get us moving the ball. We went backwards in the eighteen months Simon Amor was in the post. Matt Proudfoot just wasn't up to the job of forwards coach either. I felt sorry for the pack. He just didn't seem interested in improving players.

Then there were a whole host of Aussie coaches who came and went. One guy with an NRL background and then another would turn up and disappear just as quickly. We might have been making a bit of progress when it would all change again, and by the next time we met we would be back to square one again. There was a total lack of continuity.

The one guy I would spare from criticism would be Martin Gleeson. I respected the detail he brought, and I thought he got us playing some better rugby as an attack coach when he came in towards the end of Eddie's time. But in general, the calibre of coaches we had wasn't up to international standard.

Eddie's programme, which was so brilliant at first with England, unravelled, but despite that I never lost faith in Eddie himself. He was a rugby mastermind, without doubt, and I still backed him to get it right at the World Cup. That's what he was a proven expert at, after all.

I don't think it was the right decision to sack him, and I was genuinely gutted when he went. With France 2023 less than a year away, it was a very big stick-or-twist moment, and the RFU decided to twist.

And that meant Steve Borthwick was incoming.

11

127 AND OUT

'Fate had decided that the game that no one cares about would prove to be my last appearance for England.'

Given my experiences at Leicester, I can't say I was jumping for joy at Steve Borthwick's England appointment.

I knew he would commit everything he had to making England a force again, and that he'd work unbelievably hard, but I had concerns over the style of rugby he would bring in and where I might stand with him in charge.

His move from Leicester to England was the worst-kept secret in rugby so, when he announced it in the Tigers changing room, no one was surprised. What did wrongfoot us was when Kevin Sinfield, the club's defence coach, stepped forward after Steve's announcement and told us he was off too. We had all assumed Kev would step up and run the show at Leicester for the remainder of the season, and we were desperately keen for that to happen, but his appointment as England defence coach was a big opportunity for him as well.

For Steve's first Six Nations, Nick Evans came in as a caretaker attack coach but, as I expected, attack wasn't very high on the agenda. Steve wanted to use a very similar model to the one he'd deployed at Leicester – to play a claustrophobic pressure game with a lot of kicking. In some ways, sticking to the basics made sense – he had less than nine months to put his stamp on things ahead of the 2023 World Cup – but it really didn't get us very far initially.

There was no post-Eddie bounce. We ended the championship with two wins out of five for the third season running. I felt a little bit like I was on the outside looking in the whole time.

Steve went with Jack van Poortvliet at scrum half for his first game against Scotland, with me on the bench. His combination for the rest of the championship was JVP as the starting 9 and Alex Mitchell on the bench. After England were drilled 53–10 at Twickenham by France in the fourth match, I thought I might get back in for the last one in Ireland, but I didn't.

Still, I took at face value Steve and Kev's reassurances that England would be needing my experience down the line at the World Cup.

The warm-up Tests didn't go well.

We lost in Wales and then only just edged out what was largely their shadow team at Twickenham, in a game that saw Faz sent off and JVP injured. Alex Mitchell, who had been left out of the squad, had to be recalled to it after JVP was ruled out of the tournament.

I started against Ireland in Dublin, but that was a nightmare too. We lost the match and another player for the World Cup in Ant Watson, who had played with a tight calf and ended up tearing it. And Billy Vunipola was red-carded. Billy and Faz were now banned for the start of the tournament.

Then, in our final warm-up game at the end of August at Twickenham, we lost to Fiji for the first time in England's history. The prospects for the World Cup could not have looked more bleak.

We were struggling badly and being battered in the media. The external pressure was affecting the coaches, and that in turn was being fed through to the players. They were just so tight as they tried to drill Steve's system into us that we had no room to breathe.

Any slight system error – for example, in exiting our half efficiently – and the coaches would be all over us. It was important to set standards, yes, but the stress was counter-productive. We had a backs meeting one evening and the coaches brought up how edgy the match twenty-three looked.

'What's happening is the team is getting hammered by you guys,' I told them. 'You all need to be more vulnerable as coaches and allow a few mistakes. You need to let scenarios play out. You need to ease back.'

The direct feedback wasn't an issue with someone like Kev, but it might not have been greeted in the same way when it got back to the main man. I never really knew where I stood with him. I wasn't being disruptive; I was being constructive with my criticism. What was the point of those hundred-plus Tests I'd played if it wasn't to pass on what I had learned?

We had a lot of big-tournament knowledge in our leadership group. That was what convinced me we could salvage our campaign. I knew my experience would help on the field. I had been around the block when it came to World Cups, I knew the territory. But when we got to France, Steve went with Mitch and I had to live with that. Once he was in for the opening game and Danny had been named on the bench, I knew where I stood in the pecking order. Maybe I should have read the room more clearly from a few months out, and been better prepared for the situation, but I had always backed myself.

It was just a pity that Steve didn't feel the same.

For me personally, those weeks of the 2023 World Cup were tough.

On the one hand, I was trying to work through my issues separating rugby and personal trauma with David Priestley, but at the same time I was dealing with the realization that I wasn't going to be playing. The point was: I didn't have to be in France. I'd come so close to throwing in the towel the year before, but I'd chosen to see it through. And it felt like it had all been for nothing.

It's difficult when you're there to play and you're not involved. You're away from family for a long time. You're training hard, but you're training hard knowing that it's not getting you anywhere. It's without a purpose.

Steve did a talk once before a team announcement when he asked if anyone in the squad was an Arsenal supporter. A few hands went up. He then asked us if we knew how many times Arsenal put out what was generally accepted to be their strongest team during their 'Invincibles' season. No one knew.

I think the answer Steve gave was two or three. His point was that the incredible achievement of going through a Premier League season unbeaten and winning the title was a squad effort. We all had to be ready to do our bit.

The Invincibles became the 'Invisibles' at that World Cup. That's what the guys who didn't make the match-day twenty-three called ourselves, because that's what we became. The only dialogue we would have with Steve was on a Sunday night, when he would tell us we weren't playing. Thank God for people like Kev (who is every bit as much of a diamond bloke as you'd imagine him to be), and Aled Walters and Tom Tombleson, two of the best strength and conditioning guys I've ever worked with. They were brilliant.

The team found its way through the pool stage and past Fiji in the quarter-final. We had a lucky draw, admittedly – it couldn't have worked out much better than Argentina, Chile, Samoa and

Japan in the group, and then the Fijians – but we still had to win those games.

Guys stepped up when they needed to, like Fordy with his drop goals against Argentina when we'd had Tom Curry sent off early in the game, and Danny with his cover tackle late on against Samoa. Faz, when he returned from his ban, kicked us into the semi-final.

I tried my best to contribute in a positive way. David and I had talked about what I could do best to help the team as someone who wasn't playing but had a lot of experience to pass on. I still had a huge responsibility to the rest of the guys, and I wanted to be the ultimate team man. I prided myself on being that when I was a starter; the challenge was to persist with that in these new circumstances, but without talking over the guys who were playing.

I was used to helping to drive and direct the team in the build-up to matches and on the pitch, so I had to find the right way to keep adding value. My role changed to trying to prepare the guys who were playing as best as I could for what was coming each game. In training ahead of the semi-final against South Africa, I played on the wing as opposition, running as Cheslin Kolbe. It wasn't a very good imitation of him, but it was something.

I was still part of the leadership group too and, when we met at the start of that week, I talked to the guys about how a lot of us had been in the same place in 2019 against South Africa and how we had made a mistake in the way we had approached that final. We couldn't make that error again.

Steve named his team the next day. After he had done so, we held a players-only meeting. I stood up and spoke to the squad.

'Boys,' I told them, 'we sat here four years ago and we under-played the game in front of us. We've learned nothing if we go into this week against South Africa in the semi-final and just talk about it as another game, because it isn't. It's the most important game of your lives. It is going to take everything you've got. You're going to have to absolutely empty yourselves. But when I look at this team, I know it is a team that can beat the world champions.'

Courtney and Faz stood up after me and rammed home the message – that this was a massive, massive game and that we needed to deliver a massive performance.

You could feel the electricity in the room. It was one of the most raw and powerful team meetings I was involved in with England, and it ensured the boys were in the right mindset for that game.

If I'm being completely truthful, I think if we'd have landed any of the other quarter-finalists – New Zealand, France or Ireland – they would have blown us away. But having South Africa as our opponents, with the way the tournament had played out, gave us a chance.

The Springboks had come off a really draining quarter-final against France, which they had won by one point, and they were probably taking us lightly given the form we had been in. For once, it was us that had the mental edge against them.

The weather also came in, which suited our game plan. We played the strangling game to perfection, going to the air with the boot time after time, and in the conditions South Africa could not escape from it. With time running out, we led by two points. But the mistake we made was continuing to put up contestable kicks, rather than just hammering the ball downfield out of penalty range.

There was a good chance of a knock-on from a high ball, which meant a scrum, and a scrum was where South Africa, with their bomb squad of heavyweight forwards fresh off the bench, could squeeze out a penalty. I could see it clear as day, and I so desperately wanted to be out there influencing the game. I knew I could have helped to get us over the line, but I was totally powerless.

When Handre Pollard kicked the ball into our half with less than five minutes left, the situation was screaming for us to go long, but Freddie Steward ran it back, put the ball up and then knocked it on under pressure from Kwagga Smith just short of the halfway line. From there, we gave away the inevitable scrum penalty. In those pressure moments, you have to make the right decisions, and we made the wrong one. It gave Polly the chance to win the game.

I knew Polly would kick that penalty. With the game on the line, his mentality and his temperament were made for it. He sent it down the middle of the middle. And that was the game won for South Africa.

The boys had given it everything. They had pushed the world champions to the brink, only to have victory snatched away at the death.

I was gutted. Equally, I was so proud of them. We'd shown what it meant to be an England rugby team. We couldn't have come any closer against the world champions. That South Africa side, along with the New Zealand team of a decade earlier, were – in their different ways – the best I ever came across. But we so nearly pulled it off.

Faz, who had been booed by some England fans during the tournament, was brilliant that night. What a lead he gave the side.

I never understood the hate for him from outside. He gave everything for his country and was an outstanding England captain, the best I played under.

You could tell from the start that he was someone who set high standards for himself and for everyone around him. Straight away, when he broke into the squad, he drove training, which was unusual in a new player, particularly one so young.

Back then, if something did not go right, he would want to repeat it again and again until it did. That was a great attitude in terms of raising the bar, but sometimes it was counter-productive.

Over time he mellowed and became more patient and accepting. He was never any less driven, but it helped make him an outstanding leader.

He was one of the boys, yet he was also this inspirational talisman. Striking that balance is very hard.

He spoke very well and he had a presence, but he also had a personal side that most would have no idea about. He never felt the need to show that to the world.

We used to go for team meals out on a Tuesday after training, and a few boys would have a glass of wine – he would be one of them. If the boys were having a laugh, he wanted to have a laugh with them. I really enjoyed his company. As a team leader, I've got nothing but respect and awe for what he and Fordy did in terms of pushing the group every day while still performing themselves. It wasn't just on a game day they brought it; they did so every day. They never stopped.

For Owen, in particular as captain, it must have been exhausting. He had to check the temperature of the team and look after the individuals within it – maybe someone who was making their debut or someone who had just been dropped might need an arm round them; someone who wasn't quite giving what the team needed might need a reminder. He had so much to deal with. He was the goal-kicker and often the playmaker too, with all the extra time that entailed. He had to deal with all the media demands as well.

For all he gave to England, he should have been treasured. But he wasn't. What's that quote from the Batman film *The Dark Knight*? 'You either die a hero, or you live long enough to see yourself become the villain.' Well, that was Owen. Ultimately though, as his teammates, we all knew how much he gave to England. If anyone deserved another World Cup final, it was him. But it wasn't to be.

After our defeat, I went into the South Africa changing room and had a beer with Polly and Jasper Wiese, my Leicester teammates, and wished them luck for the final the following week.

We had a third and fourth place play-off against Argentina to look forward to instead.

Fate had decided that the game that no one cares about would prove to be my last appearance for England.

I hadn't told Steve that I was planning on retiring from international rugby after the World Cup. I didn't want a sympathy selection or a handout. But he picked me for the 'bronze match' anyway.

The game was predictably forgettable. The only thing of note about it – apart from us winning – was a spat I got into with another of my Leicester teammates, Julián Montoya, the Argentina hooker. I found myself next to him at the bottom of a ruck after being tackled, and instead of just laying the ball back, I pulled his shirt up and deliberately pressed the ball against his belly.

'He's slowing it down, his gut's in the way – it's a penalty,' I was telling the ref Nic Berry.

Julián's a great mate off the pitch, but he's a fiery guy and he didn't see the funny side. Meaningless game or not, he was fuming with me. I didn't get the penalty, but what I did get was a clip around the head from Julián a few minutes later when Argentina scored from a pick-and-go. That just set me off again.

'He's just slapped me, ref. You've got to check that with the TMO. Go to the TMO ref,' I said to Nic.

'You're in big trouble, Julián. It's going to be a yellow,' I was telling Julián. Julián was panicking, thinking he might be going off, as I giggled away.

It felt good to be taking the piss right up to the end.

When the time came to be substituted in the second half, I didn't feel any sense of emptiness or loss. As I left the field for the last time as an England player at the Stade de France, I was actually thinking: 'Thank God it's over.' Not playing for England, I loved playing for England – just that World Cup. It had been a long haul, and at that moment all I wanted was to get home.

In a pure rugby sense, I could have done without putting myself through it, but I learned a lot about myself, unpacking everything with David. Through a series of sessions at that World Cup, we got to the point where I realized it was OK to love rugby as well as love people I had lost. The two things weren't mutually incompatible.

That entire tournament was one important period of reflection for me, and I came out of it straightened out mentally. And, with the passage of time, the personal disappointment of the 2023 World Cup faded and I was able to look back fondly on the whole experience of playing international rugby.

What a truly amazing privilege it had been. I banked so many golden memories and made friends for life. Thirteen and a half years at the coalface for England had been a decent shift.

What was it that allowed me to play international rugby for so long? A few things.

It takes a huge amount of emotional energy. By the back end of your international career, you become taken for granted. Fans and critics get used to you – bored of you, even – and look forward to seeing the next cab off the rank. You need to learn how to be your own biggest cheerleader.

I guess I had an inner belief and drive that kept me going.

Some people advertise their competitiveness through their body language – Richie McCaw or Michael Hooper, say, or Faz. You'd never have said that about me. You would be more likely to mistake me for the class clown if you'd caught me laughing away at something stupid in the England dressing room half an hour before a Test match.

But you can't play top-level, international professional sport for as long as I did without that drive. I liked to keep things as light as possible on the outside but, on the inside, I loved competing. I wanted to see how good I could be. I wanted to be such a key cog in any side I played in that, if you took me out, it would be obvious that I was missing. I wanted to bring energy and influence to the team.

I was also pretty consistent. A lot of Premiership players could probably survive in a one-off international game – they might even deliver a seven out of ten performance. The trick is doing that game after game.

And I was adaptable. If it was a dry track in Australia and we were getting fast ball, I could run and play, but if the rain came down at Twickenham, I could go back to the fundamentals. That helped me to evolve and change with the game. By the end of my career, I was a tactical controlling number 9, while at the beginning of it I was anything but. That's where the game went, and I was able to go with it – even though it went against my instincts.

There was one more reason I stuck around for so long as well. I had an unbelievable support network.

My wife Char was, and is, something else. The whole time I was playing for England, she was working too, as well as looking after the kids. It must have been tempting at times to pour all the pressure of that back onto me when I was on the other end of a phone somewhere around the world, but she never did. She always allowed me to focus totally on doing the best I could for England.

What a person to have by my side.

I was proud that I got to finish what was an incredible ride with England on my terms. Whatever happened, at thirty-four, that World Cup was always going to be my end point.

It was special to wrap it up in France alongside Courtney, Joe, Jamie, Jonny May – guys who I went back to the age groups with – and a great mate in Coley. They were the ones who knew me best. They'd seen me at my highest highs and lowest lows.

As a sportsman, when it comes to the end, all you ever want is the respect of your teammates.

I think I had that.

12

TIGERS' TALES

*'Those Leicester bus journeys
back from Twickenham were utter
carnage. It would all go off, whether
we had won or lost.'*

I've played in many different stadiums and grounds around the world, but Welford Road will always hold a special place in my heart.

When you're sitting in the home changing room, waiting to take the field, and you hear all the fans in the stand above stamping their feet as Deep Purple's 'Smoke on the Water' booms out, you wouldn't want to be anywhere else in the world. It's like someone has hooked you up to an adrenaline drip.

When you walk out together, as Tigers, through the throng of supporters on the packed Crumbie Terrace, carried onto the field by their roars, you're walking in the footsteps of legends.

I maintain that no matter what the Premiership table says in any given season, Leicester remains the biggest club in England.

If you're going to be a one-club man, you might as well make it the best club in the land.

The closest I came to leaving was in 2014–15, when I almost signed for Bath. I did sign for Bath, actually – the heads of agreement on the contract, anyway – before I had a change of heart. At the time, Bath were playing a brilliant brand of rugby under Mike Ford, who I knew and liked from his time with England. They were flying, and had smashed us 45–0 early in the season. I had a meeting with Mike where he told me how keen they were to pair me up with George, his son, at half back the following season.

At the time, George had just broken into the England team. Having already played with him during his first spell at Leicester, I knew how well that combination would work. It was an exciting prospect. I could see my game improving at Bath in a way that I maybe couldn't at Leicester. Also, I'd only known life working under Richard Cockerill in club rugby, and I was wondering whether the grass was greener elsewhere. Did I need something different – a new coaching set-up and a new environment – to push me on?

So I signed the piece of paper.

The problem was that Leicester was *Leicester*. It was a trophy factory. Or it had been. I was conflicted. I rang Leicester chief executive Simon Cohen and asked him if we could catch up. I always enjoyed Simon's company, but I was never quite sure if the feeling was mutual. Being the miserable Mancunian that he is, he didn't exactly jump at my invitation.

'I suppose I can spare you some time,' he said. 'Are you treating me or am I treating you?' Everything was a negotiation with Simon – even who was paying for lunch.

'Fucking hell, Simon. Does it matter? The point is we need to chat.' We met up at Nando's in Leicester. I was straight with him.

'Look Simon, there's a good chance that I'm going to go to Bath,' I said. 'They've put forward a very tempting vision and they've offered me X.'

Simon looked on impassively, giving absolutely nothing away. 'I'll stay if you give me Y,' I said.

It was more than Bath were offering, but not by much.

Simon's negotiating skills were incredible. He could play the long game like no one else. He would rest his interlocked hands on his stomach, breathe heavily and rhythmically and just allow the awkward pause to build. He could outlast a Himalayan monk with his prolonged silences. But this one lasted about a second.

'OK', he said. 'You can have it. But you have to pay for lunch.'

Ridiculously, the debate over who would put their hand in their pocket for two wraps took considerably longer than the contract negotiations.

The truth was that, inwardly, I never wanted to leave. Where else can you play that's going to be better? Nowhere. Not in England, anyway.

The next time I renewed with Leicester, I left it to my agents Ben Lewitt and Richard Wilks (Wilksy would later go on to become the club's general manager) to sort the contract with Simon. Between us, we had a figure in mind, and Simon had a figure in mind, and this time there was a pretty big gap between the two. He really wasn't happy about what we were asking for and the conversation was going to-and-fro like a baseline tennis battle.

In the end Simon had heard enough, claimed we would destroy the club if he agreed to what we were asking, and stormed out of his own office. Wilksy and Ben were left just sitting there, a bit dumbfounded. That was awkward for them – but not half as awkward as it was for Simon when he realized he had left the keys to his snot-green VW Scirocco on the table. He had to walk back in sheepishly for them a couple of minutes later.

We settled halfway in the end.

The only other time I had my head turned by another club was in 2019, when I had just returned from the World Cup in Japan and had six months left on my Leicester contract. That time,

Toulouse were interested. And if Toulouse are interested, you listen. You think of the lifestyle and the brand of rugby, the history and the size of the club – it is a French institution – and it appeals. It appeals a lot.

I was essentially offered the chance to be back-up to Antoine Dupont, which I was fine with. But I knew if I went to France, that was it as far as England selection went, because of the RFU's ban on selecting overseas-based players. And I couldn't turn my back on England. Timing is everything, and I wasn't ready to do it at that point.

So I stayed with Leicester.

Leicester is a sporting city.

The football club is a big deal, but rugby is such a big part of the community. Go to the supermarket or a café or a shop, and people will always want to chat about the game. The players who come to Leicester quickly learn to understand that. I imagine that's what it's like in the south of France as well. The rugby club is a part of the soul of the place.

The Tigers have their own world with their own laws and traditions. The alpha male fighting culture that greeted me when I arrived did change over time, but what never changed was the expectation that you would work bloody hard. I've never been in any other club environments in England, so I don't know what they are like, but Leicester was always about graft, humility, and your responsibility to the club and your teammates.

We had this sign up at the training ground for years and all it said was: 'No dickheads here'. That was the bottom line.

The Tigers were built around a home-grown core. When I came to the club, it was underpinned by people like Martin Corry, Lewis Moody and Ben Kay, then over time that evolved to include the likes of me and my brother, Coley and Crofty – players who had come through the academy and understood the DNA of the club.

On the top of that, because of the stature of Leicester Tigers (as opposed to the money the club offered), we were able to attract some brilliant overseas talent – players like Aaron Mauger from New Zealand, Martin Castrogiovanni from Italy and Marcos Ayerza from Argentina. We had the best of both worlds.

Somewhere in the middle were the Tuilagi brothers. They were Pacific Islanders by birth, but they were around the East Midlands for so long that they became like locals. I played with four of them – Manu, Alesana, Vavae and Henry, who was so big that when he lay on his side, he was taller than when he was standing up. They were all amazing athletes and great people.

Manu was incredibly kind and thoughtful and great fun. He would always have a smile on his face. As a twelve-year-old he was parachuted into a Western culture when he moved to the UK to join his brothers. The culture was very different from the one he had grown up with in Samoa, and sometimes he did get things wrong. There were some wild moments when he got into some trouble, but he was never coming from a bad place. He was a really likeable guy. He was basically a man-child who just wanted to have a good time.

His brother Alesana was great value too. Crofty and I once bought a 3D TV set when they were all the rage. One day, at the training ground, we were talking about the novelty of watching footballs fly out of the telly towards us – while wearing those ridiculous glasses that made you feel sick after about twenty minutes – when Alesana interrupted.

'I can't get it to work,' he said.

'What do you mean?' I said.

'Every time I put the TV on, it's just like normal. I don't know what's wrong with the glasses.'

'Hang on a minute,' I said. 'What have you bought, Alesana?'

'I bought some 3D glasses, brother.'

'Not a 3D telly?'

'No, brother.'

'Alesana, you need the telly as well!'

He had just been sitting in his lounge in these ludicrous battery-powered specs, wondering why the hell nothing was happening.

Of all the Tuilagis, I would say Alesana was the best one I played with. So powerful, so skilful. Just exceptional. In his eight years at Leicester, he reduced countless opponents to rubble. Like Manu, he loved wiping people out – I think they both took more pleasure in that than in scoring tries.

There was one game against Bath at The Rec when they went after Nick Abendanon. A couple of seasons beforehand, Alesana had been cited for tackling him without the ball in a Heineken Cup quarter-final, and he had ended up missing the Premiership final after being banned. For some reason, Alesana blamed Abendanon for this, and he and Manu went after him. Steve Mafi got involved as well, so it was a full-on Polynesian manhunt.

They went out there to beat him up and poor old Abendanon was on the receiving end of some absolutely monstrous hits. There was one in particular that made me wince. Matt Banahan threw him this paper-bag-in-a-hurricane pass, Manu lined him up, arrived flat out and cleaned him up. He caught him so hard with the tackle that Abendanon made a noise like the decompression sound a tortoise makes when it goes into its shell.

I take my hat off to Abendanon because, somehow, he got up from that – and all the other Tuilagi tackles that day.

Leicester was all about physicality. The Tigers had an initiation ritual on the way back from the annual trip out to Twickenham (for the Premiership final) whereby the young guys who had just finished their first year in the squad had to try to fight their way through to the back of the bus and touch the back seat. A fingernail on it would do, that's all, to be successful – but no one ever was. You had the likes of Alesana, Julian White, Benny Kay, Cozza – Martin Corry – and Moodos to get past and, before you even reached them, you had blokes like Brett Deacon, Louis Deacon and Jim Hamilton in the way.

The senior guys would start singing very, very quietly: 'You'll never take the back seat' almost in a whisper, and the chant would get louder and louder. The young guys would be sitting there at the front discussing tactics and then someone would shout 'now' and they would all go. Some lads would go low, others high, but the end result was always the same. You got smashed.

It was a rite of passage and you would wear a few shots going through it.

I actually got out of it in my first season after playing in the Premiership final, but the following season I had to do it. I think the senior guys probably went easy on me, because I was still only eighteen, but they made sure that I was never going to get near that back seat.

You only had to do it once but there were certain lads who would do it every year regardless, just for the fun of it. They loved it. Harry Ellis did it naked one year because he thought no one would want to touch him without any clothes on. He took the high route but got held up in a sort of choke tackle, so he ended up pinned to the roof of the bus by some of the lads with his bits dangling down. It was an inviting target, and they were given a good smacking. He was screaming in agony.

Tommy Varndell once got slapped so hard on his bald head trying to fight his way to the back that there was a hand print left on top of it. The imprint rose as well when the bruise came out, so it was like some kind of weird artwork.

The 'storm the back seat' tradition was actually resurrected by England at a training camp before the 2023 World Cup. Lewis Ludlam played the Harry Ellis role, stripping down for his shot at it, which meant an unfortunate experience for Jack van Poortvliet. Lewis was held up over JVP's seat with his backside wedged on Jack's face and Jack's nose fitting perfectly into the crack. Like a Tetris puzzle piece. He just couldn't shift him.

Those Leicester bus journeys back from Twickenham were utter carnage. It would all go off, whether we had won or lost. There was one bus for the match-day squad and then another one for the players who weren't involved. That one was trouble on wheels because those boys would have been on the sauce all day.

One trip, we had this bottle of Jack Daniel's doing the rounds on the bus. We were playing eyeball shots with it – like Eyeball Paul does on *Kevin & Perry Go Large* – where you drink one shot and whack another into your eye. It didn't end well for me, and I threw up into a plastic bag. Jim Hamilton responsibly decided the best way to get rid of the bag was to throw it out of the skylight but, as he reached up to chuck the bag out, it got snagged on an armrest, ripped and the vomit poured out straight over him. He was covered in it.

The bus driver had been on the microphone quite early on in the journey, warning us he was going to pull over at the next service station and call the police if the bad behaviour continued. When we got to the services, he was on it again, saying he wouldn't drive any further unless the chaos stopped. Freddie

Tuilagi – the eldest of the clan – grabbed the mike off the driver and told him to shut the fuck up and get on with his job, otherwise he would drive us home and put the bloke in the luggage hold.

Safe to say, the driver carried on.

By the time we pulled up at Welford Road for the club's after-match party, the bus was in ruins. About ten seats were broken because of the back seat game, someone was wearing the bus toilet seat on their head, and there was a contaminated river of piss, booze and vomit flowing across the aisle. When the driver turned around to look back at the devastation after he had parked up, I just felt so sorry for him. In no other work space would some of the goings-on from that time be judged acceptable.

After one Twickenham final, Henry Tuilagi knocked Seru Rabeni out after we had got back to Welford Road.

Seru, many beers in, was being a pain in the arse, and Henry just turned round to him and said: 'Seru, you've pushed me too far, brother', and laid him out with one punch. There was silence for a couple of seconds around the room as everyone turned round to see Seru splayed out on the floor with his dreads everywhere, and then we just carried on as if nothing had happened.

That was rugby back then – well, it was Leicester rugby anyway.

I guess we took those Twickenham trips for granted to an extent because they happened every season. That run of finals – nine in a row – was an incredible record. We won four of them, including a memorable one against Saracens in 2010.

Half the team got stuck in the hotel lift on the morning of

the game, after our prop Boris Stankovich started jumping up and down inside it. It stopped between floors, leaving the lads marooned. Cockers was raging with the hotel manager, demanding an engineer arrive to let them out. Our planned morning walk-through had to be cancelled, but we still managed to win the final. Dan Hipkiss – one of the guys who had been trapped in the lift – scored the winning try four minutes from time.

The rematch the following year saw me poisoned by my own club. The catering operation at Leicester was run by two fantastic women called Jackie and Kate, but the quality of the food could sometimes leave something to be desired. We had this email from the team manager one year, just before Valentine's Day, which said that if any of us were after flowers we should speak to Kate because she was a florist. To which Ben Kay replied: 'Well that explains the food then.'

Before we travelled down for that final, we ate at the club together. I had this reheated lamb shank, which was like a wallet wrapped around a bone. I was sick in the night and felt really weak for the game. I was sin-binned by Wayne Barnes after just four minutes and we lost the game.

We always stayed in the same hotel in Chiswick ahead of the final because of its proximity to Twickenham. Despite that, we almost missed the kick-off against Harlequins in 2012.

London traffic could never be relied upon. Our bus was so badly delayed as we crawled our way to the ground that we ended up getting ready on board. By the time we reached the Twickenham perimeter, it was so close to kick-off that the route we needed to take to the car park had been closed.

Quins had announced ahead of the game that they were going to walk to the stadium from The Stoop. We could see

Twickenham in front of us and it would have made sense for us to have just hopped out with our bags and walked to the ground too, but Cockers wasn't having it. There was no way he was going to allow us to do the same as Quins – who he despised – just on a point of principle.

Instead, he made the bus driver trail all the way around the stadium in the other direction to get us to the entrance, which took ages. 'They're not going to start the game without us, are they?' said Cockers. He was right. They didn't. But we lost that one too.

The following year, 2013, we beat Northampton, our biggest rivals, pretty comprehensively at Twickenham. That was the game in which Dylan Hartley was sent off for calling the referee – Barnesy again – a cheat. He received an eleven-week ban and lost his place on the Lions tour.

The year after – 2014 – we missed out on the final for the first time in a decade.

The thing about sport is that – no matter how much you assume it will stay the same – nothing lasts forever.

Quite quickly, Leicester went from being a team that was relentlessly successful to one that wasn't. We lost the mystique we'd once had. Saracens had become the new Leicester. They were the ones setting the standards and we couldn't match them.

While we had an unbelievable starting team, as soon as the autumn internationals or the Six Nations began, all of us inter-national players would disappear. We just didn't have the cover to offset that. Saracens did. When their A-listers were away, they had such depth they would still be able to churn out the wins. Of course, it turned out that it was because they were cheating on the salary cap, and when that was eventually uncovered, they were punished for it with relegation.

A lot of people in rugby thought Sarries should have been stripped of their titles for their financial crimes. I had a different take on it.

However Saracens achieved it, England benefited from their success. The Sarries lads brought that winning mentality and big-match experience from their Premiership finals and European successes to the national side. Those guys helped take England to the top of the world rankings and to a World Cup final, and I shared in that.

So I was grateful to Sarries for what they did for England. I might have felt differently if I had lost to them in a Premiership final, but the truth is that by then we had slipped to such a degree, we weren't capable of reaching a Twickenham final any more.

It was more than just Saracens who had overtaken us.

In the past, opposition teams had come to Welford Road essentially expecting to lose, happy if they could leave with a losing bonus point. That represented a win for them. But suddenly, teams were coming and leaving disappointed if they didn't win.

We were a diminished force.

Our recruitment had gone off. One season we signed a load of lads from Treviso. They were Italian internationals, but the Italian national team tended to lose a lot, and so did Treviso. These boys were used to getting turned over every week yet, all of a sudden, they found themselves at Leicester, where the expectations are that you win every week. Winning is a habit and a culture, and they didn't know what that looked like.

The coaching at the club grew stale, too.

The fact was that a lot of us players were struggling with the same messaging that we'd had for years. It didn't matter if the greatest point was being made, everyone was just bored of the same old voice.

Every coach has his sell-by date, and Cockers had reached his.

Two years in a row, we hadn't finished high enough in the league in the regular season to earn a home play-off, and both years we had gone out in the semi-final. Midway through 2016–17, with us in fifth, it looked like we might not make the play-offs at all. So Cockers was sacked.

It was the end of an era. He was Mr Leicester in many ways. He had run Leicester with raw emotion for so long. He put his all into Leicester. He was combustible and crazy sometimes – he eventually had to have a soundproof booth put around him in the stand at Welford Road, because he would go off his head in full view of all the spectators around him – but it was only because nothing mattered to him more than the Tigers.

For all his volatility, I had a lot of respect for Cockers, but there was a kind of inevitability about him going. If we had still been reaching the Premiership final every year it might have been different, but we had slipped.

It wasn't solely the results. The other thing was that Cockers and Aaron Mauger, the head coach, were struggling to work together. They just viewed rugby so differently. Kiwi rugby mentality versus Leicester rugby mentality was like oil meeting water.

We had a pre-season inter-squad game once, where Mage took charge of one side and Cockers the other. The teams were announced three days ahead of the game. I wasn't involved, but I was at the training ground, so I walked into the Mage's dressing room.

'This week is all about getting better together for the season ahead collectively, brothers. It's not about us and them,' Mage was telling his group. As he saw it, the match was about honing our shape and structure, executing skills under pressure and then sharing a nice barbecue and a beer together afterwards. Sitting around a campfire with a guitar, singing 'Kumbaya', all being best mates . . . so wholesome.

Then I walked into the other dressing room. Cockers was coming in off his long run. 'We're going to do this to them, we're going to do that to them . . .' The works.

He was making it abundantly clear to his team that this was no knockabout friendly. And there was absolutely no mention of beer, barbies and bonding.

Two polar-opposite approaches.

When it came to game day, Cockers was mad for it, and he had revved his team up good and proper. Before you knew it, players were dropping like flies. Someone did their calf, Telusa Veainu was knocked out, and Mike Fitzgerald and Dom Barrow were having a punch-up. Fitzy punched Dom so hard he broke his hand.

Cockers' team won, so he was absolutely delighted – that was all he cared about. Mage was pretty quiet at the barbecue afterwards. Three days later, we were back at the training ground. Scott Hansen, our Kiwi skills coach, gathered us in to talk to the group. There was a long silence. Then he said: 'Put the slide up.'

An image of two dead tigers appeared on the screen. 'Right, what do you see there, boys?' he said. Then he played the noise of a great thunder crash and showed the clip of Dom and Fitzy fighting. Then, boom, it was the crash again and the screen went back to the two dead tigers. 'What do you see, boys?' he asked again. No one said anything.

'What do I see?' he said. 'Two dead Tigers. Fitzy, you're out with a bust hand. Dom, you've got concussion. We've got two dead Tigers and it's no good to anyone.'

Mage was shaking his head at the image; Cockers was grinning away in the corner.

Even though Mage had played for the club, his world view wasn't really Leicester. He once had this totally Kiwi idea of us all coming in wearing our old junior club jerseys as a way of connecting with our roots. It was a bit corny.

I thought team morale and togetherness would be better served with a good laugh together. So I went out and bought a complete Real Madrid football kit – socks, shorts, the lot – and came in wearing it the next day. Mage asked what kit it was.

'Real Madrid, Mage,' I told him. 'I was in the academy. I could have made it, you know . . .' He didn't know whether I was being genuine or not.

When Cockers was sacked, Mage was put in charge by the club, but he lasted less than three months before he got the bullet as well. The club then brought in an Australian, Matt O'Connor, who lasted one season, failed to get us into the play-offs, and was gone within one game of 2018–19 after we were drilled by Exeter.

There were far too many quick fixes being tried. Everywhere, there were shortcuts being taken and it just wasn't working. I was playing the best rugby of my career with England under Eddie, but the club stuff was going up in smoke.

The club's next bright idea was to give Geordan Murphy, who was essentially a skills coach, the reins to run the whole operation. He was a brilliant people person, but he had never been a director of rugby before, and he was suddenly in charge, with coaching staff below him who were even less experienced than he was. The club failed to equip him with the senior people around him that he needed. We fell off a cliff and in 2018–19 we came close to being relegated, which was bonkers for a club of Leicester's size.

None of us were used to this situation. The threat of relegation brought a totally different burden; it was almost like the harder we tried, the worse it got. It was such an emergency we had this guy come in from the SAS to talk to us about clarity and planning. That gave me an excuse to get a few things off my chest. I stood up and, in front of the squad, the coaches and some of the club hierarchy, I put it back to the SAS guy.

'What would you say if you were put into a situation where you had no clarity, planning or understanding of what you were trying to do? I think I speak on behalf of a lot of people in this room when I say I feel like that when I go out onto the field at the moment,' I said.

I could feel the eyes of the coaches burning into me, and literally no one came in behind me to back me up, but it had to be said for the good of the team because it was true. The club eventually brought in Mike Ford as an experienced hand on the coaching side, and I honestly believe that if he hadn't arrived to stabilize things, we would have gone down.

And, for all my love of the Tigers, I would have left if that had happened, no question.

Fortunately, it didn't.

That period really showed the Leicester fans for what they are – the best in the land.

It's all very well supporting a side when they are always winning, but it's not so easy when they are struggling. The Tigers supporters would still turn out in their thousands to back us, queuing up, come rain or shine, to run to their favourite spots on the terrace as soon as the gates opened. They really were – and are – incredible.

They were a wonderful constant throughout my Leicester

career. The other constant was the laughs. Whether we were good or bad, we always had fun. I tried to make sure of that.

My good friend Greg Bateman, the team's long-suffering prop, was quite often on the receiving end. He once made the mistake of leaving his house unguarded just after New Year. I wanted to get rid of my Christmas tree, so I drove round to his place and lobbed it into his back garden. He came into the club moaning about it the next day, wondering why on earth someone would do such a thing.

That evening, under cover of darkness, Fordy and Jonny May threw their trees over his fence too. The Bateman back garden attacks became the talk of the training ground.

When seven more of the lads did the same the next night, Greg was convinced he was being targeted. He posted a stiff message on the local community Facebook group complaining about it and appealing for witnesses. It was only when my nephew revealed to him who was behind it that he finally clocked on.

Another time, Greg was in charge of organizing our end-of-season team social, and he decided to theme it on *The Book of Mormon*. He went on the squad WhatsApp group and told every-one to wear a suit and tie.

I set up an alternative WhatsApp group with everyone but him on it, telling them to wear anything *but* a suit and tie. When he turned up for the bus to Leeds, he stood out like a sore thumb.

We tried to do the Otley Run pub crawl on that trip, and Fordy, who didn't really drink, offered to get a round in at one point. Everyone jumped in, and by the time they had finished ordering, he had been absolutely ambushed. The tray of drinks he carried back out to the beer garden was groaning. So was Fordy as he put them down on the table. 'Eighty quid,' he said, shaking his head in disbelief. 'Eighty quid. On Carling.'

Greg had a fluctuating relationship with Cockers, who once sent him inside at training because, in Cockers' words, he was 'a piece of shit'. Greg messed up a passing drill and Cockers went for him so, sensing a chance for some chaos, a few of the other lads started firing really difficult passes to him to drop. Which he did.

'You might as well fuck off to the changing room and don't bother coming back,' fumed Cockers.

He also gave him another bollocking at another training session once for being sluggish, but that one was Greg's fault. We'd decided to go for breakfast at Jones's Café Bistro near Welford Road just before the session, which was a dumb idea, but not half as dumb as taking on their legendary 666 Challenge, which Greg decided to do.

This food mountain consisted of six eggs, six sausages, six rashers of bacon, six hash browns, six slices of toast and six pancakes with maple syrup: it was colossal. If you ate it inside half an hour, you didn't have to pay – and you got a free T-shirt.

Greg was moving like a water buffalo afterwards. 'What the fuck's wrong with you, Bateman?!' Cockers was roaring at him.

On another occasion, we went out to Italy to play a pre-season friendly against Treviso. Over the course of our stay, we got through a hell of a lot of coffee at the team hotel, which we all collectively agreed to put on Greg's room bill, of course.

It was quite an eventful trip, with me having to buy a new phone for the team manager after 'accidentally' nudging him into the hotel swimming pool, fully clothed. And the Italian police were called another night when we overran a McDonald's. Afterwards, when we were back in Leicester, Cockers gave us all a dressing-down for these antics.

He took specific aim at Greg for failing to pay his bill for 200 espressos, having printed off the receipt for this lake of coffee.

Greg said he knew nothing about it. He promised that he'd pay it now that he had found out – but argued that clearly it couldn't have been his doing, since it would have been physically impossible for him to have drunk all that espresso during our stay without having a heart attack.

Cockers just wasn't having it.

'It doesn't look good, does it? It's not fucking humble, is it?' he said.

Honestly, those continental adventures – especially the Heineken Cup trips – are some of my most treasured memories with Leicester.

I loved that competition when it was in its heyday, especially those games in France against the top French clubs. They felt like real occasions. The stadiums were absolute bearpits. The French made a big thing of defending their territory, so winning there was such a challenge. We went seven years without managing it.

I remember we played in Perpignan once, during Heyneke Meyer's time. Dan Carter was making his debut and he tore us apart in the first half. Our defence coach was a guy called John McFarland, who Heyneke had brought in and who, for some reason, wore a horrible 1990s leather jacket to the game. I was travelling reserve for the game and when the lads came in at half-time John gave them a big talking-to, but I just couldn't take him seriously. It was like being addressed by Tony from *The Sopranos*.

We had a couple of attempts at cracking Stade Aimé Giral with no joy. We also had a couple of games during that run at the Stade Marcel-Michelin, which has to be one of the most atmospheric grounds in club rugby – but came out on the wrong side against Clermont Auvergne.

We lost twice in Toulouse too. We might have got a losing bonus point in one of them, except I took a quick tap from a kickable penalty towards the back end of the game and got turned over by Thierry Dusautoir. I walked into the changing room afterwards and was greeted by a clip around the ear from Cockers and a full-on blast from him.

We still reached the quarter-final that season, but Jonny Wilkinson kicked us to defeat in Toulon.

It was all to play for going into the last ten minutes. The ref, George Clancy, got the two captains together and told them he didn't want a penalty settling a great game. So, for the last ten minutes, Toulon did nothing except infringe, including one blatant push on Ant Allen when he chased his own chip with a couple of minutes left, and Clancy didn't give anything.

Toulon won 21–15.

We finally got over the line in Montpellier the following season, in 2013–14. There was a dramatic finish, with a last-minute try from Niki Goneva and a nerveless conversion from Ryan Lamb, who had come off the bench, winning it by a point.

There were a few seconds on the clock when Lamby took the conversion, so we still had to receive the kick-off but we closed the game out. We got back into the dressing room in great spirits, only for Cockers to go at Lamby for five minutes for not running the clock down to zero before the conversion.

'We did win, you know,' said Lamby, after the storm had blown out.

We reached the Heineken Cup quarter-final again that season – the last before it became the Champions Cup – only to lose in Clermont again.

I had watched on as a teenager when we reached the 2009 Heineken Cup final, and I played in the semi-final defeat to Racing seven years later. But the only European final I ever played in was against Montpellier in the second-tier Challenge Cup in 2021, which showed how far we had fallen. We lost.

Silverware finally returned to Welford Road the following season, when that Freddie Burns drop goal at Twickenham won us the 2022 Premiership final. After coming off the bench when Fordy did his Achilles, that one act gave Freddie legendary status among the Tigers. In his own mind, anyway.

Freddie was a great character and, in fairness, he nailed his moment and turned the celebrations into a one-man show. He led the singing at the reception afterwards with a rendition of 'Take Me Home, Country Roads' that John Denver would never have recognized, telling anyone who would listen that he had essentially beaten Saracens on his own.

His girlfriend at the time told him it wasn't all about him. 'That's where you're wrong,' he told her.

The old order had been restored, with the Tigers back at the top of the tree.

Could that 2021–2 season have been the forerunner for another period of sustained dominance if Steve Borthwick hadn't gone off to coach England? Honestly, I don't think so. By the time he left, midway through the following season, we had lost more league games than we had won and we were struggling a bit. Sides had worked out our one-dimensional rugby.

Richard Wigglesworth, Steve's replacement, actually did a really good job in starting to move our game on. He got us to the Premiership semi-finals, and created a much more enjoyable environment in his six months in charge. But then he went off to join Steve at England too, so it was back to square one.

The next guy through the revolving door, Australian Dan McKellar, was a disaster. We were really, really poor under him and finished in eighth. He couldn't go quickly enough as far as I was concerned – especially as it cleared the way for Michael Cheika.

Another Aussie, Cheika had an impressive coaching CV, including a five-year stint in charge of the Wallabies. It was a real coup for the club to land someone of his standing, and he lived up to all the expectations. He was a great fit for the club because he had that fighting Leicester mentality and a great way of selling his message. And playing under Cheik in my last season was a breath of fresh air. He got me excited about playing rugby – even at the age of thirty-five. When he arrived, I was a Bunsen burner on its last spluttering gasp, but he opened up the valve in me again.

When you're an older player, coaches often leave you to do your own thing – they assume you just do what you do – but I loved how Cheik refused to do that. He would challenge me to think about things in different ways and he didn't mind being direct about it. That was what I was used to with Cockers and Eddie and that's what I had always wanted – honesty.

Cheik was a pleasure to work with, although we'd hardly got to say hello before I was being booked in for heart surgery.

During a game at Sale back in 2021, I was substituted off and had sat down on the bench when suddenly my heart started going crazy. I told the doctor something was wrong. He took my pulse and checked me out, but then everything settled down.

While the feeling of my heart pounding out of my chest was disconcerting, I put it to the back of my mind. A heart examination before the 2023 World Cup flagged up a couple of potential issues, but after some more tests I was told there was nothing to worry about.

Then, nine months later, after an open training session at Leicester, I was doing some sprint drills with our S and C coach Will Findlay in the rain when it happened again. This time, it was worse. I really thought I was going to black out. I had to sit down at first, then lie down on the pitch while Will rushed off to get a medic. There must have been about thirty people watching, wondering what was going on. I was wondering myself.

I was fine within a few minutes, but when there was another episode a couple of weeks later during a game at Northampton, I knew I had to get it dealt with. When it happened, I thought I was going to have to ask the referee to stop the game, but Saints scored a try that gave me some recovery time, after which I was able to finish the match.

I went to see a specialist, who told me this sort of thing was quite common in sports people. That may well have been true, but in my experience it wasn't something that was often or openly talked about.

I had a small device about the size of a pen lid fitted underneath my pectoral muscle to monitor my heart, which forwarded on the data to a receiver under my bed at the end of each day. I hadn't had it in long when my heart went haywire again on the treadmill at home.

The doctor rang me the next day to tell me the data had confirmed what the issue was. He told me I had a condition called supraventricular tachycardia, which basically meant my heart was prone to racing extremely fast and out of rhythm, and reassured me that they could sort it and there was no risk of me having a heart attack.

I was booked in for an ablation procedure. The surgeon went in through my groin, then stimulated my heart to 250 beats per minute to identify the misfiring nerve endings that were causing the problem, and then, having done so, he burned them out. I was awake during all this, but sedated, and I can't actually remember anything about it. Apparently, I talked a lot. No change there, then.

All things considered, I got away pretty lightly with physical problems over the course of my career – two shoulder surgeries and a knee op – so maybe I was overdue something else.

When I was back to full fitness, Cheik started using me as a 'closer', coming off the bench in the second half of games and using my experience to try to get the side over the line.

I could accept that by this point. It was the reality of my stage of rugby life. I was still a good player, I just used to be a better one – physically, anyway. I could see opportunities quicker than ever because I'd seen all the pictures before, I just couldn't exploit them like I was once able to, because I wasn't as fast as I once had been.

Ageing is an interesting thing for a sportsman to deal with. The numbers don't lie. As a player, you're monitored all the time, and in your mid-thirties the GPS tracker doesn't come up with the same numbers as it once did. Some players just can't accept the blow to the ego, but my way of dealing with it was to laugh about it.

We had a game at Newcastle early that season where I broke out of our 22 right at the end of the match. A few years beforehand I'd have gone all the way – I had scored an eighty-metre individual try against Bath in a Premiership match eleven years prior, from a similar position. This time I got to halfway and realized that, instead of me pulling away, everyone (including the opposing front row) was catching me up.

I booted the ball out to end the match instead and, when I eventually got my breath back, just started laughing out loud at myself.

The stuck-in-treacle ruck dart against Exeter Chiefs in January 2025 that won me the Topps Tiles Triumph of the Month honour at Leicester, I trademarked as the 'Show and Slow' try. Thank God I only had twelve metres to cover rather than fifty.

Fortunately, I was able to add to Cheik's set-up in other ways. I was almost like a player/coach in some respects. The experience I had gained meant I was able to drive training, build the mindset of the team and help the coaches tactically.

Cheik and I would have some really stimulating discussions about the game and strategy, bouncing ideas off each other.

I combined the last stretch of my career with a new podcast with Coley – *For the Love of Rugby* – which has been a really enjoyable departure. It's good to have the chance to talk rugby with a great mate, and for us to reveal a bit of our personalities.

People have a perception of you from what they see on their screens. I remember Jim Telfer having a go at me once for coming across as arrogant. But really you never see how people truly are until you spend some time with them. I think Coley has been a revelation to most listeners. Anyone who saw him on the field, moaning about scrum decisions while looking like one of the Mitchell brothers in *EastEnders*, would probably imagine he is a monosyllabic misery, but he is such a dry and amusing character.

I hope I come across as the bloke I am – energetic, glass-half-full and someone who just enjoys being around people.

When we set the podcast up, Coley was still part of the England squad, about to play in the 2024 Six Nations; obviously I wasn't . . .

At first, it was strange to leave England behind. I'd watch Test matches, living every moment and feeling every tackle. I'd be looking out for opportunities and for ways to gain an advantage.

That first championship was all a bit like that. I was so desperate for the boys – a lot of whom were great mates – to do well. But, over time, the situation normalized, and it sank in that it wasn't my team any more. I became an England fan again.

In the April of that final season, we moved back to Norfolk, where I had taken on an athlete mentoring role at Gresham's as head of performance sport. The kids were about to start school there. Full circle.

I commuted for the last few weeks, staying at Crofty's place when I needed to be at Leicester. Just like the old days.

Coley decided to call it a day too at the end of that season, and Cheik chose to let us start the last game of the regular season against Newcastle in front of a full house at Welford Road. When we were taken off together early in the second half, the whole stadium rose to applaud us. It was a lovely ovation and I was welling up as I left the pitch. At that moment, I really did feel appreciated.

It was even more special because in the crowd that afternoon were almost seventy of my friends and family, who had travelled all the way from Norfolk to attend the game. Fifty-two of them were on a bus that left the farm at 9 a.m. That included my brother, Tom, and his new partner, Kate.

Those few weeks turned into a sort of farewell tour. After the play-off semi-final win over Sale, I walked around Welford Road, drinking it all in for the last time.

For it all to finish at Twickenham in a seventh Premiership final, eighteen years on from my first, was wonderful. It was testament to how Cheik had turned Leicester into Leicester again. But you don't get to write your own ending. My 338th and last first-team game for the Tigers saw Bath edge us out by two points to take the league title.

Coley's last act on a rugby pitch was to be sin-binned, which was somehow appropriate given how much time he had spent moaning at refs throughout the years. If the yellow was cruel, it was also irrelevant in the grand scheme of a great career.

Bath deserved their trophy.

After they had been presented with it, I walked over to see my family on the sidelines. Tom was there and, as we embraced, we both shed a tear in each other's arms. It wasn't just the end of my rugby journey; it was the end of *our* rugby journey.

But that was OK.

It was strange saying goodbye to all the teammates I'd developed such a strong bond with in training, on the pitch and socially, not knowing for sure if I'd see some of them again. But for me it was time to go.

For so much of my life, rugby had been the all-important presence, but by this point, given everything that had happened to me outside the white lines, I saw rugby for what it was: a great game that I got to play at the weekend, but not what defined who I am.

I tried just as hard to win, but I was able to accept when we didn't. It stung to have come so close in that final – but, when the ink dried on my career, I was at peace.

13

STATE OF PLAY

'Rugby needs to be willing to embrace change on the scale I've outlined above. The traditionalist powers-that-be need to become revolutionaries.'

Rugby union faces some big challenges as it looks to the future.

During my career, the sport has been through a turbulent time, with clubs going bust, a class action lawsuit lodged over head injuries, and a drop in playing numbers. The game is not as robust and strong as we would all want it to be. It is vulnerable. Financially, it is struggling. Player salaries increased above what the game could realistically afford, then along came Covid, the income dried up, and the chickens came home to roost.

It was pretty scary when London Irish, Wasps and Worcester folded, because you didn't know where it was going to end. Even a club of Leicester's size was in trouble. We accepted wage cuts to keep the Tigers going. The ten-club league the bloodletting left is too small. We need to go back up to twelve clubs as soon as possible.

We need a healthy Premiership, not just for its own sake, but for Europe's too. The Champions Cup has lost some of its appeal, with the dominance of the wealthy French clubs and Leinster. The English game is now trying to keep its head above water.

Despite this, some of the rugby we see every weekend is incredible. The athleticism and intensity make for great spectacles. Some of the attacking rugby on show is brilliant. It is this that convinces me that rugby has a rosy future – if it has the courage to make some big decisions.

I think it is time to press the accelerator and open rugby union up. I'm not talking about tinkering. Rugby needs to be radical. To future-proof the game, it needs to think outside the box.

What follows is my eight-point plan for rugby union's future.

Step one: Go to fourteen-a-side

It's claustrophobic out there.

Professionalism has changed the game. It isn't the same sport it was during the amateur era. There are players in every position who are trained athletes.

When I first played for Leicester, defence was about just having bodies strung out in a line. Then Shaun Edwards reinvented it with his blitz defence. Now every team, to one degree or another, is flying off the line. There's less space, and way less time, so it's a lot harder to attack now.

Rugby's authorities have tried various ways to try to create more space. The 50:22 law – which gives a side the line-out throw if they kick the ball from their own half and it bounces into touch in their opponents' 22 – has led to teams putting extra defenders in the back field. But I would go much further. To create more space there are two big-picture options: either make the pitch wider or lose a player.

Rugby pitches vary in size. Twickenham is 125 x 70 metres, whereas Welford Road is 97 x 66 metres. Changing those dimensions has obvious practical problems. You can't just move a stand or a terrace back five metres.

Losing a player, however, could be done. And it would make a big difference. Who would you get rid of? It would have to be a number 8 or a winger, I reckon.

I'd lose a winger.

It is a big step, I know, but we need to be bold – fourteen-a-side is the way ahead.

Step two: No half-time

A rugby match is two halves of forty minutes with a fifteen-minute break in the middle.

Half-time is an accepted part of the game, but I'm curious to know whether you need one. Couldn't we just do a continuous eighty minutes? That would bring more fatigue into the game, and fatigue is what cracks well-organized defences.

Take that fifteen-minute recovery period away, and it would be a game-changer.

Step three: Introduce no-kicking zones

I wonder whether in certain zones of the field, kicking should be outlawed.

I don't mind kicking to clear your lines, or as an attacking weapon in the opposition half, but what about banning it between a team's 22 and the halfway line? Force teams to counter-attack from there, instead of robotically going to the box-kick, and the mindset change would be liberating.

Step four: Make kicks worth a point

Rugby's points system is out of balance.

Five points for a try and three points for a penalty, or a drop goal, doesn't give teams enough of an incentive to be bold. If a shot at goal was reduced to a single point, you would see teams run a lot more penalties with the ball.

Over the eighty minutes of a game, the ball is in play for an average of thirty-five minutes at the moment. That's just not enough. This would be one way to increase it.

Step five: Speed up the set piece

I'd speed up every lineout, so that once the ball has gone out of play, you've got twenty seconds to get the ball back in play, rather than thirty. I would get rid of reset scrums too – if the scrum goes down, the team with possession has to play.

I don't want rugby union to look like rugby league – we still need the scrum and the lineout – but teams have to be encouraged to play the game at a quicker pace. We want viewers thinking: 'I can't take my eyes off this.'

There are times where rugby is like that, but then it shoots itself in the foot with the parts of the game that are plodding.

Step six: Ban catch tackles

I'd get rid of the catch tackle – or choke tackle, as they're sometimes known. They just slow the game down.

Instead of the dynamic ruck that follows a normal tackle, we end up with the game stationary. Then a scrum is awarded.

Get rid of the catch tackle and you also discourage upright tackling, which surely has to be a benefit safety-wise too, as we try to reduce the number of head impacts in the game.

Step seven: Scrap goal-line dropouts

World Rugby tried to deal with the repetitiveness of pick-and-go-fests by introducing a goal-line dropout if the attacking team is held up over the line.

I get the idea, but I would bring in a tap-and-go on the 22 instead. Chuck the ball to your quickest guy, he taps and he's off.

What's going to bring people to watch the game? What's going to make people tune in? It has to be around making the game quicker and making it flow better.

Step eight: Switch to summer

If we want club rugby to thrive, a change of season would help deliver a more entertaining product and provide a more welcoming environment for fans. Playing in the depths of winter sometimes leaves you with little choice but to play up-the-jumper rugby, because of the conditions.

There would be a marketing benefit too. Switching to summer would also take rugby union out of the shadow that Premier League football casts in the winter, and the blanket media coverage it receives.

I understand that to get such a change over the line is going to be difficult. Practically it would be hard to change because of the global calendar. The Premiership isn't powerful enough to just unilaterally move and demand that everyone else falls into line. But there is nothing to stop us moving junior rugby in this country to the summer as a start.

I'm a rugby dad now and I watch my eldest Boris playing on filthy winter Sunday mornings, and I'm just amazed that we haven't made rugby union into a summer sport. For three or four months of the year, it's cold and wet and horrible – and that's just the experience standing on the touchline.

I really think that we're missing a trick. Why can't rugby start at Easter time and run through until the end of October, at least at minis level? If kids weren't handling the ball with frozen fingers, it would improve skills and give them a better version of the game to play.

In the summer months, you're only competing against sports like cricket and tennis rather than football. There are lots of talented kids who play football in the winter who have never even discovered rugby, but a change of season would give them that chance.

People worry whether the ground would be too hard in summer, but that doesn't seem to be a problem for rugby league. I think it would reverse the numbers drain and get a lot more people into the game.

Rugby needs to be willing to embrace change on the scale I've outlined above. The traditionalist powers-that-be need to become revolutionaries.

Some of my ideas might not work – you always can change those parts back – but we don't know until we try. I suppose the biggest question facing rugby as it looks forward is the existential one. Is it a game fit for purpose in the twenty-first century, knowing what we know now?

The concussion issue is a real one.

There will always be an element of risk in rugby. It is a physical contact sport with a lot of moving parts, and accidents will happen. But it is important to make the point, given all the negative publicity rugby has faced, that the game has never been safer in terms of the treatment of head injuries.

When I first started out, there was very little in place to protect us as players. If you got knocked out, no one thought anything of it. You would be expected to play – and you would expect to play – the following week. Now you're removed from the pitch, you go through the protocols and, if you fail your head injury assessment, you're out of the game. Often it doesn't even get that far before you're subbed.

When I copped one on the jaw playing against Sale in the 2023 Premiership semi-final, the medics came over to attend to me.

They asked me some questions and, from my answers, they knew straight away I wasn't right. They were straight onto the coaching staff to tell them I would be going off and I wouldn't be returning.

There was no thought that it was a big game with a place at Twickenham on the line and that I might be all right in ten minutes. They had my best interests at heart.

There has been a huge culture change in my time in the game. Unfortunately for those former players who are fighting their battles because of brain injuries, they played during a less enlightened time. A bang on the head was deemed to be no different to a bang on the knee back then. It's anything but now.

You have an independent doctor there, you've got your own club doctor, you've got the opposition doctor – there are a lot of people looking out for concussion. And if one is confirmed, it's now a mandatory twelve-day stand-down.

Without doubt, there have been a lot of advances in this area.

That said, I still don't think we are there yet. I think there are more improvements that can be made, specifically in the amount of contact training we do. It's still too much.

It's not necessarily the big impacts that cause the damage, it's all the little ones that add up. To mitigate that risk, I would suggest that players need to stay away from contact almost entirely during the training week. Of course, there are elements of training where you can't really avoid it – scrummaging and mauling being the big two. But I think when it comes to bone-on-bone tackling practice, that needs to be either scrapped or monitored by neutral observers to make sure clubs stick to very strict limits.

What will happen, I believe, is that one league will introduce something like that, and then everyone else will follow suit. So why not start with the Premiership? Why would you not want to be leading the world on one of the biggest issues facing the game?

I guess the million-dollar question is whether I am happy for my children to play rugby as it stands now. And for all that it can be improved and taken to the next level, the answer is categorically: yes.

When I watch Boris play, I see how much the game gives him. It's not just the fresh air and running around outdoors. It's the teamwork, the respect, the camaraderie; all those great things about rugby. I want him to experience and benefit from the sport like I have done.

Rugby has allowed me to share so many priceless moments with so many wonderful people.

For me, that happens to have been in a Leicester and an England shirt with my brother, with Crofty, with Coley and with all the rest. But when you strip it back, the relationships that rugby builds and the fun at its heart are the same whether it's Holt, North Walsham or the Lions.

The game is the game, and it is a special one.

I have had my ups and downs with rugby but, honestly, when I look at it now, as an ex-player and fan, I do so with nothing but warmth.

It has been the game of my life.

POSTSCRIPT

I always said I'd include this in a book if I ever wrote one.

Throughout my career, I was lucky to play with so many great players at Leicester and with England. If I was to have one more game for each team, these would be the players I would pick to play alongside.

Thanks for reading.

Ben Youngs' Leicester XV

15 Geordan Murphy
14 Niki Goneva
13 Manu Tuilagi
12 Anthony Allen
11 Alesana Tuilagi
10 George Ford
9 Me
1 Marcos Ayerza
2 Tom Youngs
3 Dan Cole
4 Calum Green
5 Louis Deacon

6   Tom Croft

7   Lewis Moody

8   Jasper Wiese

Ben Youngs' England XV

15 Elliot Daly

14 Anthony Watson

13 Manu Tuilagi

12 Owen Farrell

11 Jonny May

10 George Ford

9   Me

1   Ellis Genge

2   Tom Youngs

3   Dan Cole

4   Simon Shaw

5   Maro Itoje

6   Tom Croft

7   Sam Underhill

8   Tom Curry

ACKNOWLEDGEMENTS

Writing this book has allowed me to reflect on my career and what an awesome time I've had in rugby. I'm indebted to so many people for helping me along the way.

So thanks to . . .

My mum and dad, for all their love and support and for always being there for me. I couldn't have wished for better parents.

Tom, for being my brother, for paving the way for me in rugby and for creating so many great memories on the field together.

Char and the kids – I'm so glad that I got to share so many of these experiences with you. I'm a lucky man.

My in-laws, Nick and Kate – thanks for all the support you've given the family when I have been away. And my wider family – thanks for your constant backing over the years. Especially Auntie Lulu, my number one fan and my main kit beneficiary. Also, my cousin Monty, for all those carefree hours chasing each other in the garden, trying to emulate our heroes, and for then being there every step of the way throughout my career. And James Knight, a great friend – you have been such a brilliant sounding board for me and I have been so grateful for your searing honesty.

Thanks also to . . .

ACKNOWLEDGEMENTS

My first coach Mike Bush, for showing me your infectious enthusiasm for the game. And Gresham's, for giving me the opportunity to play so much sport, especially my rugby coaches there, Richard Brearley and Simon Worrall.

Andy Key, my coach at the Tigers academy, for your early guidance. And the one-off that is Richard Cockerill, for all the time you put into me and for the number of stories you have equipped me with for after-dinner speaking!

Alex Martin and Tom Tombleson, for their dedication in helping me try to become a better athlete. And psychologist Matt Thombs, for all the work you did with me away from the pitch to equip me for top-level sport.

Tom Scott and Peter Tom, who have invested so much into the Tigers down the years – thanks for your continued support.

My teammates. There are too many of you to mention, but I have to give a special shoutout to Dan Cole, George Ford and Tom Croft – great friends as well as great players.

My England coaches, especially Eddie Jones and John Mitchell – thanks for taking me to another level as a scrum half.

Ben Lewitt, my outstanding agent, who took over from the equally excellent Richard Wilks, now Leicester's general manager. Thank you for all your hard work on my behalf. Ben helped to put this project together along with both Nick Walters – top book agent at David Luxton Associates – and Simon Cohen, to whom I remain indebted to for so many things . . . the Nando's, the brooding negotiation silences and, most of all, his wise counsel.

Neil Squires, my ghostwriter on this book – thanks for helping to tell my story. Having sat on opposite sides of the table throughout my career as you chronicled it as a journalist, it was great to work together on this trip down memory lane.

The brilliant editors at Pan Macmillan – Ause Abdelhaq,

ACKNOWLEDGEMENTS

Melissa Bond and Sara Cywinski – and the rest of the team – Nick Griffiths, Penny Isaac, Neeharika Nene, Vera Pirri, Holly Sheldrake, Natasha Tullett, Josie Turner and Rachel Vale – thanks so much for bringing this book to fruition.

Lastly, all the supporters out there – the Leicester fans, the England fans, the rugby fans who have backed me over the years. I want to say a massive thank you from the bottom of my heart. We have a special game and you are a huge part of why it is so special.